Home Work

HISTORICAL STUDIES OF URBAN AMERICA

Edited by Lilia Fernández, Timothy J. Gilfoyle, and Amanda I. Seligman
James R. Grossman, Editor Emeritus

RECENT TITLES IN THE SERIES

Emily Lieb, *Road to Nowhere: How a Highway Map Wrecked Baltimore*

Stephen M. Koeth, *Crabgrass Catholicism: How Suburbanization Transformed Faith and Politics in Postwar America*

Daniel Wortel-London, *The Menace of Prosperity: New York City and the Struggle for Economic Development, 1865–1981*

A. K. Sandoval-Strausz, ed., *Metropolitan Latinidad: Transforming American Urban History*

Alexander Wood, *Building the Metropolis: Architecture, Construction, and Labor in New York City, 1880–1935*

Leslie M. Harris, *In the Shadow of Slavery: African Americans in New York City, 1626–1863*, With a New Afterword by the Author

Tim Keogh, *In Levittown's Shadow: Poverty in America's Wealthiest Postwar Suburb*

Nicholas Dagen Bloom, *The Great American Transit Disaster: A Century of Austerity, Auto-Centric Planning, and White Flight*

Sean T. Dempsey, *City of Dignity: Christianity, Liberalism, and the Making of Global Los Angeles*

Claire Dunning, *Nonprofit Neighborhoods: An Urban History of Inequality and the American State*

Tracy E. K'Meyer, *To Live Peaceably Together: The American Friends Service Committee's Campaign for Open Housing*

Mike Amezcua, *Making Mexican Chicago: From Postwar Settlement to the Age of Gentrification*

Arnold R. Hirsch, *Making the Second Ghetto: Race and Housing in Chicago, 1940–1960*, With a New Afterword by N. D. B. Connolly

William Sites, *Sun Ra's Chicago: Afrofuturism and the City*

A complete list of series titles is available on the University of Chicago Press website.

Home Work

GENDER, CHILD LABOR,
AND EDUCATION FOR GIRLS IN
URBAN AMERICA, 1870–1930

Ruby Oram

THE UNIVERSITY OF CHICAGO PRESS
CHICAGO AND LONDON

The University of Chicago Press, Chicago 60637
The University of Chicago Press, Ltd., London
© 2025 by The University of Chicago
All rights reserved. No part of this book may be used or reproduced in any manner whatsoever without written permission, except in the case of brief quotations in critical articles and reviews. For more information, contact the University of Chicago Press, 1427 E. 60th St., Chicago, IL 60637.
Published 2025

34 33 32 31 30 29 28 27 26 25   1 2 3 4 5

ISBN-13: 978-0-226-84431-2 (cloth)
ISBN-13: 978-0-226-84433-6 (paper)
ISBN-13: 978-0-226-84432-9 (ebook)
DOI: https://doi.org/10.7208/chicago/9780226844329.001.0001

Library of Congress Cataloging-in-Publication Data

Names: Oram, Ruby, author.
Title: Home work : gender, child labor, and education for girls in urban America, 1870–1930 / Ruby Oram.
Description: Chicago : The University of Chicago Press, 2025. | Series: Historical studies of urban America | Includes bibliographical references and index.
Identifiers: LCCN 2025010978 | ISBN 9780226844312 (cloth) | ISBN 9780226844336 (paperback) | ISBN 9780226844329 (ebook)
Subjects: LCSH: Girls—Education—Illinois—Chicago—History—19th century. | Girls—Education—Illinois—Chicago—History—20th century. | Discrimination in education—Illinois—Chicago—History—19th century. | Discrimination in education—Illinois—Chicago—History—20th century. | Child labor—Illinois—Chicago—History—19th century. | Child labor—Illinois—Chicago—History—20th century. | Home economics—Study and teaching—Illinois—Chicago—History—19th century. | Home economics—Study and teaching—Illinois—Chicago—History—19th century. | Educational equalization—United States—History.
Classification: LCC LC1481 .O73 2025 | DDC 371.8220973/1109034—dc23/eng/20250403
LC record available at https://lccn.loc.gov/2025010978

Authorized Representative for EU General Product Safety Regulation (GPSR) queries: **Easy Access System Europe**—Mustamäe tee 50, 10621 Tallinn, Estonia, gpsr.requests@easproject.com
Any other queries: https://press.uchicago.edu/press/contact.html

For my mother,
Renee LeBoeuf

Contents

Group Abbreviations ix

INTRODUCTION
The Girl Problem · 1

CHAPTER ONE
The "Girl Problem" or the "Servant Problem"?: Policing Girlhood Labor in Illinois Carceral Schools, 1870–1910 · 15

CHAPTER TWO
Fit for Motherhood: Regulating Girlhood Health and Labor in Chicago Public Schools, 1888–1915 · 41

CHAPTER THREE
The Bane of the Tenement: Educating Immigrant Daughters for Scientific Housekeeping, 1890–1910 · 71

CHAPTER FOUR
A School Built Around the Girl: Education for Paid and Unpaid Labor in Chicago High Schools, 1900–1915 · 97

CHAPTER FIVE
Sex, Spending, and "Going Astray": Vocational Guidance Counseling for Girls of Legal Working Age, 1910–1920s · 125

CHAPTER SIX
A Nation of Good Homes: Labor, Citizenship, and Home Economics for American Girls, 1917–1930 · 157

CONCLUSION · 185

Acknowledgments 193
Archive Abbreviations 195
Notes 197
Index 247

Group Abbreviations

ACA	Association of Collegiate Alumnae
AFL	American Federation of Labor
AHEA	American Home Economics Association
BOE	Board of Education
CWC	Chicago Woman's Club
GFWC	General Federation of Women's Clubs
IWA	Illinois Woman's Alliance
LISA	Ladies' Industrial Schools Association
LWV	League of Women Voters
NCLC	National Child Labor Committee
NHEA	National Household Economic Association
NSPIE	National Society for the Promotion of Industrial Education
VSL	Vocational Supervision League
WCTU	Woman's Christian Temperance Union
WTUL	Women's Trade Union League

[INTRODUCTION]

"The Girl Problem"

> The girl problem is the most pressing one before the public. The consequences of a girl's mistakes are so much more far-reaching, so much more disastrous for the family.
>
> Ellen Martin Henrotin, president of the Chicago Woman's Club, 1909[1]

A twenty-five-year-old "lady reporter" for the *Chicago Times*, Helen Cusack, went undercover as a factory girl in 1888. Disguised in "the rags of poverty," Cusack spent a month supporting Chicago's garment industry alongside immigrant girls who stitched corsets, trimmed winter cloaks, and sewed buttons on blouses. Cusack spoke to girl seamstresses with "deathly pale faces" who worked elbow to elbow on a diet of cold coffee and black bread. She worked with teenage girls like Annie from immigrant families who made sixty-five cents a day cutting dress reeds to support her younger siblings and widowed mother. Cusack met a group of twelve-year-old girls in a "slave-grinding hell-hole" who worked ten-hour days wearing shoes held together with thread and tape. For one month, Cusack's accounts of "miserable girlhood" appeared daily on the front pages of the *Chicago Times* and the *New York World* under the sensational title: "City Slave Girls."[2]

Cusack's "City Slave Girls" exposé brought national attention to the brutal factory conditions endured by working-class girls in industrial cities.[3] Cusack, however, said little about labor legislation. She did not demand factory inspections or a ban on child labor at the end of her twenty-three-part series. Instead, Cusack concluded "City Slave Girls" with a call to reform Chicago's public schools. She warned readers that factory girls would exit the workforce completely unprepared for motherhood without "practical education" for the home. She urged school officials to introduce hands-on classes that taught girls "to cook, to sew, to mend, to mind their children, and care for their own health." In her final article, Cusack argued that public schools had a responsibility to reform their curriculum in service of the urban working girl. "What the shop-girl and factory-girl needs is training," she wrote, "training that the scholastic stuffing of our public schools does not supply."[4]

Home Work is a history of how white women reformers used public education to police the labor lives of working-class girls in the urban North. In 1870, most working women and girls over the age of ten earned wages in private homes or rooming houses as domestic servants. White American-born girls left domestic service for new opportunities in the public workforce over the proceeding decades. By 1910, 70 percent of white working women and girls labored outside the home in factories, shops, and offices. Because of racial discrimination in the urban workforce, Black women and girls who migrated out of the Jim Crow South earned wages as domestic servants and factory hands. In total, the number of female wage earners in Chicago increased elevenfold between 1880 and 1930. Girls under the age of eighteen made the lowest wages and held the least stable positions in all lines of work. Young domestic servants experienced sexual assault in an unregulated industry. Girl "sewing serfs" worked seasonal jobs with workplace hazards due to the lack of labor laws. Observers like Cusack also worried about the moral dangers awaiting girl workers who ultimately needed to prepare for marriage and motherhood. "In no place I worked did I see any incentive to decency, honesty, or respectability," wrote Cusack.[5]

Reform groups of mostly middle- and upper-class white women expanded urban education between 1870 and 1930 to redirect urban girls toward housekeeping, motherhood, and "respectable" employment. In Chicago, wealthy clubwomen lobbied for state-funded carceral schools that trained "wayward" girls to work in private homes rather than public shops and factories. Social reformers like Jane Addams helped pass mandatory school attendance laws to protect the "the growing girl" from industrial labor after Cusack's reporting. Clubwomen demanded seats on Chicago's Board of Education (BOE) and introduced new courses like domestic science, hygiene, and childcare into the girls' curriculum. After World War I, college-educated white women secured new positions with federal agencies to bring wage-earning girls back into the school system through mandatory continuation schools. Women education reformers created careers for themselves through segregating public education by gender and policing girls' transition from school to work.

The American-born daughters of European immigrants were the focus of these reform initiatives. Nearly 25 million immigrants from southern, central, and eastern Europe passed through Ellis Island by World War I. Industrial cities like Chicago were immigrant cities populated by white ethnic communities from the empires of Germany, Russia, Italy, and Austria-Hungary. Including their American-born children, immigrant families accounted for 80 percent of New Yorkers and 78 percent of Chicago's population in 1890.⁶ Public education expanded alongside mass immigration from eastern and southern Europe. School reformers argued that the American-born children of the "new immigrants" required public intervention to ensure their training for citizenship, productivity, and good health. The immigrant cities of New York, Boston, and Chicago had the largest public school systems (in that order) by the turn of the century. Chicago had 225 public elementary schools and 15 public high schools in 1900. Roughly 300,000 children attended Chicago public schools each day, 88 percent of whom were first- and second-generation immigrants.⁷

Public schools regulated the labor lives of immigrant children during the Progressive Era. First- and second-generation immigrants were the least likely to attend public school beyond the lower grades in industrial cities. Less than 5 percent of all urban children continued on to high school in 1900. While school enrollment rose over the next two decades, 60 percent of urban children still left school by age sixteen in 1922. Many European immigrant families relied on their children to earn wages by sixteen to supplement the family income. Others expected children to stay home during the day to take care of younger siblings and ill relatives on behalf of working parents. Tens of thousands of Chicago children spent their school days loitering on street corners and playing games in alleys because their industrial work was inconsistent and their domestic duties unsupervised. Child labor reformers used school attendance laws to guide these children into the classroom for their physical and moral protection. Public schools hired truancy officers to arrest children who skipped class and criminalized parents who relied on their labor. These new regulations allowed school officials to enforce normative expectations of childhood through mandatory attendance, vocational education, health classes, and lessons in good citizenship.⁸

School officials often ignored Black children during this expansion of public education. Chicago's Black population accounted for less than 2 percent of total residents in the early twentieth century. The number of African Americans across the industrial North grew dramatically after 1910 as families migrated out of the Jim Crow South in pursuit of more economic opportunity, civic freedom, and physical safety. Chicago's Black population doubled between 1910 and 1920. The Black population doubled again by 1940 to account for 8.2 percent of all Chicagoans. Black migrant parents encouraged their children to take full advantage of interracial and modern school systems in northern cities to promote respectability and racial uplift. But white school officials neglected Black children when enforcing new school regulations like attendance laws, health exams, and guidance counseling. As historian Moira Elizabeth Hinderer argues, Chicago school reformers engaged in a politics of "racial containment" through informal exclusion and segregation of school resources.[9]

White women reformers contributed to racial inequality in urban education through their demands for girl-centered schooling. Anti–child labor activists in the settlement house movement positioned American-born daughters of immigrants as the most vulnerable children in industrial cities throughout the early decades of the Great Migration. They rendered the labor of Black girls invisible or, at the very least, outside the scope of public school investment. Women-led school initiatives that did acknowledge the presence of Black migrant girls from the Jim Crow South reinforced racial disparities in Chicago's female workforce by training Black girls for paid domestic service while encouraging immigrant daughters to envision futures as full-time American homemakers. Using education to solve the "the girl problem" between 1870 and 1930 helped segregate urban schools by both gender and race.

Home Work focuses on Chicago as a case study of women-led school initiatives that took place across the industrial North between 1870 and 1930. Chicago industrialized after 1870 and experienced rapid population growth alongside other midwestern and northeastern cities. Industrialism redefined the urban North as America's "manufacturing belt," where working-class families made, sold, and shipped industrial and consumer goods across the country. The expansion of railroad transportation after the Civil War made Chicago both a manufacturing center and a commercial hub by the turn of the century. Working-class families in Chicago supported the nation's second largest garment industry after New York City. They worked in stockyards and warehouses for the nation's largest meatpacking and mail-order catalog companies. Chicago was a destination for the Great Migration that attracted more than 44,000 Black residents by 1910, 90 percent of whom lived in Chicago's South Side "Black Metropolis." The employment and educational opportunities in Chicago contributed to the city's meteoric growth at the turn of the twentieth century. In 1890, Chicago was the nation's second largest city after New York, with 1.1 million residents. Chicago's population doubled by 1910.[10]

Chicago was home to a thriving urban reform movement led by white women's groups. Chicago women organized reform groups to address a host of social issues linked to the rise of cities, industry, and European immigration after the Civil War. Among them were the first generation of college-educated women who founded social settlements like Hull House from which they spearheaded political campaigns to regulate women's working hours and outlaw child labor. These social reformers worked with wealthy white "clubwomen"—the wives of bankers, lawyers, and politicians—who funded progressive initiatives in public schools and settlement houses. Influential clubs like the Chicago Woman's Club (CWC) welcomed a few Black members by the turn of the century. Yet Chicago's urban reform community was largely segregated by race. Black social reformers organized their own relief agencies, social services, and settlement houses for Black migrant families while white women focused on European immigrants and demanded public investment in their American-born children.[11]

Home Work complicates the class politics of white women in Chicago's urban reform movement. Historians of women and gender have demonstrated how these reformers built cross-class coalitions to achieve important policy changes, including factory inspections and shorter workdays for women by the 1910s.[12] But middle-class labor supporters like Jane Addams and Florence Kelley simultaneously promoted narrow work expectations for girls through their public school reform. They supported the women's labor movement but ignored working-class girls who wanted to study stenography rather than dressmaking in neighborhood high schools. While lobbying against child labor, they still expected immigrant daughters to perform caretaking and housekeeping labor on behalf of busy mothers in tenement districts. Women in the settlement house and club movements viewed public education as a powerful tool for social reform that could uplift working-class girls and immigrant families. Many of their initiatives, however, placed new labor burdens on working-class daughters and denied girls the education they actually wanted.

Class, then, is an important category of analysis in this history. I use "working class" to describe the men, women, and children whose livelihood depended on the daily wage. Working-class mothers earned wages outside the home in factories and warehouses or inside the home in apartment sweatshops. Their working-class children also earned wages or supported wage-earning parents through unpaid domestic labor (caregiving, housekeeping). The middle-class reformers highlighted in this book often grew up in traditional American families with breadwinning fathers and were not expected to work as children. Many had college degrees, or at least high school diplomas, and used these credentials to work in school administration and government agencies. Middle-class reformers promoted the expectation that working-class girls should prepare for unpaid service to their future homes, husbands, and children. Many of these reformers contradicted this vision of family life by remaining single and childless. They gained power through asserting control over working-class girlhood and expanded the regulatory power of public schools in the lives of *all* working-class children in the process.

I refer to these women as "school reformers" and "education reformers" throughout *Home Work*. Some of the figures highlighted in this book—like Ella Flagg Young, the nation's first female superintendent of schools—are familiar to scholars of American education. Activists like Jane Addams are well documented in the history of women's political reform but rarely contextualized within the history of urban education.[13] Most scholarship on school reform in the Gilded Age and Progressive Era revolves around men. Historians in the 1970s first highlighted the work of male school officials who created "one best system" of urban public schools by reforming the instruction of male students. More recent studies continue this tradition, drawing attention to the male "district progressives" who consolidated school power and professionalized school governance in the early twentieth century. Women working outside the school system, like Florence Kelley, viewed public education as a collective site for women to forward "the nation's work" of solving urban social issues. This book encourages scholars to expand our definition of a "school reformer" by exploring how clubwomen, nurses, and labor activists altered urban education from the outside in.[14]

Women reformers looked beyond the public school to police/protect working-class girls through education. A network of carceral schools for troublesome children grew in tandem with public schooling in the industrial North. Women's groups helped build bridges between public education and the burgeoning juvenile legal system to guide girls back to school and arrest those who challenged sexual norms. I define "urban education" broadly to encompass the training and guidance directed toward girls in all publicly funded institutions. Networks of private schools—most notably, urban Catholic schools—are not the focus of this book. Instead, *Home Work* uncovers how women school reformers directed public resources toward girls' education and used the state to promote their vision of domesticity and respectability.[15]

Women school reformers relied on "maternalism" to remake girls' education in industrial cities. The logic of maternalism suggested that women were better fit than men to oversee programs and institutions geared toward children because of their "natural" motherly instincts. Black women also embraced maternalism to fund institutions for poor children and organize mutual aid for Black families in the industrial North. *Home Work* highlights how white women leveraged their gender to gain supervisory control over public resources between 1870 and 1930. In Chicago, white education reformers used maternalism to oversee state-funded carceral schools for girls and secure representation on the BOE. Maternalism empowered white college-educated women to run juvenile courtrooms and access federal funding for home economics after World War I. Maternalism helped white women advance their own careers by asserting a gendered responsibility to guide white American-born girls toward respectable womanhood.[16]

In sum, *Home Work* uncovers how Chicago's "female dominion of reform" shaped one of the city's most important urban institutions: the school.[17] Similar groups of school reformers altered urban education across the industrial North. Clubwomen in Boston and New York established carceral schools for white girls and funded domestic science classes for immigrant daughters. Middle-class social reformers organized vocational guidance services and scholarship programs to keep working-class girls in school. Women school reformers shared their concerns for the working girl and commitment to education reform at national conferences. They traveled to different cities to learn from successful reforms in sister school districts. *Home Work* highlights these broader trends while centering local reforms in Chicago. This local lens allows for greater attention to individual reformers, schools, and acts of resistance from girls who often rejected women-led initiatives on the community level.

Home Work places girlhood at the center of public school reform and the creation of educational bureaucracy between 1870 and 1930. Historians often generalize the subjects of urban school reform as "children" and "students." But school reformers rarely, if ever, designed new course requirements for "children" or "students"; rather, reformers catered to the perceived needs of "boys" or "girls" who required gendered education for gendered work roles in adulthood. As historian Julia Grant argues, male school officials viewed working-class immigrant boys as criminally dangerous and prone to delinquency. They promoted shop classes to curb boyhood behavior by instilling the values of hard work and productivity in the next generation of American workmen. Important scholarship on boyhood and urban school reform—particularly in the history of vocational education— has obscured the centrality of girlhood. In Chicago, the first state-funded carceral schools catered to white American-born girls. Child labor activists helped keep girls in school longer than boys to protect their reproductive health as "mothers of the race." The first vocational guidance counselors entered Chicago schools due to moral hysteria about sexual delinquency and "white slavery." A desire to protect the white working girl shaped some of the most important school reform achievements of the Progressive Era.[18]

School reformers used urban education to place new boundaries around modern childhood. The concept of "childhood" was a mid-nineteenth-century invention. Intellectuals, doctors, and educators in both Europe and the United States argued that childhood was a distinct life stage that required different accommodations from the state. Legal and medical institutions adapted to the idea that children were in a state of development that left them vulnerable to outside influences. Reformers described children as partially formed citizens who needed special protection to ensure their future morality and productivity. By the Progressive Era, most reformers took for granted the new logic that boys and girls had a "right to childhood," which should be protected by the state. That right included access to leisure, play, and public education. Working-class children who earned wages, cared for family members, or played unsupervised on city streets challenged burgeoning ideas about adolescence. Self-appointed "child savers"—mostly white middle-class Protestants—sought to protect the right to childhood through mandatory schooling and safe recreation. They also policed urban childhood by removing boys and girls from "dangerous" surroundings and creating new categories of deviant childhood behavior (like juvenile delinquency).[19]

State institutions and child welfare groups often racialized childhood as white. The white "worthy poor" children of European immigrants were the face of anti–child labor campaigns, child health initiatives, and foster care programs. Medical professionals denied Black boys their right to childhood by calling them "men" based on racial stereotypes about Black male aggression and physical strength. Black girls were also deemed "women" at earlier ages due to racist assumptions about their sexual maturity. Black reformers asserted the rights of Black children by emphasizing the respectability of their dress and speech. Black settlement house workers invested in Black children's right to play and leisure through recreational opportunities like music and art classes. But the systemic denial of Black childhood during the Progressive Era led to inequitable state investments in child welfare and racial disparities in public education.[20]

Like "childhood," "girlhood" is a socially constructed idea that was in flux during the Gilded Age and Progressive Era. The legal boundaries between "girl" and "woman" shifted as reformers rewrote age-of-consent laws and created new criminal systems specifically for child offenders. Most northern state governments placed the divide between a girl "delinquent" from a woman "criminal" at age eighteen. Boyhood "delinquency" often ended earlier by age sixteen. Throughout *Home Work*, I refer to female students and workers under the age of eighteen as "girls" due to this legal boundary. White women reformers helped define girlhood differently than boyhood through their education reform. They argued that extending the age boundary of girlhood would keep girls in school longer and protect them from the amorphous dangers of public life and labor. The protected category of "girl" was not equally extended to Black girls. Like childhood in general, state actors often associated the vulnerable and dependent state of girlhood with whiteness.[21]

Reformers connected "womanhood" with the social responsibilities of marriage and motherhood that presumably began in a woman's early twenties (if not earlier). School reformers suggested that girls—especially white girls—had a right to childhood before taking on these womanly duties. Earning wages or caring for younger siblings at home disrupted their childhood right to rest, play, and learn during girlhood. Yet reformers also suggested that girls had serious responsibilities as future mothers and homemakers, which required greater demands on their education. Girls needed to learn homemaking skills before they married and reared children of their own. They needed to appreciate the value of chastity and importance of protecting their bodies for healthy reproduction. Working-class girls challenged these girlhood expectations by rejecting domestic education. They pursued classes in stenography so they could work in mixed-sex offices rather than studying traditionally feminine needle trades. They chose to leave school early to make their own wages and spend money independently in the public world of consumerism and nightlife. *Home Work* argues that women school reformers used education to direct working-class girls away from these choices and place them on the path toward respectable American womanhood.[22]

∴

Home Work is organized into six chapters. Chapter 1 introduces the wealthy clubwomen and middle-class social reformers who founded state-funded carceral schools for "problem girls" in Chicago. The Illinois Industrial School for Girls (est. 1877) confined white girls under eighteen years old and mandated domestic training as moral reform. Administrators also required domestic education for inmates to address a labor shortage affecting their own homes known as the "servant problem." Court officials sentenced a growing minority of Black girls to a second institution, the remote Illinois State Training School for Girls (est. 1893), where they also received domestic instruction and "indenture" from the school as live-in servants. The shifting racial demographics of juvenile incarceration by the 1910s led reformers in both schools to argue that domestic education prepared Black girls for paid domestic labor and white inmates for homemaking and motherhood. Through carceral school reform, women's groups in Chicago used domestic education to redirect the labor of white working-class girls, reinforce racial segregation in women's housework, and place new legal barriers between urban girls deemed "dependent" or "delinquent" by county courts.

Some of these same women reformers pursued seats on the Chicago BOE to keep working-class white girls enrolled in school and protect their bodies from industrialized labor. Chapter 2 argues that white clubwomen and social reformers in the settlement house movement used public education not only to curb child labor, but white girlhood labor specifically. They viewed white American-born girls as the most vulnerable workers in the urban economy and lobbied for tighter school attendance laws to ensure girls' physical health. Anti–child labor activists in Chicago reformed the elementary school curriculum by supporting mandatory medical screenings and courses for "little mothers," both of which promoted healthy reproduction among future "mothers of the race." Child labor activists like Florence Kelley used the growing power of public education to invest in the health of all urban children and protect young workers from physical harm. But the racialization of the vulnerable girl worker as "white" promoted narrow norms of healthy girlhood in the curriculum and placed Black girls outside the scope of new school investments in child welfare.

Women also used new leadership roles in school governance to teach domestic skills like sewing, cooking, and housekeeping to the American-born daughters of immigrants. Chapter 3 highlights how turn-of-the-century assumptions about working-class motherhood gendered the elementary school curriculum through the addition of "domestic science centers" for girls in immigrant neighborhoods. Galvanized by the domestic science movement, reform-minded women demanded "scientific housekeeping" courses to help second-generation girls safely care for younger siblings while their mothers earned wages. They argued that domestic science could solve serious public health issues in the tenement districts by teaching girls to sew warm clothing, cook nutritious meals, and stop the spread of disease with good sanitation. This faith in domestic science placed unrealistic labor burdens on young girls and suggested that poor domestic health was the result of insufficient education rather than a lack of public services. Furthermore, these women school reformers sometimes contradicted their own child labor activism by requiring that immigrant girls train for the twin vocations of educated housekeeper and public health informant.

Chapter 4 explores competing efforts to reform how urban high schools prepared girls of legal working age (fourteen to sixteen) for labor in Chicago. At the height of the vocational education movement, women labor activists lobbied school officials to create trade programs for future dressmakers and milliners. They compromised their vision of girls-only vocational education with the interests of college-educated reformers who wanted girls to study "household arts" for unpaid domestic work in their future homes. These school reformers worked together to lobby for the city's only all-girls public school, the Lucy Flower Technical School for Girls (Flower Tech), which opened in 1911. Flower Tech taught needle trades *and* household arts, reflecting a social agenda to educate white working-class girls for respectable labor. Flower Tech's curriculum neglected the actual interests of working-class girls who wanted a traditional liberal arts education and white-collar skills. This chapter relies on archived oral histories of former Flower Tech students to show how Black students remade Flower Tech's reputation to serve their own academic interests.[23]

Women school reformers also promoted vocational guidance counseling to control the sexual autonomy and spending habits of white working-class girls. Chicago clubwomen and college-educated social reformers organized the Vocational Supervision League (VSL) to investigate employment opportunities for girls of legal working age and offer counseling before they exited the school system for work. The Chicago BOE incorporated their counseling services into the public schools by 1915. In chapter 5, I argue that racialized anxiety about the white working girl's sexual purity inspired women's vocational guidance reform in Chicago. VSL members believed that the teen years were a dangerous age for white girls, who could "drift" into the sex trade or be corrupted by alleged "white slave traffickers" in mixed-sex offices. This chapter explores how school reformers used juvenile probation in the courts, school counseling, and scholarship services to guide white working-class girls back into the public school system. I argue that white American-born girls ultimately benefited from this investment in their continued education by using scholarship support to learn white-collar skills when office work was culturally femininized, desexualized, and recast as "American" work during World War I.

These first five chapters highlight the conflicting goals of women school reformers and the girls they hoped to reform. In the late nineteenth century, working-class girls rejected education for live-in domestic service and chose to pursue more independent positions in the public workforce. High school students ignored needle trades and household arts programs because they wanted to work as stenographers and teachers. The women highlighted in this book used education to promote their social reform agendas of protecting childhood health, sexual normality, and middle-class domesticity. They neglected the interests of working-class students who desired urban freedom, consumerism, and upward class mobility. *Home Work* relies on letters to newspapers, archived oral histories, and juvenile court testimony to uncover how generations of Chicago girls challenged women's effort to reform their labor lives through education reform.[24] These sources point to the autonomy of urban girls and the limitations of school reform as a tool for social control.

Educating the American working girl for respectable labor became a national priority after World War I through the Smith-Hughes Act of 1917. Chapter 6 covers how urban women's groups shaped this landmark policy that provided federal aid to vocational programs at the high school level for the next half century. While labor women fought to keep domestic education out of the original Smith-Hughes bill, urban clubwomen successfully demanded federal aid for "vocational home economics" to prepare the daughters of immigrants for American homemaking. The inclusion of home economics in the Smith-Hughes Act empowered a generation of white college-educated women to advance their careers using new government resources. In the urban North, these women relied on government aid to require wage-earning girls to return to school and study American homemaking in public "continuation schools" under their leadership. They promoted racialized assumptions about gender, labor, and citizenship by suggesting that only white girls should prepare for the American expectations of full-time homemaking with government aid. National women's groups supported federal investment in home economics as "equalization for women" in the post-suffrage decade. But government support for home economics increased gender and racial segregation in public education by spreading a narrow vision of women's respectable labor far beyond the urban school system.

Chapter 6, then, demonstrates how women education reformers nationalized their urban school initiatives to direct girlhood labor toward home work. This history complicates redemptive scholarship on "the secret history of home economics," which credits the field for women's advancement in higher education, advertising, and public policy.[25] I argue that the achievements of women in the home economics movement were made possible through their regulation of girlhood labor. Members of lobbying groups like the American Home Economics Association (AHEA) leveraged their expertise to prepare the next generation of white American women for citizenship. They promoted racial segregation in women's education by excluding Black home economists from the AHEA and encouraging state agencies to prepare all non-white girls for the double burden of homemaking and wage earning. The home economics movement did, indeed, allow important advancements for women within colleges and government agencies. The movement also inscribed new racial and class boundaries between girls as education for the work of American womanhood.

Centering girlhood in the history of Progressive Era school reform uncovers new roots in the history of educational inequality. Certain schools and groups of students became "doubly advantaged," to use Erica M. Kitzmiller's term, by both public resources and charitable investment during the Progressive Era.[26] Some students—such as white American-born girls—also gained additional resources by being doubly policed. Scholars can better understand the history of urban education through greater attention to gender ideology and women's school reform initiatives. Social anxieties about white working girls fueled the expansion of urban education at the turn of the twentieth century and the inequalities embedded in school policy and curriculum. Through reforming girlhood education, local women reformers in cities like Chicago helped stratify schooling by race, class, and gender.

[CHAPTER ONE]

The "Girl Problem" or the "Servant Problem"?

Policing Girlhood Labor in Illinois
Carceral Schools, 1870–1910

Fourteen-year-old Mamie Davis, the daughter of white American-born parents, was the alleged ringleader of a riot that erupted at the Illinois State Training School for Girls in 1895. According to administrators, Davis led a group of girls through the three-story building in Chicago as they splintered doors open with broken table legs, smashed windows, and threw books and dishes onto the street below. The police took Davis to the Harrison Street station around eight o'clock that night and asked the reason for her rebellion. Davis explained that she hated her mandatory domestic service to the carceral institution. Administrators confined Davis in the school's sewing room, where she spent hours mending household items like bedsheets and nightgowns for fellow inmates. After four years of domestic training—cooking, laundry, sewing—Davis and her fellow rebels had enough. "We didn't like to sew all the time," she explained at the police station. "We got tired of it."[1]

County courts sentenced thousands of girls between the ages of ten and eighteen to state-funded carceral schools in the late nineteenth century. Wealthy white philanthropist women and middle-class social reformers ran these institutions across the industrial North. They confined girls picked up by local law enforcement for petty crimes like pickpocketing, wandering city streets, or skipping school. Carceral schools for troublesome children were part of a broader shift in state responses to crime. State governments invested in "reformatories" for both adults and children where administrators emphasized education and vocational training to rehabilitate rather than punish wrongdoers.[2] Domestic labor defined the daily activities of women and girls in reform-centered institutions that confined mostly (if not exclusively) white inmates in their early decades.[3] In Illinois, women's groups lobbied for state laws mandating that "problem girls" study cooking, sewing, and laundry work during their sentences. White women involved in carceral reform viewed domesticity as moral protection for the poor and working-class girls sentenced to their care. They argued that domesticity would solve the "girl problem" by teaching values like chastity and helpfulness for their inmates' future marriageability. Through required domestic education, carceral schools enforced a narrow vision of normative womanhood on a growing population of incarcerated girls.[4]

Women in carceral school reform also made domestic education a requisite of juvenile justice to address a labor shortage known as the "servant problem." Upper- and middle-class women relied on the labor of working-class girls in their homes as live-in servants in the late nineteenth century. Over 70 percent of wage-earning women and girls worked as domestic servants in 1870. But their numbers drastically decreased by the turn of the century as women and girls entered the public workforce in shops, factories, and downtown offices. Women in the employing classes complained about the shrinking pool of well-trained servants in their desired demographic (white, American, English speaking). In the late nineteenth century, Illinois carceral schools trained their mostly white inmates for live-in service and placed girls out in private homes. Even after her rebellion, Davis was paroled from the Illinois State Training School as a live-in servant for a carpenter and his housewife in Chicago. Domestic education served the dual purpose of moral protection and labor control in state-funded carceral schools.[5]

Women reformers helped design these new state institutions to meet the needs of white middle-class homes and the labor expectations of white middle-class womanhood. Administrators hoped to protect who they viewed as "worthy" white daughters like Davis from sexual immorality and industrial poverty by directing their labor toward live-in service. They did so at the exact moment white working-class girls were leaving the field behind. Women reformers created new legal categories that stratified urban girlhood by race in the process. County courts in Illinois often deemed white problem girls "dependents" to suggest their need of state protection at the whites-only Illinois Industrial School for Girls. They more often categorized Black girls as "delinquents" by the turn of the century and sentenced them to the remote State Training School for Girls in Geneva, Illinois. The history of these two Illinois institutions reveals how influential white women's groups reinforced a racial hierarchy of domestic labor in their efforts to police white girlhood sexuality and employment through carceral schooling.[6]

Protecting the "Helpless Potato Sprout"

A devastating fire swept through Chicago in 1871 that rendered one-third of residents homeless. The Great Chicago Fire galvanized wealthy society women to organize clubs and relief agencies in the years that followed. Frustrated with the slow response of male-led reform groups, philanthropic women raised funds to provide shelter, medical aid, and childcare support for those living amid the ashes. Their participation in relief work launched the women's club movement in Illinois. As historian Maureen Flanagan argues, the Great Chicago Fire "gave prominent Chicago women a totally new urban experience." The fire convinced wealthy clubwomen that the city's poor required charitable public investment in their housing and education. Many of the women's clubs founded after the fire—like the Chicago Woman's Club (CWC)—continued to lead major municipal reforms in the city for the next fifty years.[7]

One such women's group was the Ladies' Industrial Schools Association (LISA), which organized in 1871 to provide housing and education for girls who appeared "homeless and dependent" after the fire. LISA represented an elite group of politically active women in the Midwest. Helen Mar Judson Beveridge, the daughter of one of Evanston's founders, Philo Judson, served as LISA president. Her husband, John Lourie Beveridge, served as governor of Illinois from 1873 to 1877. Other prominent members included Myra Bradwell, the first woman to pass the bar exam in Illinois, and suffragist Elizabeth Boynton Harbert, president of the Illinois Woman's Suffrage Association. Elite members of LISA were concerned about the increased public presence of women and children in Chicago after the Civil War. But the Great Chicago Fire exacerbated their fears about the physical safety and sexual purity of girls who appeared to roam the city in search of work, shelter, and charity. Prevailing gender norms of Victorian culture mandated that girls remain shielded from public life to preserve their innocence and sexual purity before marriage. Unsupervised urban girls therefore signaled social chaos to these nineteenth-century reformers. Following the fire, one LISA member argued that young girls wandering Chicago were "a blot upon our civilization."[8]

Women-led relief groups across the industrial North suggested that girls required greater public investment than their male counterparts. Eliza Archard, a Boston social reformer, wrote in 1867 that city girls who lacked sufficient guardianship or stable housing could not fend for themselves because of "their puny bodies." The public needed to invest in the city girl's shelter, moral guidance, and vocational training while the typical "active, muscular boy" could find housing or work on his own. Concerns about physical frailty and sexual vulnerability point to why states like Massachusetts and Illinois established state reformatories for girls years before making similar investments in boys. "Help the weaker side," Archard urged, "the stronger can take care of itself."[9]

LISA initially focused their relief effort on girls in their teens. They considered girls in this age group too old for housing services provided by Protestant orphanages but too young for marriage. LISA members asserted that teen girls needed the protection and motherly care of "women of influence" to ensure their physical and moral safety in industrial cities. Of chief concern was that girls in their teens would inevitably turn to prostitution without women's maternal protection. In the popular imagination, the young prospective sex worker was weak, unsupervised, and easily corrupted. "Take an average city girl with her weak, white hands," worried Archard of the public girls in Boston. "What will become of this helpless potato sprout?" As Archard suggested, nineteenth-century relief organizations assumed the most vulnerable "street waifs" had "white hands." Those worthy of relief were imagined as white, chaste, and English-speaking girls who were innocent victims of parental poverty or death.[10]

The politically connected leadership of LISA spent five years raising funds among fellow clubwomen to open a home and training school for "homeless and dependent" girls. In 1877, they opened the Illinois Industrial School for Girls in a former Union veterans' home on the border between Chicago and Evanston. Nineteenth-century reformers often used the term "industrial school" to convey vocational training as well as modern values of industriousness and efficiency. The two-story brick building originally had beds for sixty girls, who had two hours of regular school instruction in the afternoon. The remainder of their days were devoted to prayer and domestic instruction in cooking, sewing, and housekeeping. Financial donations by Chicago clubwomen with illustrious last names like Van Buren, Pullman, McCormick, and Palmer supported maintenance of the school—building renovations, food supplies, teacher salaries—for the next half century.[11]

The Illinois Industrial School was designed for white urban girls who lacked housing or sufficient parental guardianship for a variety of reasons. Girls in their teens were brought to the institution by local police officers, teachers, or sometimes their own parents, who needed temporary caretaking for their daughters while they found better housing or stable work. Some girls had lost their caretakers. Others were children of widowed single parents who relied on the entire family to sell candy on street corners or beg for change. Nearly all these girls were daughters of white American or European immigrant parents. These were girls like Mamie Davis, who at age eleven was sentenced to the school by a county judge for parental neglect. Young white girls like Davis epitomized the popular image of the racialized "worthy poor" street waif in need of shelter and education for her own safety and sexual purity. LISA enforced a quota on Black girls when they first opened before banning non-white girls entirely at the turn of the century.[12]

As school president, Beveridge structured the institution as both an educational and carceral institution from its founding. LISA members paid the salary of a former Chicago public school teacher who taught the standard curriculum offered in the city's primary schools for two hours a day. But girls could not come and go or see their families as they pleased. Beveridge and her colleagues referred to girls not as students but as their "inmates." In the early years of the institution, LISA members had no legal right to incarcerate girls dropped off by police officers, school officials, or parents. No state law restricted parents from retrieving their daughters or prevented girls from leaving the school of their own accord. Administrators incarcerated girls for two years despite lacking legal grounds to do so.[13]

Beveridge helped draft a bill for the state legislature to keep girls legally confined to the school. The Girls' Industrial Schools Act of 1879 required institutional oversight by a majority-female board of trustees (formerly, LISA) who assumed parental rights over girls once they were formally sentenced to the institution by county courts. The act mandated at least six-month sentences for girls under the age of eighteen. The Girls' Industrial Schools Act kept the school under LISA's private leadership but provided a public funding stream from local counties to support their work. Illinois counties paid $10 a month per girl in support of her clothing, food, and education supplies. The institution underwent regular inspections from the State Board of Charities to retain its accreditation and funding. The Girls' Industrial Schools Act gave Beveridge and her colleagues leadership over the first state-funded carceral school for Illinois children.[14]

The Girls' Industrial Schools Act also cemented normative behaviors of urban girlhood in Illinois law. The act provided the state's earliest definition of a "dependent child" two decades before the nation's first juvenile court opened in Chicago at the turn of the century. The 1879 law defined a girl as "dependent" on the state—and therefore in need of institutional care—if she lacked parental guardianship due to abandonment, drunkenness, or death. The state also classified girls as dependents for a list of ambiguous public behaviors like wandering alleys, hanging out in brothels, and "consorting with vicious persons." Girls found begging on street corners or "selling any article in public" could also be deemed dependent on the state by county court officials. This definition of dependency encompassed nearly all seemingly unsupervised activities of urban girls. The act placed new boundaries around girlhood by restricting girls' legal access to urban spaces.[15]

Illinois state law placed looser boundaries around urban boyhood. Four years later, women's groups helped accredit a brother institution for white wayward boys in the farming town of Glenwood, Illinois. The Boys' Manual Training School Act of 1883 reiterated the earlier definition of a dependent child, thus cementing the state's ability to incarcerate boys who challenged the middle-class ideal of a protected childhood. Yet the state placed fewer restrictions on boys' confinement to the Illinois Manual Training School for Boys (later the Glenwood Manual Training School). County courts could sentence dependent boys between the ages of ten and sixteen to the institution. Girls, in contrast, were sentenced up to age eighteen. School trustees could legally discharge boys from the Glenwood school at any age if doing so was "for the good of the boy." Administrators released boys if they found an apprenticeship opportunity, a job, or if they wanted to return to school. In other words, boys could prove their lack of dependency—their manhood—at varying ages. Girls could not do likewise. Under state law, girls were only released into the "respectable home" of an employer, relative, adoptive family, or husband. School trustees could otherwise retain parental control over female inmates until their twenty-first birthdays. Both conditions of release lengthening their period of girlhood dependency on the state.[16]

These first state-funded schools for dependent children joined a growing number of institutions designed to "protect" urban children from negative social conditions associated with poor and working-class urban families. In the late nineteenth century, states invested more resources into institutions for girls than boys. By 1880, at least a dozen states funded "industrial schools" for girls run by women. Almost all were in the Northeast and Midwest near large manufacturing centers in Massachusetts, New York, Pennsylvania, and Ohio. These state governments founded industrial schools on a centuries-old legal doctrine exported from English common law known as *parens patriae*. Translated roughly as "parent of the nation," *parens patriae* justifies a state's power to assume parental control over those deemed incapable of caring for themselves. For urban reformers, signs of non-normative childhood—loitering on public streets, playing in dirty alleyways, earning wages—justified the transference of parental power away from actual parents to maternal state actors like Beveridge and LISA. Illinois officials accredited additional carceral schools for boys and girls over the next three decades to expand the state's parental power over urban children. By 1909, Illinois carceral schools confined roughly 7,700 children on any given day.[17]

LISA established the first state-funded carceral school for children in Illinois to protect "worthy poor" white girls from urban disorder. Their school reform required legal reform through the new category of "dependent" childhood. Women's groups used schools like the Illinois Industrial School for Girls and sister institutions across the urban North to both invest in child welfare and police urban girlhood through incarceration.

Little Housekeepers

Carceral schools for girls emphasized domestic instruction as the cornerstone of their curriculum. The board of trustees of the Illinois Industrial School for Girls was responsible for providing inmates with basic public school training in reading, writing, and arithmetic. Under the Girls' Industrial Schools Act, they also offered mandatory training in "domestic vocations" so girls could "assist in their own support" when released. Trustees emphasized cooking and housekeeping skills for "dependent" inmates. These were considered essential skills for girls to perform paid labor as live-in domestic servants or unpaid domestic work as helpful daughters and future wives. Across the urban North, women who ran girls' industrial schools also suggested that domestic education could counteract their exposure to the "vice" associated with city street culture. The founder of the first industrial school for girls in Manhattan, Protestant reformer Emily Huntington, argued that domestic education kept girls focused on "the womanly virtues of the future" rather than "the questionable amusements of the streets." Domestic education provided moral order for girls by keeping them disciplined against unstructured urban leisure.[18]

Training girls for domesticity also solved a major labor anxiety of middle- and upper-class white women known as the "servant problem." The employment of house staff was a hallmark of middle- and upper-class domestic life in the nineteenth century. In the 1870s, however, women and girls in the most desirable demographic for live-in servants—young, white, English speaking—were quickly leaving the field behind. These working-class women and girls preferred the structured hours and regular pay of the public workforce, which opened rapidly for women across the northern Manufacturing Belt. Young women and girls who migrated to northern cities in the 1870s and 1880s pursued new opportunities in the light manufacturing and clerical sectors. Between 1870 and 1900, the number of wage-earning women who worked as domestic servants dropped from nearly 70 percent to 33 percent. Meanwhile, the number of women and girls in light manufacturing quadrupled.[19]

Young working girls were happy to leave domestic service behind. Living under the constant supervision of employers was grueling and demoralizing. The round-the-clock expectations of live-in service provided little free time for urban workers to spend with family and friends. An 1889 survey of nearly seven hundred New York City servants found that a lack of free evenings was a primary reason for women's distaste for the work. As one young servant explained, tending to employer needs day and night was degrading for "self-respecting girls" who wanted control over their leisure time on evenings and weekends. The wages were also low, averaging around three dollars a week for most full-time domestics. But some young workers chose to make even less in factories and warehouses in exchange for more freedom. As one young servant explained: "The reason why more women choose other work is they would rather work all day and be done with it and have evenings for themselves." Another summarized why working girls preferred factory work to live-in service: "so that her life may be her own."[20]

This rejection of domestic service raised a series of cultural concerns for women in the employing classes. Urban housewives feared that working-class girls had alienated themselves from domesticity and lost the opportunity to practice homemaking skills they would later need as mothers. "I don't see how they could perform their household duties as wives, or understand what sort of mothers they would make," worried one Chicago housewife in 1873. Wealthier women also felt their own domestic lives destabilized by the exodus of servants from their homes. They lamented that the shrinking pool of available live-in servants lacked the training and social customs they expected from staff in efficiently run households. One Chicago woman complained in 1876 about "the countless number of girls offering their service in the city" who were not "competent" in household responsibilities or manners. "This class of girl possess such a remarkably small amount of skill," she wrote to the *Chicago Tribune*.[21]

Carceral schools for girls mandated domestic service training at the exact moment that white working-class girls pursued wages elsewhere. At the Illinois Industrial School, inmates devoted at least half their school days to domestic training and domestic service to the institution. Trustees and donors equipped the building with workrooms where girls practiced cooking, place setting, laundry, canning, and sewing. After morning prayers, girls received a "common school education" from a former Chicago public school teacher whose salary was partially paid by clubwomen on the board of trustees. After lunch, girls continued cooking, housekeeping, and table-setting lessons that stretched into the evenings with institutional chores like laundry and meal prep for fellow inmates.

Domestic lesson plans were explicitly linked to the desired duties of a well-trained and well-mannered servant. Chicago clubwoman Harriet J. Willard published domestic service textbooks between 1880 and 1882 for use at the Illinois Industrial School. Willard was a member of the most influential women's club in Chicago, the Chicago Woman's Club (CWC). The book series, titled Familiar Lessons for Little Girls: For Industrial Schools and for Homes, devoted chapters of instruction to subjects like place setting, bed making, cooking, washing kitchen dishes, and lighting kerosene lamps. A chapter titled "How to Talk" instructed girls to never use slang or "loud speaking," and to cultivate "quiet, gentle tones of voice" in the home. The second volume of Willard's textbook series devoted an entire chapter to the proper custom of answering a doorbell. Willard advised future servant girls to make sure their hands were clean before opening the door to inquire: "Who shall I say wishes to see the lady?"[22]

The youngest girls practiced these skills during "kitchen garden" classes. A play on the term "kindergarten," Emily Huntington pioneered the kitchen garden class at the Wilson Industrial School for Girls in Manhattan in the 1870s. Huntington argued that industrial schools could use games and play to prepare girls as young as three for domesticity. Girls in kitchen gardens practiced setting the table for a tea party, served pretend meals to dolls, and swept the floor to the beat of music. Competitive games where girls raced through domestic duties while singing were common in kitchen garden classes. At the Illinois Industrial School, girls under the age of fourteen practiced setting the table in the evening as quickly as possible while singing the lyrics: "As quick as you're able; / Set neatly the table . . . / First lay the table cloth square; / Napkins arranged with due care."[23]

This instruction for "little housekeepers" extended beyond carceral schools in American cities. The nation's largest women's group, the Woman's Christian Temperance Union (WCTU), funded free kitchen garden schools in at least fifteen cities during the 1880s. President of the WCTU's Kitchen Garden Committee, Mary McClees, explained in an 1883 article that protecting urban girls from moral corruption was "the special aim" of the evening schools. Kitchen gardens taught girls that idleness was "sinful" and instilled values of cleanliness, virtue, and hard work. She wrote of one kitchen garden school in which working-class girls arrived "untidy and rude." Just one evening of education reformed the girls as "neat and polite." She explained how a group of aimless girls who loitered on street corners attended one of their Baltimore kitchen gardens. The girls found jobs as domestic servants after their education and were "saved from vice." Like industrial schools for dependent girls, McClees suggested that the WCTU's kitchen gardens were an investment in protecting worthy poor white daughters from sexual corruption.[24]

Clubwomen invested their own money in kitchen garden programs to solve this "girl problem" and the "servant problem." One of Chicago's most influential clubwomen and philanthropic reformers, Ellen Martin Henrotin, founded the Kitchen Garden Association in 1883. Henrotin was president of the CWC and wife to the late founder of the Chicago Stock Exchange. Funded by CWC members, Henrotin's network of kitchen garden

Little Kitchen Garden Maids

"Little Kitchen Garden Maids" in a Kitchen Garden Association school, 1893 (*Chicago Tribune*, courtesy of ProQuest Historical Newspapers)

schools convened in Protestant churches and elementary schoolhouses on weekday evenings. Henrotin also viewed kitchen gardens as an investment in girlhood "morality." Fellow clubwomen supported the schools to ensure the next generation of well-trained house staff. Dr. Annie Hungerford White, a physician and Chicago clubwoman, argued in 1891 that Chicago homes were "dominated by ignorance" due to the lack of dedicated training for live-in servants. Writing in the *Journal of Industrial Education*, White complained that the only schools that taught girls "to earn an honest living" were carceral like the Illinois Industrial School. All urban girls should have access to domestic training so every urban home could benefit from expert service. "We want cooks and maids for the masses," she wrote. "We want a hundred women who can cook a beef-steak or boil a potato."[25]

Clubwomen like White did not want "maids for the masses," however. They wanted well-trained white staff for middle- and upper-class homes like their own. In the industrial North, the WCTU opened kitchen garden schools near European immigrant communities hoping to attract American-born daughters. Only two WCTU kitchen garden schools—both in Louisville, Kentucky—trained Black girls for service. Almost all of these schools, however, were poorly attended because girls and their families were uninterested in professionalizing the service field. In 1890, for example, the Kitchen Garden Association established an evening school specifically for girls already employed in their homes as servants. Members encouraged fellow clubwomen to send their servants to the school to learn new cooking skills, sewing techniques, and "civilized" decorum for middle-class service. The school closed after less than a year because clubwomen's servants refused to attend.[26]

By rejecting domestic service, working-class girls claimed their right to some of the privileges of a middle-class life. They prioritized free weekday evenings to spend with friends, shop, and experience leisure. They pursued jobs in shops and offices for more autonomy with their time and to feel less degraded while they labored. During the kitchen garden movement, women in the employing classes noticed these preferences and criticized working-class white girls for their sense of entitlement to a higher status of employment. In an 1876 letter to the *Chicago Tribune*, a Chicago housewife blamed the "servant problem" on the arrogance of white American girls. These girls thought too highly of themselves, feeling "so *genteel* to stand behind a counter." The woman argued that domestic labor would keep girls respectable and prepare them to later care for their own homes. But these were not working girls' priorities.[27]

Wealthy white women founded the Illinois Industrial School to remove "worthy poor" girls from their urban communities and direct their labor toward housekeeping. Working-class girls in Chicago recognized these efforts as self-serving. In 1876, a former domestic servant weighed in on the so-called "servant problem" in a letter to the *Chicago Tribune*. She explained that she left her job as a live-in servant because of grueling working conditions under the employment of a woman she identified as "Mrs. F." Her pay was less than three dollars a week, and she had no free weekday evenings. The writer did not know exactly how Mrs. F spent her days, but suspected she was "the head of some charitable institution" where "lady friends" provided for the city's poor. She argued that women like Mrs. F were wrong to imply that training could solve the servant problem. Servants pursued wages elsewhere because women like Mrs. F had no regard "for poor girls' feelings."[28]

The kitchen garden movement was largely unsuccessful due to the unpopularity of domestic work among women's target audience of young white American-born girls from the working class. No record exists of the Kitchen Garden Association in the twentieth century. The WCTU schools also shuttered during the 1890s. Similar efforts at professional "schools of housekeeping" for domestic servants were poorly attended in northern cities like Boston, Philadelphia, and New York. Women across the industrial North failed to convince girls to give up weekday evenings to train for a job they did not want. Only in carceral schools where girls were forced to perform domestic labor did the kitchen garden model persist into the twentieth century.²⁹

Domesticating the Delinquent Girl

Clubwomen argued that education for domestic service could also reform girls convicted of crimes in the industrial North. During the 1890s, neighbors of the Illinois Industrial School complained about the increase of girls with "unruly conduct" confined to the institution. A nearby woman wrote a letter to the governor alleging that girls flirted with men through the windows using "very foul and indecent" language. One neighbor expressed her concern that some of the girls confined to the institution were sexually immoral—"a disgrace to the neighborhood"—and another claimed the school was "a breeding place for vice." Clubwomen shared these concerns. They argued that county courts had increasingly sent girls to the institution who were not vulnerable "dependents" in need of care but "delinquents" who required reform. In 1893, clubwomen Ellen Martin Henrotin and Emma Gilson Wallace spearheaded an effort to open a separate institution for delinquent girls. Henrotin and Wallace were both well-connected CWC members who served on the prestigious Women's Auxiliary of the World's Columbian Exposition that year. Two months after the Chicago's World's Fair opened in 1893, Henrotin and Wallace secured $75,000 from the state legislature to open a new "training school" for the "female juvenile offender."³⁰

Henrotin and Wallace organized the State Guardians for Girls to oversee this new institution. Like LISA, the State Guardians helped craft a new legal category of urban girlhood in their promotion of a separate carceral school for delinquent girls. An 1893 state law authorized the State Guardians to select and purchase land for the Illinois State Training School for Girls. "Delinquent" inmates of the Illinois State Training School were defined as girls between ages ten and eighteen who committed crimes that would result in imprisonment if committed by adult women. Many behaviors associated with criminal offenses, however, were indistinguishable from behaviors listed as signs of "dependency" in the Girls' Industrial Schools Act of 1879. For example, the 1879 law described the dependent girl as "a wanderer through streets and alleys, and in other public places." Virtually the same definition defined the criminal offense of "vagrancy." The 1879 law classified girls "found in a house of ill-fame" (brothel) as dependents in need of state protection. Yet sex work ("prostitution") or sexual activity ("incorrigibility") were crimes that resulted in imprisonment. What distinguished a girl

Ellen Martin Henrotin (1847–1922), c. 1890 (Library of Congress, Manuscript Division, National American Woman Suffrage Association records)

found in a brothel (dependent) from a girl deemed to be working in one (delinquent)?[31]

Legal distinction between dependency and delinquency often hinged on the subjective judgments of police officers and court officers. In an all-white legal system, racial bias dictated this assessment. Court officials consistently found Black girls "delinquent" for circumstances construed as signs of dependency among white children, such as wandering the streets unsupervised (vagrancy) or begging on street corners (public nuisance). Less than 2 percent of Illinois residents were Black when the Illinois State Training School opened in 1893. Yet ten of the fifty-nine girls confined to the school in its inaugural year were Black (17 percent). The Illinois Industrial School, which always catered to white American-born girls, banned Black girls after the State Guardians established their separate reformatory for "delinquents" in 1893. The industrial school for "dependent" girls remained whites-only at least through the 1920s. Illinois women's groups therefore contributed to the criminalization of Black girlhood at the turn of the twentieth century. Discrimination from court officials was only half the issue. Often, court officials sent Black children to institutions for "delinquents" because the women who ran schools for "dependents" enforced racial quotas or outright bans.[32]

The State Guardians for Girls assumed parental control over delinquents sentenced to the Illinois State Training School after 1893. As trustees of the institution, they were also required to train inmates for "domestic vocations" so girls could "earn an honest livelihood" when released or paroled from the institution. Court officials sentenced girls for a minimum of one year, during which time they received "a good English education" from two former Chicago public school teachers for three hours each day. The rest of their time was devoted to domestic work in one of five departments: sewing, laundry, cooking, meal serving, and housekeeping. The forced domestic service of inmates provided necessary labor to keep the institution running and save taxpayer money. This labor also supported the social reform goals of the State Guardians, who viewed domestic training as both morally and economically essential for white urban girls during the servant crisis. Indeed, most inmates were white with American or European immigrant parents despite the disproportionate percentage of Black inmates.[33]

Members of the State Guardians for Girls argued that delinquent girls needed to learn "laws of the home" far away from the distractions of industrial Chicago. The Illinois State Training School for Girls was housed in a former elementary school in the South Loop of Chicago from 1893 to 1898 while the State Guardians searched for a site to build the state reformatory. Members complained about frequent rebellions and acts of resistance by inmates at the downtown location. In addition to Mamie Davis's rebellion in 1895, the State Guardians reported that girls hung out the windows during class and asked men to throw them cigarettes. Some inmates started small fires in the sewing and laundry rooms to avoid domestic service. They snuck out of their windows at night and ran away to families and friends. These acts of resistance, documented in state archives, offer glimpses of how girls pushed back against a growing system of state-funded juvenile detention. For the State Guardians, the rebellions showed the necessity of moving the institution to a remote location where girls had fewer opportunities to escape. In an 1893 interview with social worker Julia Lathrop, Charlotte Holt of the State Guardians argued these discipline problems stemmed from the school's location on a busy intersection with "street windows on all sides" where "passersby may look and speak." Holt reasoned that the city presented too many distractions and temptations for girls prone to rowdy behavior and flirtation. She wanted the school to reopen on a large campus in the rural countryside, where girls could focus on "the comforts of home life."[34]

Relocating the Illinois State Training School addressed twin problems associated with girlhood delinquency at the turn of the century. The State Guardians echoed earlier women's groups that the city posed moral dangers to delinquent girls that could derail their transition into respectable womanhood through sexual corruption. On the other hand, reformers viewed delinquent girls as socially dangerous in themselves due to presumptions about their sexual immorality. Into the twentieth century, county courts sentenced inmates to the State Training School for Girls on vague criminal charges like "immorality" or "incorrigibility," which were legal euphemisms for sexual activity. Between 1904 and 1927, over 80 percent of girls who appeared before Chicago court officials were convicted of these crimes. Victims of rape and incest were also criminalized by county courts for their own abuse and incarcerated for "moral offenses." Reformers and city officials associated premarital sex—whether consensual or coerced—with vice, prostitution, the spread of sexually transmitted diseases, and the breakdown of urban families. One Cook County judge therefore blamed delinquent girls for bringing "crime, disease, sin and misery" to the city of Chicago. The Illinois State Training School protected delinquent girls from the city and protected the city from delinquent girls.[35]

The Illinois State Training School reopened in 1898 in the farming town of Geneva, Illinois, thirty-five miles west of Chicago on the Fox River. The State Guardians organized the school in a "cottage plan" in which groups of inmates—called "families"—lived in cottages scattered across the rural school grounds. The cottage plan was used in the nation's first state school for delinquent girls, Lancaster Industrial School for Girls in Massachusetts, and became the model for incarcerating delinquent girls and adult women by the turn of the century. Residential quarters were often racially segregated. In Geneva, administrators reserved two cottages by the turn of the century for Black inmates located on the opposite side of the grounds. At the center of the ninety-four-acre campus sat a schoolhouse and chapel for Sunday services. Administrative buildings and workrooms for sewing,

Postcard from the State Training School for Girls in
Geneva, Illinois, c. 1910 (author's collection)

cooking, laundry, and canning sat on the periphery of the campus. The State Training School at Geneva was the only state-run institution for delinquent girls in Illinois for the next eighty-five years.[36]

School officials argued that education for "domestic vocations" had the power to reform girlhood delinquency. Margaret Ray Wickens, a wealthy philanthropist and temperance activist, served as the institution's first superintendent. She explained in 1895 that daily domestic work refined girls' character by teaching values like "moral discipline," "self-restraint," and "the maintenance of order." Wickens asserted that this training could help the "moral offender" prepare for respectable womanhood. Inmates sentenced to the State Training School were not yet "hardened criminals" incapable of change. Rather, inmates were "girls of mistakes" who could become decent women under the right moral supervision and vocational guidance.[37]

The State Guardians' trust in education to reform girlhood delinquency was a departure from the strategies of earlier Protestant reformers. Antebellum reform groups generally viewed sexually active girls as inherently immoral and incapable of uplift. The State Guardians did not describe their inmates as "ruined women" requiring removal from society. Rather, they emphasized girls' inchoate state of development—their girlhood— which required protection and educational support. The State Guardians described their work as forward-thinking, even radical, in a legal system that continued to punish children as adults and offered few public resources for the "fallen" woman. In a letter to the governor, the State Guardians explained that the Illinois State Training School was a new type of institution infused with "a liberal and progressive spirit" that cultivated "the latent good" in delinquent girls.³⁸

Members defended their practice of incarcerating girls as essential to this progressive initiative. But parents resisted their daughters' confinement to the State Training School and made attempts to free them from the institution. Chicago mothers wrote to the governor's office defending their parenting abilities and asked local aldermen and lawyers to write character references on their behalf. According to the State Guardians, these requests caused "a great deal of annoyance." In the 1890s, progressive governor John Peter Altgeld often sided with mothers and ordered the State Guardians to release girls into the care of their families when requested. Administrators urged him to reconsider. Ophelia Amigh, another temperance activist born in the Midwest, served as superintendent when the institution relocated to Geneva in the 1890s. She ran the institution for nearly two decades. In an 1896 letter to Governor Altgeld, Amigh argued that removing girls from "their old dangerous surroundings" helped ensure they were "educated in the right direction." In one exchange preserved in the state archives, she protested Altgeld's pardon of a sixteen-year-old girl named Nora. According to Amigh, Nora became delinquent while working in a factory, where she "fell into bad company." Amigh blamed Nora's mother for her sexual delinquency, explaining that Nora was unsupervised because her mother worked outside the home. She argued that Nora would be "thrust in the way of temptation" if released into the care of her wage-earning mother. Nora could only become "a respectable woman" under the maternal guidance of the State Guardians for Girls.³⁹

Amigh's letters to Governor Altgeld conveyed a common assumption that the moral failings of girls were the result of their negligent working-class mothers. Under the logic of *parens patriae*, this practice of "mother blame" justified the transference of parental care away from actual mothers to maternal state actors like Amigh. Doing so had real consequences for urban families. Nora worked in a factory before her delinquency charge, likely because her family relied on her wages to help pay for housing, food, and clothing. Amigh ignored this material reality. She suggested that Nora's domestic education and moral reform were more important than Nora's contributions to her family.⁴⁰

The Illinois State Training School reinforced state investment in reforming troublesome girls through forced domestic education and labor. The law establishing this carceral school outlined a new category of urban girlhood—the "delinquent"—that city officials used to remove girls from their families and urban surroundings. The State Guardians for Girls also mandated that their inmates engage in domestic service to counteract delinquency and encourage chastity. As members of the employing class, it is no surprise that the State Guardians viewed their own homes as the model environment to teach respectable womanhood. Amigh employed one white American-born servant at the turn of the century. Henrotin oversaw the work of three Irish girls who lived with her family in 1900. For the State Guardians, girls who moved outside this labor system were socially dangerous and in need of redirection toward supervised wage earning in the private home.[41]

Sexuality and Indentured Servitude

Women in carceral school management also controlled girls' labor outside their institutions through employment placement and "indentured" parole. Throughout the 1880s, Helen Mar Judson Beveridge oversaw the placement of girls as head of the Home and Indenture Committee at the Illinois Industrial School for "dependent" girls. This use of the word "indenture" is telling. Beveridge paroled girls from the institution as literal "indentured servants" in private homes. Girls were not free agents who could set their own wages or employment conditions once they were on parole. Rather, employers made contracts with the institution for the indenture of paroled inmates as house staff. According to Beveridge's annual reports, some girls attended night school or worked in stores and offices while paroled from the institution. But Beveridge released most girls into positions as live-in servants or indentured them through contract with the institution. In 1888, thirty-one of the forty-eight girls were placed in "respectable homes" as paid house staff (65 percent). Prospective employers wrote letters to Beveridge requesting she refer well-trained servants from the carceral school. One letter requested Beveridge send "a young, good girl" to a couple in the countryside "who wish a good servant." Letters of request and "help wanted" ads for domestic servants often specified desired personality traits like "neat" and "respectable," which were code words for white and chaste. Beveridge was overwhelmed by the abundance of requests from prospective employers seeking white American-born servants from the school. "Many applications for girls cannot be met at all," she admitted in 1886.[42]

Beveridge also reviewed requests from couples hoping to adopt younger "dependent" girls and men interested in marrying them. Prospective parents also requested white and English-speaking girls who would serve as helpful daughters in their home. Like prospective employers, couples stressed their interest in adopting a white daughter who would perform domestic tasks like laundry and housekeeping for free. A Civil War veteran wrote to Beveridge requesting "a bright, intelligent girl, 12 years old, American" to help his wife with chores. Men looking for young housewives made similar requests to Beveridge to release girls into their care, promising financial support in exchange for their wife's unpaid labor as housekeeper and cook. These letters reveal that Beveridge did not merely serve as president of a benevolent home and training school for destitute girls. She also worked as a labor and marriage broker for the institution. She used her leadership role to connect middle- and upper-class families with domestic help, both paid and unpaid, on the assumption that inquiring men and women would offer financial security to dependent girls in exchange for their labor.[43]

Amigh extended her maternal control over delinquent girls by instituting a parole system at the State Training School for Girls in Geneva, Illinois. Reformers in the industrial North promoted parole as a progressive reform that helped incarcerated men and women transition back into society. By the turn of the century, trustees of the Illinois State Training School allowed some inmates to live with parents or relatives while on parole and attending public school, night classes, or working in family businesses. Annual reports suggest most parolees were placed as live-in domestic servants. Amigh viewed the public workforce as morally dangerous for girls, especially those suspected of "sexual delinquency." Female workers in factories, shops, and warehouses interacted with male coworkers and managers with whom they could engage in coerced or consensual sex. These workplaces were also located near sites of commercialized nightlife and "vice," another moral threat to the working-class girl. For these reasons, reformers like Amigh assumed the domestic sphere was the safest work environment for girl parolees.[44]

The State Guardians had a strict protocol for paroling delinquent girls as live-in servants. Due to their fears of sexual impropriety, Amigh gave employers a pamphlet with advice on how to keep their servants "moral." Titled "Suggestions for Employers," the pamphlet asked employing women to submit monthly reports on whether girls were "improving morally" while working in their homes. The State Guardians instructed women to keep girls focused on their futures by suggesting: "don't talk about the past with her" and "don't tempt her." They warned employers that girls should have limited interaction with men. If men lived in the house where a girl was paroled to work, school officials advised that her room be as far away as possible from the man and inaccessible without the employing matron's knowledge. The pamphlet stressed the importance of protecting girls' sexual purity: "This is the most important feature in all your duties."[45]

These suggestions may reflect the State Guardians' genuine interest in protecting girls from sexual violence. Working in a private home created ample opportunity for sexual abuse. Yet the State Guardians did not openly discuss this reality. On the contrary, their records reveal a blind faith in the heightened security of the home for working girls. Amigh often included letters from parolees and released inmates in her annual reports as evidence that domestic service reformed delinquent girls into "useful respectable women." These letters implied chastity, such as one parolee's letter describing her life as a live-in servant with descriptors like "pure" and "sweet." A former inmate wrote in 1906 that she "would never think of working in a factory again" because factory girls "get in with all kinds of people and go to the bad if they are not careful.... I write this because I have found it out to be true." The former inmate concluded: "Give me house work above all other kinds ... the girl is always respected." The letters—each strategically chosen by Amigh for publication—conveyed the message that domestic service work supervised by women could protect girls' sexual purity.[46]

Women's anxieties about sexual purity led them to police the labor of girls both inside and outside the institution. The parole system also allowed school administrators to outsource inmate labor to women in need of live-in help. Like the Illinois Industrial School, the State Training School addressed the "servant problem" by connecting employers with trained workers. Employers paid parolee wages directly to the institution. The State Guardians returned only some of these wages to girls "for her own uses." Annual reports of the State Training School suggest that the amount returned to paroled workers varied based on the position and the girl. In one report, Amigh implied that the amount returned to parolees was determined by her subjective assessment of the girl's trustworthiness to spend the wages wisely. She justified the withholding of wages as necessary to cover expenses like parolee travel from the institution to their workplace. The institution likely profited from this system of outsourced domestic labor as well.[47]

Race and "Respectable" Labor

Women in carceral school reform stopped promoting live-in service work for white "problem girls" in the early twentieth century as the field increasingly became associated with Black women's labor. The first wave of Great Migration families left the Jim Crow South for northern cities in the 1910s. They moved to access better jobs, schools, and the ballot along with freedom from legalized segregation and racial terror. By 1920, more than 50,000

Black southerners settled in Chicago. Black workers faced racial discrimination in hiring despite more civil freedom in the urban North. Outside of Black-owned businesses, migrant women and girls rarely worked in Chicago's shops or offices. Most found jobs in the service field as cooks or maids in private homes, hotels, and institutions. Three out of four wage-earning Black women in Chicago filled these positions by 1920. Like working-class white women, Black migrant women tried to avoid live-in service work due to the lack of autonomy. One Black migrant told a social worker she was "disgusted" when resigned to take a job as a live-in servant in Chicago because she lost her sense of personal freedom.[48]

Urban clubwomen implied that live-in service work was no longer respectable for white working girls as the Great Migration accelerated. Instead, they encouraged white working-class girls to "live out." In 1908, a group of Boston clubwomen organized the Women's Municipal League to train white girls as live-in servants. Ten years later, members actively dissuaded white Boston girls from living in private homes due to their lack of "freedom." One of the group's members, social reformer Marguerite Stockman Dickson, wrote a popular vocational guidance textbook for girls in 1918. Each chapter explored available employment choices for girls and young women like teaching, dressmaking, and nursing. The title of the final chapter, "Marriage," inferred the final stage of a woman's career as well as the expectation that female workers leave paid work behind for the duties of wifedom. In her chapter on domestic service, Dickson cautioned girls against "living in" with their employers, which had become "particularly hard for a self-respecting girl to bear." If girls decided to pursue service work, she recommended they live outside their employer's home to maintain independence and respectability. Dickson did not explicitly link this recommendation to the racialization of live-in service work in northern cities. She did not need to. Across the industrial North, other observers commented on the anti-modern nature of live-in service work with racialized descriptors like "primitive" and "slavery."[49]

In the early twentieth century, a racial division in waged domestic labor emerged between Black servants who "lived in" and white servants who "lived out." White domestic professionals lived outside their employer's home and held domestic titles like nanny, decorator, or social secretary for an employing housewife. Black domestic professionals continued to fill the round-the-clock obligations of live-in cook and parlor maid. Essie Octavia Crockett, who worked as a live-in servant in Washington, DC, in 1918, remembered this racial division of labor between service women in an oral history with historian Elizabeth Clark-Lewis. She recalled that the matron would hire "a white lady to make up her menu for her fancy parties" or hire white women "to do fancy writing for Christmas cards." But these white servants did not really "work" in Crockett's view. "In that house only colored people worked," she explained. Nettie Bass, who migrated to DC from North Carolina in 1909, recalled how white girls were leaving their service jobs as quickly as possible when she arrived to the city. "Young ones? They'd only stay 'til a better job would come along—a store, factory, or office—somewhere would take them." Racial discrimination in the public workforce kept Black migrants like Crockett and Bass out of the public workforce. De facto segregation in the women's workforce also allowed white employers to pay Black servants lower wages, knowing they had limited alternatives for employment.[50]

In the 1910s, social reformers encouraged white working-class girls to enter public fields of labor that were dominated by other white women to maintain their respectability. Jane Addams, who cofounded the Hull House settlement in Chicago's West Side tenement district, wrote in 1912 that men were uninterested in marrying girls who worked as live-in domestic servants due to the social stigma surrounding their labor. Middle-class men did not want a wife who worked "in someone else's kitchen," she wrote, because they found "the entire situation embarrassing." Girls who worked as live-in servants thus threatened their prospects for marriage, the cornerstone of respectable womanhood. Addams suggested that working-class girls pursue positions in dressmaking and millinery shops instead, two needle trades dominated by white American and European women in the 1910s.[51]

Women reformers who ran carceral schools also dissuaded white girls from pursuing live-in service due to increased reports of sexual violence in private homes. Addams, who served on the board of trustees of the Illinois Industrial School for Girls, heard horror stories from former servants through her social work at Hull House. In *A New Conscience and an Ancient Evil* (1912), Addams explained that live-in servants were "easy victims" of sexual assault. She suggested that the threat alone of sexual abuse led to anxiety and even higher suicide rates among live-in servants. These conditions also hurt girls' respectability as potential wives. Addams argued that some men found dating a domestic servant "embarrassing" because they presumed these girls were "ruined" during their employment. Addams encouraged fellow women reformers to reconsider their assumption that private homes were inherently safe for working girls.[52]

Mounting concern for the sexual purity of white domestic servants led to institutional changes in Illinois carceral schools. The whites-only Illinois Industrial School stopped placing girls out as domestic servants by 1906 after reports that some of their former inmates had been sexually assaulted. The State Board of Charities investigated these reports and blamed administrators for their "culpably lax" review of domestic employers. The school also relocated after the state's investigation of their placement policies. In 1908, the board of trustees expanded the institution to a forty-acre campus in Park Ridge, a northwest suburb of Chicago, where inmates lived in "cottages" similar to the Illinois State Training School. Trustees continued to accept only white dependent girls between the ages of ten and eighteen who devoted half their school day to the study of "domestic vocations." But administrators disassociated the goals of this domestic training from the wage-earning duties of a domestic servant. Instead, they argued that domestic education strengthened girls' character and prepared them for marriage and motherhood. Ellen Martin Henrotin served as superintendent when the Illinois Industrial School relocated to Park Ridge. In her first annual report, she explained that the new purpose of teaching "domestic vocations" was to "educate these girls to be good wives, mothers and useful citizens."[53]

Carceral school reformers ignored the threat of sexual violence for Black live-in servants. In fact, many continued to recommend live-in service as a form of moral protection and even delinquency prevention for Black girls in the 1910s. In Chicago, many Black women and girls preferred to pick up "day work" shifts in hotels and rooming houses rather than live with their employers. Day work shifts as cooks and housekeepers offered less stability but more free time and independence. White social reformers in Chicago suggested that these day work shifts were sexually dangerous for Black women and girls. The work seemed morally treacherous because day workers could encounter sex workers or drunken men while housekeeping in hotels and rooming houses. In 1911, a group of Chicago child welfare reformers argued that higher rates of delinquency among Black girls were the result of their preference for day work in "vicious surroundings" like rooming houses. "The colored women . . . do not realize the need of careful training," wrote one reformer. "The fact remains that they will accept a lower wage and live under far less advantageous conditions for the sake of being free at night." In the 1910s, then, some women reformers argued that live-in service was dangerous for white girls but safe for Black girls. Urban independence was recast as acceptable for white working girls, something that could even promote respectably and good character. But working outside the home remained a potential sign of sexual delinquency for Black working-class girls in the minds of white women reformers.[54]

Administrators at the Illinois State Training School reinforced this racialization of working-class girlhood in the 1910s. School administrators made a "radical departure" in the vocational curriculum by introducing new programs for needle trades and office work in 1916, two sectors of the workforce populated by white female workers. Trustees outfitted a new residential cottage for "business girls," who studied shorthand, typing, and published a school newspaper called *The Training School Chat*. They dedicated another residential cottage to "trade girls," who learned dressmaking and millinery skills to earn wages in shops when paroled from the institution. The new vocational programs reflected growing acceptance that white working-class girls would live outside the home before marriage and were entitled to some level of personal financial freedom. Trustees still required these inmates to spend three hours a day in various domestic departments on campus. Much like the Illinois Industrial School, administrators justified this training as useful for future homemaking when girls presumably exited the workforce for marriage.[55]

Domestic service continued to define the mandatory vocational training of Black girls confined to the State Training School in Geneva, Illinois. Black girls made up a growing minority of inmates during the Great Migration of the 1910s and 1920s. Most Black girls sentenced to the institution were arrested on poverty charges or convicted of sexual immorality. By 1920, Black girls accounted for 20 percent of inmates. Administrators housed Black girls in two crowded and segregated residence halls—the Faith and Lincoln cottages—where they did not have access to new vocational classes like office work. Known as the "industrial department," the Faith and Lincoln cottages engaged Black girls in domestic service and institutional housekeeping. These girls spent their days weaving, sewing, and making baskets by the 1910s. They cooked in the school cafeteria and made paper flowers and table decorations to beautify the institution. Their work kept the carceral school running and saved Illinois taxpayers money. When some of the white cottages switched over to trade and white-collar training, trustees renovated girls' residential housing. White inmates not only had new vocational programs but fresh paint, polished floors, and refinished furniture in their living quarters. The furnishings of the Faith and Lincoln cottages—like their curriculum—remained firmly in the past.[56]

Black women reformers established their own institution for "dependent" girls in Illinois during this period of change. Their goal was to protect Black girls from being deemed "delinquent" and sentenced to the remote Illinois State Training School due to lack of alternatives in the juvenile court system. A Black preacher and temperance activist, Amanda Smith, first opened an orphanage for dependent Black children in 1893 about twenty miles south of Chicago in the temperance town of Harvey, Illinois. Under the leadership of social reformer Adah M. Waters, the orphanage became an industrial school in 1912 for Black girls under age eighteen. Waters secured state accreditation of the Amanda Smith Industrial School for Colored Girls under the Girls' Industrial School Act of 1879 so the institution could admit "dependent" girls processed through county courts. Under state law, the Amanda Smith Industrial School also taught girls "domestic vocations" through required courses like cooking and housekeeping. School trustees also modeled the Amanda Smith Industrial School after the principles of Booker T. Washington, who emphasized pragmatic industrial training and cultural respectability at the Tuskegee Institute. By the 1910s, the Amanda Smith Industrial School also offered courses in nursing, hairdressing, and stenography along with domestic instruction. Girls studied a liberal arts curriculum including literature, geography, and African American history. The Amanda Smith Industrial School was the only institution for dependent Black girls in the state that was run by Black women.[57]

Members of LISA and the State Guardians secured government investment in their institutions by leveraging class and racial privileges in defense of white girlhood. The Amanda Smith Industrial School, in contrast, relied on community support through mutual aid organized by local Black women's clubs. The institution was short-lived due to lack of state support. The Amanda Smith Industrial School closed after suffering a devastating electrical fire in 1924 that killed two children. Administrators blamed the fire on an insufficient inspection by the State Board of Charities. When the institution shuttered, Black girls accounted for over 30 percent of inmates confined to the Illinois State Training School. Between 1937 and 1938, Black girls between ages fifteen and eighteen accounted for 75 percent of "delinquents" sentenced to the Illinois State Training School by the Cook County Juvenile Court despite representing less than 5 percent of Chicago's population.[58]

Conclusion

Women carceral school reformers established new state-funded institutions that limited girls' access to urban space and controlled girlhood labor during the Gilded Age and Progressive Era. Reform groups like LISA and the State Guardians for Girls made domestic education a requisite of juvenile justice by arguing that live-in service provided moral protection for white working-class girls. As one LISA member put it, domestic training helped vulnerable girls find work in "comfortable homes" under "good influences."[59] Their interest in protecting urban girls was coupled with a desire to police how and where girls labored during a servant shortage. These institutions—and the new legal categories that supported them—demonstrate the importance of centering girlhood in histories of child welfare, education, and juvenile justice reform. Anxieties about urban working girls specifically fueled the development of carceral institution building across the industrial North.

The women who ran carceral institutions viewed education as their primary engine of reform. They argued that educating girls for domestic labor would have a profound impact on moral development and prepare girls for respectable womanhood. These reformers also used education as a justification for their carceral practices. Ophelia Amigh argued that she *had* to incarcerate girls away from their families to achieve the progressive goals of moral uplift and respectable employment for inmates sent to Geneva, Illinois. Furthermore, these schools blurred the boundary between education and forced labor. "Educating" girls for domestic work involved mandatory and unpaid service to the institution. During the Great Migration, administrators increasingly placed the burden of that unpaid labor to the institution on Black girls.

These women reformers did not achieve their goal of redirecting the labor of white working girls through carceral education. Educating "dependents" for servitude did not solve the servant problem because white women and girls had already exited the field in rapid numbers. Efforts to bring domestic instruction out of the carceral school through kitchen garden programs were short-lived for this reason. Groups like the Kitchen Garden Association could not use education to change worker preferences. They could not control girlhood sexuality or curb large-scale trends in the female labor market. This is not to say, however, that their carceral school reform did not have serious consequences for working-class girls. These carceral schools removed girls from their families, sometimes depriving the families of an essential labor source. Women reformers placed boundaries around girls' legal access to urban space by criminalizing their "dependent" and "delinquent" behaviors. By the 1910s, women in carceral school reform invested in protecting white working girls from sexual abuse in private homes while ignoring the sexual vulnerability of Black girls in domestic spaces. They supported a racial division of domestic labor by encouraging white girls to consider their "dependent" futures as wives while enforcing domestic servitude for Black inmates.

This history of carceral school building highlights the fixation of many white women's groups on policing working-class girlhood through education. Wealthy clubwomen and middle-class social reformers alike demanded educational investment in young white girls to guide them toward what they considered a respectable labor market. Carceral schools were one of a series of educational and institutional reforms targeting white urban girls in this period. In the late nineteenth century, some of these same women gained leadership positions on Chicago's school board to control when and how white working-class girls made their legal transition from school to work.

[CHAPTER TWO]

Fit for Motherhood

Regulating Girlhood Health and Labor in
Chicago Public Schools, 1888–1915

A social worker at the University of Chicago Settlement House, Louise Montgomery, interviewed five hundred American-born girls laboring in the stockyards with their immigrant parents. Her book, *The American Girl in the Stockyards District* (1913), highlighted the physical toll suffered by second-generation girls who worked as meat-packers and factory hands instead of attending public school. Girls as young as twelve suffered from swollen feet, crooked backs, and physical exhaustion from standing all day in packing-houses. Montgomery described one girl who was initially "strong, vigorous, solid" before joining the workforce. After one year in a factory, the girl lost ten pounds and became "nervous, listless." She met another fourteen-year-old girl who was "broken in health" after one year of wage-earning and required bed rest to save her reproductive health. Montgomery concluded that girls under age sixteen were unfit for the physical strain of industrialized labor. In fact, she warned, many American-born girls might never bear children as women after spending "their girlhood employed."[1]

The number of second-generation girls in the industrial workforce skyrocketed at the turn of twentieth century. The children of recent immigrants were most likely to earn wages in their teen years to support their family income under the pressure of urban poverty. Montgomery's study found that 65 percent of immigrant families in the stockyards district took their American-born daughters out of school as soon as they could—often before the legal age of fourteen—because of economic necessity. "You are not a rich American," Montgomery overheard one immigrant mother tell her wage-earning daughter. "You need no education beyond the law." Some immigrant daughters continued to find work as domestic servants in private homes at the time of Montgomery's study. Most filled jobs in the "light" manufacturing sector as seamstresses, milliners, confectioners, machine hands, and meat-packers. These child workers held some of the least stable, poorest paid, and most dangerous positions in the industrial economy.[2]

Child labor reformers looked to public school systems to help protect immigrant daughters from industrial labor across the northern Manufacturing Belt. Women labor activists lobbied for compulsory school attendance laws to curb child employment by keeping students in school until the age of sixteen. These reformers promoted the modern assumption that regular school attendance was essential for a normal, healthy childhood. Their use of public school policy as a child labor deterrent placed distinct boundaries around working-class girls who faced special scrutiny from school officials before entering the workforce. In Chicago, health experts shared the concern of reformers like Montgomery that entering the workforce could wreak havoc on the reproductive health of the "growing girl." Their desire to protect the bodies of working-class immigrant daughters supported the expansion of urban education at the turn of the century through new state attendance laws and public school bureaucracies.[3]

Women labor activists often gendered the child worker and racialized her as white and American born. Montgomery relied on mainstream scientific ideas about eugenics and degeneration to suggest that white American-born girls had the most physically vulnerable bodies because they were the most "civilized." These young workers therefore required the highest protection from the state as future mothers of "the race" who would rear white American citizens. In Chicago, women reformers lobbied for anti–child labor and mandatory school attendance laws that hinged on this logic. Their racialization of the girl worker as "white" suggested that Black girlhood exploitation was nonexistent or, at the very least, outside the scope of public school investment in child welfare.[4]

Education officials reformed the elementary school curriculum to support anti–child labor initiatives and invest in gendered notions of childhood health. The first "physical culture" (physical education) programs taught second-generation girls to avoid strenuous labor and conserve their strength for motherhood. Women health professionals led "hygiene" classes during which immigrant daughters learned the threat of manufacturing jobs to their potential offspring. These curricular reforms relied on narrow metrics of "normal" health to ensure the fitness of American-born girls and their future children. Emerging in concert with child labor restrictions, courses like physical culture demonstrate how urban reformers used both law and curriculum to police girlhood labor at the turn of the twentieth century.[5]

The Failure of the Schools

A group of reform-minded women organized the Illinois Woman's Alliance (IWA) in 1888 to address the brutal work conditions of girls in garment factories. The IWA's first meeting was called by Corrine Stubbs Brown, a public school teacher and socialist reformer who grew up in Chicago before the Civil War. Brown was galvanized to protect young girls from garment factories after reading the "City Slave Girls" exposé in the *Chicago Times* earlier that year. Helen Cusack's undercover reporting drew national attention to the mass employment of first- and second-generation immigrant girls who supported the "ready-made" fashion industry. Chicago had the nation's second largest ready-made clothing industry after New York. Garment factories in these two cities were the largest employers of girl workers under age sixteen. At their organizing meeting, Brown thanked Cusack's journalism for exposing "the conditions surrounding our working girls." She announced: "The exposure of these truths touches us." The meeting attracted a cross-class coalition of women similarly moved by the disturbing press coverage of young girls toiling as underpaid seamstresses. Teachers, wealthy clubwomen, and socialist labor activists joined the IWA to protect working girls from Chicago's "slave-grinding hell holes" through legal reform. They spent the next five years lobbying for state laws that would keep girls out of garment factories and enrolled in public schools.[6]

The IWA worked with Chicago's most politically powerful women's club, the Chicago Woman's Club (CWC), to pass a statewide school attendance law in 1889. The CWC pressured the Chicago Board of Education (BOE) to take school attendance seriously as a child labor preventive throughout the 1880s. The BOE was founded in 1872 to manage school funds and oversee the construction of new schoolhouses as the city expanded. Appointed annually by the mayor, early board members were all wealthy merchants, lawyers, and bankers, whose actions were notoriously corrupt in Gilded Age Chicago. Members were accused of lining their own pockets during construction deals and using public funds to purchase school properties from their personal real estate empires. The CWC petitioned the mayor of Chicago, Republican John A. Roche, to give women seats on the school board in 1887. Ellen Martin Henrotin, who served as CWC president that year, told the press that public schools deserved "the best women in the community" who understood the needs of children better than businessmen.[7]

Urban women in the club movement argued that they were naturally suited to oversee organizations and institutions focused on children by virtue of their socially prescribed roles as mothers. White women's clubs like the CWC successfully leveraged the logic of maternalism to enter new areas of municipal governance at the turn of the twentieth century. CWC members argued that they were naturally fit for leadership in schools, factories, and sanitation services as an extension of their maternal caretaking duties to keep spaces clean, safe, and moral. Henrotin relied on maternalism to gain CWC membership to the Chicago BOE. In 1888, Mayor Roche designated a seat on the BOE for a "woman representative" from the CWC. At least one member of the CWC (sometimes two) sat on the Chicago BOE into the twentieth century. Roche also created new positions for women in school governance at Henrotin's request. He appointed several women as assistant superintendents—including the future first female superintendent of schools, Ella Flagg Young—to oversee the city's growing network of neighborhood public schools.[8]

The IWA successfully strengthened school attendance laws as part of their child labor activism. The state legislature passed the first mandatory attendance law six years earlier that required children between the ages of seven and fourteen to attend school for at least twelve weeks of the year. Chicago's BOE never enforced this law, however, and most parents did not know it existed. With seats on the school board, the CWC worked with the IWA to draft a new state law enforcing regular school attendance. Named after Chicago's Superintendent of Schools Richard Edwards, the Edwards Law of 1889 empowered school boards to hire the first truant officers. These new school officials made house visits, tallied attendance, and even arrested children under the age of fourteen who wandered the streets or earned wages during the school day. The Edwards Law was the state's first serious step toward universal school attendance for children in the primary grades. Truancy enforcement also established a new relationship between public school officials and the state's burgeoning juvenile carceral system. After 1889, children arrested by truant officers could be sentenced to carceral schools if found guilty of dependency or delinquency.[9]

The IWA lobbied for the nation's first anti-sweatshop policy following the Edwards Law, which banned all children under fourteen years old from manufacturing jobs. The Workshop and Factories Act of 1893 did not restrict the working hours of men or boys. The original law did, however, limit the working hours of all women and girls to eight hours a day. The Workshop and Factories Act charged employers who hired children under fourteen or employed girl workers for more than eight hours of a day with a misdemeanor. The law also empowered the governor to enforce these labor restrictions through appointing a state factory inspector. The IWA argued that women factory inspectors were best suited to protect child workers and respond to the complaints of women workers, who were likely victims of sexual harassment and violence in the workplace. In addition to a state factory inspector, Illinois had at least ten assistant factory inspectors by the following year, and at least half of them were women.[10]

Republican Governor John Peter Altgeld appointed Florence Kelley as the first state factory inspector in 1893. Kelley was the thirty-four-year-old

Florence Kelley, ca. 1910–1916 (Records of the National Woman's Party, Manuscript Division, Library of Congress, Washington, DC)

daughter of a Philadelphia abolitionist who helped organize the Republican Party in the 1850s. Like IWA founder Brown, Kelley was a member of the Socialist Labor Party and an outspoken critic of both child labor and industrial capitalism. Kelley was the first woman to hold state-level office in Illinois. She joined a small but growing group of women factory inspectors recently appointed in northern states, including Pennsylvania, New York, and Massachusetts.[11]

Kelley shared the political and social commitments of fellow middle-class women in the urban settlement house movement. Kelley lived at Chicago's Hull House, the nation's first social settlement, while working as state factory inspector. Cofounded by social reformers Jane Addams and Ellen Gates Starr in 1889, Hull House provided a range of social services for immigrant families in Chicago's crowded Nineteenth Ward tenement district. Immigrants could take English classes, use daycare services for their infants, and attend vocational courses in the evenings. In the early twentieth century, Black social reformers founded their own settlement houses that provided social services for Black migrants from the Jim Crow South. Black and white women in the settlement house movement devoted particular attention to addressing child welfare. They worried about high rates of childhood employment and vagrancy, offering opportunities for young people to have recreational opportunities under their guidance. The settlement house movement was largely segregated. White social workers at Hull House invested heaviest in services for eastern and southern Europeans, who represented the city's largest minority groups. They placed the American-born children of immigrants at the center of their reform agendas.[12]

Kelley argued that child labor was physically dangerous for the children of new immigrant families from eastern and southern Europe. In her first report as state factory inspector, Kelley explained that over 20,000 "toiling children" in Chicago continued to leave school for manufacturing jobs despite the IWA's success with the Edwards Law of 1889 and Workshop and Factories Act of 1893. Most of these children were "undersized, rachitic, deformed" from factory labor. Kelley suggested that the physical toll was greatest on girl workers, who spent "their strength beyond reason" resulting in "nervous exhaustion." Kelley recommended the Chicago BOE hire more truant officers and the state hire additional factory inspectors to remove children from industrial workplaces. She worried that working children would be "permanently enfeebled" without greater investment from school and state officials alike. "Children will inevitably fail in the early years of manhood and womanhood," she warned.[13]

Child labor activists like Kelley viewed girls as the most physically and morally vulnerable workers in the industrial economy. Reformers argued that girls could be more easily injured and faced the gendered threat of sexual abuse. In demanding tighter attendance laws, the IWA stated that child labor both "dwarfed the physique" of girls and jeopardized their "womanly purity." Kelley's early reports as state factory inspector included numerous examples of girlhood health problems and physical injury in Chicago factories. In her 1894 report, Kelley compared the health conditions of eighty-five girls and fifty boys working in Chicago at the age of fourteen. Factory workers of both genders suffered from poor sight, anemia, and skin rashes. Girls suffered additional ailments, according to Kelley. They had swollen hands and feet from crimping fabric and using foot-powered sewing machines. Kelley referenced one girl with a "mutilated forefinger" from a sewing machine accident.[14]

Child labor activists highlighted the vulnerability of white girl workers in lobbying for federal anti–child labor legislation in the following decades. Photojournalist Lewis Hine's famous photographs of child mill workers for the National Child Labor Committee (NCLC) in 1908 demonstrate gendered perceptions of the child labor problem. As historian Julia Grant argues, Hine often photographed groups of boys standing together, shoulder to shoulder, staring collectively into the camera lens. While these group shots suggested the magnitude of the child labor problem, they also conveyed a sense of "boys' camaraderie, shrewdness, and even pride." In contrast, Hine usually photographed girls alone on the factory floor surrounded by rows of heavy machinery. These images implied the isolation, vulnerability, and immense physical burdens of industrialized labor experienced by girl workers.[15]

The national anti–child labor movement also racialized the child worker as "white." Hine's famed photographs of the child labor problem depicted white children, rendering the labor of Black children invisible. The young workers highlighted in anti–child labor campaigns reflected a white middle-class vision of vulnerable "worthy poor" children who were deserving of state protection. This racialized conception of child labor was not unique to the industrial North. Southern reformers also agitated to remove white children from manufacturing jobs beginning in the 1880s and lobbied for school attendance laws. Southern child labor and school attendance laws left loopholes that enabled the continued employment of Black children. In 1903, for example, the state legislature of Alabama criminalized the employment of children under twelve in manufacturing jobs unless they were "children of dependent families." Manufacturers in Alabama could legally employ children under the age of twelve if their parents showed signs of "dependency," such as lack of housing, unstable employment, drunkenness, or vagrancy. These poverty markers disproportionately affected Black families in the Jim

Child mill workers photographed by Lewis W. Hine for the National Child Labor Committee, 1908 (Library of Congress, Prints & Photographs Division, National Child Labor Committee Collection)

Crow South. Black children, then, both fell outside the bounds of child labor reform and were deprived the legal privilege of a protected childhood in the process.[16]

Concern for the physical and moral safety of white girl workers galvanized anti-child labor activism in the late nineteenth century. Chicago women's groups like the IWA and CWC viewed child labor as a gendered problem that demanded gendered legal solutions. They argued that state and school officials must work together to keep "worthy poor" girls out of industrial workplaces for their physical safety. Their efforts were part of a growing national movement that centered on white American children. In the years that followed, public schools became a primary site of child labor reform efforts. "Children under 14 years can never be wholly kept out of the factories and workshops until they are kept in school," Kelley argued in 1893. "Surely the weakest point in our whole child labor legislation is the failure of the schools."[17]

Mothers of the Race

The IWA's concern for white working girls also reflected popular medical assumptions about reproductive health and heredity. In the late nineteenth century, medical professionals assumed that female bodies were naturally weaker than male bodies because they had finite reserves of energy. Young women and girls who spent their days standing in factories depleted their limited energy reserves needed for the work of reproduction. Medical professionals encouraged women and girls to conserve their limited strength for the presumed labor of future motherhood. Overextending one's strength could lead to physical and mental ailments that mothers might pass down to their offspring. By the nineteenth-century logic of "degenerative theory," girl workers who depleted their strength in factories not only threatened their own health but the health of future generations.[18]

Medical experts argued that girls going through puberty needed the most rest to protect their reproductive health and avoid degeneration. State Factory Inspector Kelley argued that girls should not work during their "critical years of development" (puberty) for this reason. She suggested that doing so could lead to "pelvic disorders" among girls that were "ruinous to their children in the future." Kelley viewed child labor as dangerous for all children. But child labor was dangerous for girls *and* their future families. In the nineteenth century, doctors advised against working while menstruating due to the depletion of finite energy. They described menstruation as a disability, illness, or temporary disease affecting women and girls. "Every woman should look upon herself as an invalid once a month," wrote one American doctor in an 1871 health book for women. The treatment for the "monthly disability" was rest. Without rest, medical experts assumed that girls would struggle to have healthy pregnancies.[19]

Protecting working girls from degeneration supported the eugenics movement dedicated to encouraging better breeding. Francis Galton, who coined the term "eugenics" in 1883, defined the field as "the science of improving the stock." Eugenics encompassed a wide range of activities in the late nineteenth and early twentieth centuries. Most notorious were restrictive initiatives pushed by white state actors such as forced sterilization and institutionalization. By 1937, thirty-two states passed eugenics laws that led to the forced sterilization of at least 63,000 Americans who were deemed physically or mentally "unfit." But a range of more innocuous policies also fell under the eugenics tent. These additive reforms included medical screenings, advice literature on child welfare, and education programs intended to encourage good breeding.[20]

Eugenics and degenerative theory were malleable ideologies that reformers relied on to promote diverse social agendas in the Progressive Era. White doctors and sociologists used eugenics as the answer to a host of turn-of-the-century racial anxieties. These included fears that mass immigration threatened "the American stock" and panic over the preservation of white "civilization" during US imperialism abroad. As historian Michele Mitchell argues, Black educators and intellectuals also promoted eugenic ideas to avoid "race suicide" by encouraging the biological health of Black families. Conduct manuals and health advice in Black periodicals implied that social factors like poor marital relations, intemperance, or unsanitary homes could lead to degenerative Black children. Child labor reformers also relied on eugenics to promote their goals for social improvement. They argued that school and state officials must protect the American-born daughters of immigrants because they were future "mothers of the race" who would raise white American citizens.[21]

Chicago reformers embraced this logic in defense of the eight-hour workday restriction for women and girls in the Workshop and Factories Act of 1893. State officials argued that "medical investigations" proved that working more than eight hours a day caused "injury to a girl or woman in her sexual function." Overstrained women would rear "mentally degenerate offspring, for whom society must afterward care." This was especially true for "girls and delicate women" who were "deprived of the power to bear children" if forced to work more than eight hours a day. The owner of a box factory in Chicago who relied on girl workers sued the state over this section of the 1893 law. His lawyers argued that limiting the working hours of women and girls violated their Fourteenth Amendment right to personal freedom. The state lost the case against the box factory and that section of the law was overturned. Kelley and her colleagues hoped this attention to physical degeneration would improve the labor lives of women and girls through a shorter workday. She called the court's decision to let girls work more than eight hours a day "cruel and anti-social."[22]

Women labor activists relied on degenerative theory to make arguments for shorter workday laws for women and girls into the twentieth century. In the 1910s, members of the National Women's Trade Union League (WTUL) successfully passed ten-hour workday laws at the state level to protect the reproductive health of women and girls. "A woman's body is unable to withstand strain, fatigue, and privations as well as a man's," argued labor activist Violet Pike in favor of a shortened workday law for women. "The nervous strain resulting from monotonous work can only result in undermining the whole physical structure of the woman.... [It] can destroy the health of women and render them unfit to perform their functions as mothers." As Pike suggested, long hours spent hunching over worktables was considered particularly ruinous for reproductive health by depleting finite energy reserves. "I can't help feeling that no woman should be allowed in the packing houses," agreed Chicago WTUL president Mary Dreier Robinson in 1912. "Having them stand all day working.... It seems too terrible for words."[23]

Child labor reformers asserted that white American-born girls were the most vulnerable to degeneration in the workforce because they were the most civilized. In her study of girl workers in the stockyards, Louise Montgomery argued that immigrant women from eastern and southern Europe ("the hardy immigrant") were naturally better fit for strenuous factory labor. Their American-born daughters, however, faced greater injury not only because of their vulnerable age but because of their "American temperament." Montgomery suggested that American girls were both weaker and more civilized than their parents by virtue of their birthright citizenship. Their need for rest was the result of environmental factors—growing up in America—rather than innate biology as immigrant offspring. According to Montgomery, American-born girls lacked the "vigorous foreign stock" of their parents and therefore needed to reserve their energy for motherhood. For Montgomery, white American-born girls had the weakest physical capacity for industrial labor and therefore required the most protection from the state.[24]

This racialized notion reinforced neglect for the safety of Black girl workers. Century-old stereotypes born out of the enslaving economy shaped white perceptions of Black bodies as inherently stronger and fortified for hard work. White medical professionals also argued that Black girls matured faster, falling back on racist myths about Black women's strength and sexual promiscuity. For these reasons, white observers often assigned greater maturity to Black girls than white girls of the same age. They deemed Black girls physically strong and sexually advanced while white girls were physically weak and sexually vulnerable. As Montgomery alluded, physical weakness and sexual vulnerability were two traits associated with civilized American womanhood. By centering the vulnerability of "civilized" white girls, Montgomery asserted their worthiness of state protection in the workplace and implied that Black girls were thus less vulnerable and less civilized.[25]

The industrial workforce was unquestionably dangerous for all workers at the turn of the century, especially young girls. Roughly 35,000 factory workers died each year in work-related accidents between 1880 and 1900. Some of the era's most notorious tragedies befell industries that employed the youngest and most vulnerable child workers like garment factories. The deadliest example occurred in 1911 when 146 garment workers—mostly Russian and Italian girls in their teens—died in a fire at the Triangle Shirtwaist Factory in New York. Public health officials would document the long-term health consequences of poor ventilation and industrial pollution decades after women like Florence Kelley demanded state investment in the physical well-being of industrial capitalism's youngest workers. But the early legal system that addressed these problems is also significant for promoting flawed science about the physical inferiority of female bodies and the dangers of "strain" to girlhood reproductive health. Child labor activists relied on eugenic ideology to encourage sympathy for the future mothers of white American children who toiled in shops and factories. In doing so, they suggested that the white working girl had the most value to the state and required its greatest investment.[26]

The Work Certificate System

Kelley left Chicago for New York at the turn of the century, where she continued her child labor activism. After she moved, Kelley's colleagues at Hull House continued her fight to strengthen school and labor laws in protection of girl workers. In 1901, Jane Addams organized a Women's Committee on Child Labor to investigate Chicago industries that employed girl workers in violation of the Edwards Law and Workshop and Factories Act. The committee of Hull House social workers and clubwomen visited factories, shops, and warehouses employing workers under fourteen and published a report detailing the physical dangers in their workplaces. Their study devoted particular attention to girl workers in box and garment factories. They visited one box factory that employed 400 girls in their early teens and were outraged to see girls stand all day assembling boxes. Standing all day in hunched positions, they wrote in their report, caused girls to "dwarf their physical and mental growth."[27]

Addams's committee drafted two bills based on their report, both of which passed the state legislature in 1903. The Compulsory Attendance Law of 1903 required students to attend either public or parochial school until the age of fourteen. The Child Labor Law of 1903 barred most employers from hiring children until the age of fourteen. Notably, the laws introduced a new partnership between state and school officials to regulate the employment of children between the ages of fourteen and sixteen. To work at the legal age of fourteen, child laborers needed a "school-to-work certificate" that verified their age and history of school attendance. The state required work certificates for all compensated labor, whether industrial or work in a store, office, or hotel. The Chicago BOE issued work certificates to prospective child workers. The certificates required the signature of both the superintendent of schools and the state factory inspector. Without a valid certificate, children "of the working paper class" could not legally leave school until the age of sixteen.[28]

The new laws supported women's interest in protecting the reproductive health of girl workers through greater regulation of their labor. Members of the Illinois Federation of Women's Clubs drafted a section of the 1903 Child Labor Law that further restricted the employment of girl workers between the ages of fourteen and sixteen. Unlike boys, girls could not leave school at age fourteen for jobs that required "constant standing." This section of the act allowed school officials to deny work certification to a girl if they considered the job too strenuous for her physical health. For some child welfare reformers, this restriction did not go far enough. Kelley argued that school officials should deny all girls their "working papers" until at least age sixteen. "We do not really value the health of our children if we let little girls just fourteen years of age leave school," she wrote in 1912.[29]

The Compulsory Attendance Law of 1903 applied to all Illinois cities with populations of over 100,000 residents, of which there was only one: Chicago. Students in rural districts also left school at young ages to work on farms and in family shops. Reformers suggested that rural and industrial workplaces were inherently different. Work on farms provided children and adults with more bodily autonomy, unstructured work hours, and access to fresh air and sunshine. Reformers associated work in the industrial city, in contrast, with lack of bodily autonomy as workers completed monotonous tasks in cramped environments. Industrial workplaces were poorly lit and unventilated, posing additional health risks to urban workers. The distinct contexts of urban and rural work shaped how reformers responded to the social issue of child labor at the turn of the twentieth century. Child labor reformers understood "child labor" as not only a gendered and racialized problem, but a distinctly urban one.[30]

Most of the nation's industrial centers relied on urban school boards to help regulate the employment of children under sixteen years old. State legislatures in Massachusetts and New York also passed compulsory attendance laws that regulated the employment of urban children by 1905. Like Chicago, these school systems issued work certificates and dispatched truant officers to track down wage-earning children who lacked school-issued working papers. The New York City Board of Health issued work certificates to 40,000 children each year, half of whom were girls. State laws placed further restrictions on girl workers to protect their health, adding greater barriers for immigrant families who relied on their daughters' wages to make ends meet. Truant officers with the school system—as well as state officials like factory inspectors and the police—could arrest girls who worked without proper certification and bring them to court as law-breaking "delinquents."[31]

In 1903, the Chicago BOE issued more than 14,000 certificates to students between the ages of fourteen and sixteen, allowing them to legally leave school for work. Girls accounted for one-third of students issued work certificates by the 1910s. Most girls who left school for work legally—over 70 percent in 1915—were the American-born daughters of immigrants from Germany, Russia, "Bohemia," and Italy. Unknown numbers of girls left school before the age of fourteen with forged work certificates. Children under fourteen frequently lied about their age to receive certification or had their certificates forged by parents who relied on their wages. When Louise Montgomery interviewed American-born girls in the meatpacking district, she discovered that most distinguished between giving their "working age" and "real age."[32]

Many immigrant families who could afford to keep children in school chose their sons, whose breadwinning power would presumably benefit from extra years of education. Pearl was among the many girls in her West Side neighborhood "sent into the shops" with a forged work certificate in the 1910s. Pearl was born in Russia and immigrated to Chicago with her parents when she was twelve. She sewed men's suits in a garment factory with a forged work certificate for two years. Later in life, Pearl recalled that many Russian parents in her neighborhood relied on their daughters' wages to support the family income. "Parents would be shamed if the daughter had to go out and work," she recalled. "They wanted their children to get an education, but it was impossible." Sophie Kosciolowski immigrated to Chicago from Poland shortly after Pearl in 1911. She worked in the stockyards at age twelve with a forged work certificate, making $3.50 a week, all of which she gave to her mother. In some immigrant enclaves, first-generation daughters like Pearl and Sophie were more likely to earn wages than their brothers and often entered the workforce at earlier ages.[33]

Families circumvented the work certificate system in numerous ways so their daughters could enter the workforce. In 1907, the state factory inspector uncovered a so-called "certificate mill" at St. Joseph's Polish School, where police allegedly found 1,300 forged work certificates issued to children who were under the legal working age. The school's parishioner signed all the certificates and was charged with violating the Child Labor Law of 1903. Observers often blamed fraud on the "greed" of immigrant parents. But the lengthy paperwork of the work certificate system was difficult to navigate legally for any parent with limited English skills.[34]

Furthermore, school officials required parents to prove the accuracy of their children's work certificates by showing either a birth certificate or baptismal documents confirming their child's age. Parents could initially bring these documents to their neighborhood school for approval. Addams and the Women's Committee on Child Labor centralized this system so that all parents had to visit the BOE's downtown offices for approval. In the opening weeks of school, the press reported the long lines of mothers waiting for hours outside the Chicago BOE offices to secure certification for their working-age children. If they did not have access to birth records, parents made another lengthy appearance before the Cook County Juvenile Court to verify their child's age under oath. No wonder many families evaded this system altogether.[35]

The Compulsory Attendance Law and Child Labor Law of 1903 were major advancements in the continued education and physical protection of working-class children. Tighter age restrictions extended the school lives of girls in particular, which was an investment in the public education of girls from working-class immigrant families who were often pulled out of school sooner than boys. These laws also marked an expansion of the regulatory power of school officials over the lives of all urban students. Child labor activists like Kelley and Addams helped state actors make decisions about working-class children that often defied the needs of immigrant parents. These laws reveal a central assumption undergirding the child labor reform movement: that American school and state officials—not immigrant families—should decide what was best for their children.

A school-to-work certificate issued by the Chicago Board of Education, 1906 (Chicago Board of Education Archives)

Fitness for Work

Urban school officials used health assessments to further regulate when children could leave school for work at the turn of the twentieth century. A group of Chicago BOE members organized one of the nation's first health screenings of public school students in 1899. Led by a school board member and physician, Dr. Walter Scott Christopher, the Child Study Committee evaluated students "from the physical side" by measuring their height, weight, strength, and "vital capacity" (lungs). Christopher selected a neighborhood school populated with "normal American children" with white American-born parents for the study. These students provided a control group of "normal" childhood health, according to Christopher. In later studies, school officials would compare students with "hereditary tendencies" (immigrants) to the control group. This eugenic study of white American boys and girls conveyed anxieties about the impact of mass immigration from eastern and southern Europe on American breeding. Christopher argued that studying the physical health of immigrant children would help medical professionals understand how the unique physiology of immigrants would "blend" into "a common America type."[36]

Christopher's report led school officials to establish a permanent Department of Child Study in 1900. The department used Christopher's 1899 study to conduct regular exams of "normal" (white and American) children and issuing reports on their average height, weight, posture, grip strength, hearing, memory, balance, and more. The department also kept track of contagious diseases like smallpox and issued reports on rates of epilepsy. Their work was not unique to Chicago. Urban school systems across the industrial North created bureaucracies charged with monitoring and treating student health conditions around the turn of the twentieth century. These departments promoted a new public school responsibility: caring not only for the education of children, but for their health and vitality.[37]

Studies by the Department of Child Study encouraged school officials to make additional investments in bettering the "physical culture" of students. The professional bodybuilder and health educator Bernarr Macfadden popularized physical culture education when he launched the men's magazine *Physical Culture* in 1899. His monthly magazine was one of the most widely read publications in the Midwest and sparked a range of new health fads for men, including weightlifting, running, and intermittent fasting. Macfadden suggested that structured exercise and gymnasium training would protect the future of white American manhood. The first issue of *Physical Culture* opened with a singular declaration: "Weakness is a crime." Macfadden argued that living in "civilized country" could lead male bodies to degenerate because men were no longer worked according to "nature's laws." City life threatened their health and virility. Strength and health—"the natural condition of man"—were devalued in industrial cities, where men stood or sat all day in cramped offices and crowded factories. Macfadden argued that physical culture education would return white men in "civilized" society back to "health, strength and power."[38]

Macfadden embraced the eugenics argument that physical education prepared white American boys for better breeding in adulthood. In *The Virile Powers of Superb Manhood* (1900), Macfadden argued that sedentary city jobs led to unsymmetrical bodies that were "unnatural" and weakened men's "sexual organs." Regular exercise—particularly bodybuilding—would increase circulation and enhance "the sexual power of man." Macfadden and his followers were explicit that physical education was important for Anglo-American boys and men to make the most of their virile capabilities. "It is one of Nature's unfailing laws that the best of her species shall possess the greatest powers of transmitting their kind," he wrote in 1900. Physical education helped boys and men of the "most advanced races" improve their reproductive capacity. As Macfadden's writing confirms, eugenic anxieties about reproduction were not limited to women and girls in turn-of-the-century health movements.[39]

Male fitness experts relied on contradictory rhetoric to promote physical education. On one hand, they argued that industrialism was bad for male bodies and turned boys into "sissies" through lack of autonomy. American masculinity was deeply connected to the rural economy in the nineteenth century. What made men "men" was their agrarian self-sufficiency and dominance over the land. The world of machines stifled masculinity by requiring male bodies to conform to the monotony of machine operating and limiting their independent movement. On the other hand, turn-of-the-century health educators relied on the language of industrialism to describe the ideal male body. Male bodies needed to be strengthened into machines. They could be optimized for maximum performance. Health reformers applied the industrial language of "efficiency" to the male body by referring to its various "systems" that required equal input and output of energy. Proponents of physical education relied on the language of industrial capitalism to describe the physical problems of industrial capitalism.[40]

Most urban school officials embraced the physical culture movement by building gymnasiums for boyhood exercise at the turn of the century. They echoed Macfadden, espousing that urban boys needed physical education to protect their manhood from degeneration. "Children who attend school in large cities should be given ample opportunity for bodily exercise," wrote

Chicago's first director of physical culture, Christian Meier, in 1901. Meier argued that the schoolboy "in rural districts" could keep fit through farm labor and the freedom of recreation in nature. But boys "in a great city" became sedentary and weak. The Chicago BOE equipped twenty elementary schools with ladders, swinging rings, and balance beams for boys' gymnastics classes in 1898. Within two years, the number of elementary schools with gymnastic equipment tripled. By 1913, all of Chicago's twenty-one high schools had dedicated gymnasiums with tracks for running and bodybuilding equipment like weights and dumbbells.[41]

Clubwomen encouraged school officials to consider the physical education of female students as well. The CWC organized the Society for the Promotion of Physical Culture and Correct Dress when members joined the BOE in 1888. These clubwomen shared medical information about women's physical health and encouraged women to avoid physically restrictive fashions like the corset and the bustle. Members argued that girls should engage in some (but not all) of the physical cultural exercises open to boys to promote "graceful expression." By the turn of the century, both boys and girls took fifty minutes of physical culture each week that included drills with balls and dumbbells, running, and calisthenics.[42]

Physical culture education for girls was slower to enter public school systems due to medical doctrine about female "energy conservation." Women's physical culture clubs and fitness experts, most of whom worked in women's colleges, encouraged young women and girls to exercise in moderation and emphasized gracefulness. The director of physical training at Wellesley College, Lucille Eaton Hill, argued that popular sports like basketball placed too much "excitement" on the "emotional and nervous feminine nature." Her 1903 textbook *Athletics and Out-Door Sports for Women* warned readers that competitive sports could "wreak havoc" on reproductive health. Instead, Hill recommended that young women improve their physical "gracefulness" through calisthenics and stretching. Swimming and cycling could also encourage good posture and symmetrical development. Women's turn-of-the-century exercise advice for girls reflected more modern ideas about feminine beauty. Hill suggested that the "New Woman" could be active and athletic, but only in moderation. Ultimately, Hill reiterated mainstream medical advice that women and girls should exercise in moderation for healthy reproduction. The purpose of physical culture, she argued, was to train "healthy girls to make good mothers."[43]

Officials with the Department of Child Study used physical culture classes to evaluate gendered norms of physical and mental ability. By 1910, school officials separated primary school students by gender for weekly physical education classes under the guidance of male or female gym teachers. Alongside exercise, students were evaluated based on attributes of height, sight, strength, and arm span. The "normal" metrics of these exams were rooted in the subjective cultural assessments from Christopher's 1899 study of white American children. Exam results therefore led school officials to deem immigrant children non-normative, particularly in mental acuity. For example, first-generation children often scored poorly in reading comprehension and on reading speed evaluations that assessed "normal" mental age. New to the English language, these students could be classified as mentally slow or "dull" and placed in special education classrooms for "subnormal" children.[44]

Child Study officials used health exams to keep children out of the workforce for non-normative ability. School officials required children to pass a health evaluation before receiving their work certificate to leave school between ages fourteen and sixteen. Officials denied boys and girls work certificates after failing their exams for a range of serious public health issues. Health exams likely saved lives and protected children from spreading typhoid and the mumps. According to the director of the Department of Child Study in 1912, Dr. Daniel MacMillan, these evaluations also revealed the general "unfitness of a boy or girl" to engage in the "occupational line to which he or she fancies." MacMillan and his colleagues used an "age test" to determine the fitness of children who planned to leave school for work by age fourteen. Age tests assessed whether a student's physical and mental abilities corresponded with the norms for their age. A girl might be the legal age of fourteen, but was she as tall or heavy as the "average" fourteen-year-old girl evaluated by the Department of Child Study? Did she have the average hand strength or vital capacity as a "normal" girl?[45]

School officials used medical expertise to extend the boundaries of childhood and to further restrict child labor based on gendered and racialized metrics of "normal" ability. Their use of "age tests" complicates some historical assumptions about child labor. In Chicago, the objective marker of age was not the only metric of restricting child labor. School officials made subjective assessments of health and body normativity that also restricted child labor in the early twentieth century. This physical evaluation and labor restriction of working-class children increased in the 1910s. The Chicago BOE enlisted a hundred health officials with the Chicago Department of Health to conduct routine medical exams of schoolchildren in 1910. The number of nurses increased over the next few years to meet the needs of the city's 330 neighborhood schools. Nurses with the Department of Health were mostly concerned with stopping the spread of contagious diseases and quarantining students for smallpox and measles. But they, too, relied on the age test to determine eligibility for employment. During the 1914–15 school year, health officials denied nearly one-third of students work certificates for failing their health exams.[46]

The results of these health exams reveal gendered anxieties about child labor. Between 1912 and 1914, health examiners most often denied boys work certification for reasons that fell under the category of "low mentality." These included students deemed mentally slow, "feeble-minded," or lacking the normal reading or writing skills of their age group. A 1915 study of Chicago neighborhood schools found that boys were 22 percent more likely deemed "retarded" than girls after examination. The sons of immigrants fell under this category and were the most likely placed in new special education classes for "subnormal" children. Social reformers and medical professionals of the period argued that low mentality was a sign of pre-delinquency among boys. "Many dull children left untrained, shifting from job to job, are potential delinquents," explained one Chicago social worker in 1909. These children were considered the most likely to enter vagrant or criminal lifestyles due to their lack of good judgment. Ensuring that mentally slow "laggards" remain in school was thus "preventative of juvenile and adult delinquency." Denying working papers to working-class boys based on mental aptitude was not simply a matter of child wellness. The practice also addressed a social problem linked to unsupervised urban boyhood.[47]

Girls were more often denied work certification under classifications of "physically unfit for work." Medical examiners argued that many fourteen- to sixteen-year-old girls were weak for their age and should stay in school to protect their bodies for reproduction. These included girls like fourteen-year-old Ellen, who found a job in an ice-cream cone factory making $2.50 a week. She applied for a work certificate to leave school and support her widowed mother, who was caring for three younger children at home. Ellen failed her health screening. The examiner deemed Ellen too "physically weak" for work despite her legal age and advised Ellen to stay in school "until she was older and stronger." The Department of Child Study thus extended Ellen's childhood—her girlhood—by denying her working papers. She could not embark on the adult responsibilities of wage earning at age fourteen as outlined by law. Instead, her physical health mandated an extension of schooling until age sixteen.[48]

Medical screenings confirmed the beliefs of child labor activists that immigrant daughters like Ellen were the least fit for industrial labor. School officials trapped these girls between two contradictory ideas about girlhood health and physical activity. Ellen was deemed abnormally weak and therefore in danger of overstraining herself in the industrial workforce. Ellen had to stay in school and strengthen her body—but not too much!—to protect healthy growth. School officials codified weakness as an unavoidable fact of her girlhood.

A Right to Childhood's Joys

The accelerating pace of mass production only heightened concern for the working girl's health in the early twentieth century. By the 1910s, most manufacturers in the ready-made clothing industry adopted the piecework system to maximize output. Pieceworkers earned wages based on the number of pieces they produced in a day rather than the number of hours they worked. Attaching earnings to speed made factories more dangerous and increased workplace accidents. Child labor reformers argued that the system was also dangerous because it drained girlhood "vitality." Louise Montgomery argued that piecework created a physical condition of "permanent rush" that was "physiologically dangerous" for white American-born girls. She reported that the average American-born pieceworker—weaker than her immigrant counterpart—could only work under the stress for three years before depleting her "nervous energy." Montgomery attributed troubling mental conditions to piecework that today might be classified as anxiety disorders. She also made sweeping presumptions that mental stress could prohibit healthy pregnancy. Piecework would undoubtedly create "inefficient motherhood," Montgomery posited, through "heightened infant mortality, a lowered birth-rate, and an impaired second generation."[49]

In 1910, women school officials enlisted Dr. Caroline Hedger to warn girls against pursuing manufacturing work as part of their physical education. Hedger lived and worked from the Chicago Commons settlement house in the 1910s. Born in Ohio to white American-born parents, she held medical degrees from Northwestern University Women's Medical School and Rush Medical College. She taught "hygiene" to girls in grades six through eight and gave public lectures on childhood health open to all parents. Her hygiene lessons to girls included important public health habits like washing hands to stop the spread of contagious illness. Many of her health lectures stressed the threat of child labor for girls specifically. In one lecture for elementary school parents, Hedger described the condition of a group of 4,000 American-born girls working in the stockyards district. She argued that half of the girls inspected by the Department of Health required monthly treatment for work-related ailments. "One fourth of them had headache caused by eye strain," she told parents. "Others had hysteria from nerve drain." Hedger warned parents that girls who left school for such employment could damage their reproductive health. She lamented that "this class of girls" could not have healthy children due to degeneration. She also told parents that girlhood employment decreased "the quality of the mother's milk."[50]

Female students encountered this advice in physical culture and health classes across the industrial North. A 1910 hygiene lesson plan used in New York City schools made a similar recommendation for girls to avoid factory labor for their vitality. Students read that a healthy girl was one "who takes care of her body" by avoiding "sedentary occupations." Long days spent sitting or standing in confined positions could damage a girl's growing lungs, heart, and spine. Instead, health classes instructed girls to incorporate "walking, pure air, gymnastics" into their daily routine. These recommendations reveal middle-class assumptions about the worthy use of leisure time for girls. A respectable, healthy girl was one who spent her time strolling through the park or playing with her friends. Earning wages in crowded workplaces fell outside the realm of respectable feminine movement.[51]

Hedger argued that leisure and play were essential environmental factors to protect girlhood health and encourage good breeding. Hedger often invoked eugenic language about "race suicide" when discussing industrial labor for white American-born girls. Like other health experts, Hedger assumed that girls could pass down work-related ailments—nervous strain, poor eyesight, curved spines—to their children and dilute the American stock. Allowing "their kind" to have children, she argued in 1913, would be bad for the future of "the race." But Hedger did not suggest that the American-born daughters of immigrants were already degenerate as the children of "inferior" minority ethnic groups. Rather, she implied that American-born children of immigrants were white and responsible for carrying white children. The physical and mental stress of earning wages—not innate biology—posed the greatest threat to good breeding. Industrial capitalism was the problem. Public education was a solution. As Hedger argued in one lecture, American-born girls could develop the right "material of womanhood" if they stayed in school and avoided "the stress of Chicago life."[52]

Settlement house workers also argued that access to recreation and play could protect working-class children from physical ruin. In the early twentieth century, settlement houses offered a more diverse range of physical culture opportunities for both boys and girls than public schools. Hull House hosted a popular Girls' Basketball League whose members were mostly the American-born daughters of Italian and Russian immigrants. Chicago Commons also offered basketball, dance, and gym classes for boys and girls from eastern European families on the city's Northwest Side. At least two Black settlement houses, the Wendell Phillips Settlement and Emanuel Settlement, offered gymnastics and regularly took children to parks to play sports. Social workers in the settlement house movement were also concerned about the healthy physical growth of gendered bodies. But they were more driven by a desire to provide working-class children with leisure, fun, and stress relief.[53]

Exercise and recreation programs for working-class children reflect a central principle of the labor movement. Labor activists demanded shorter workdays and higher wages on the grounds that working people had a right to leisure and recreation ("eight hours for what we will"). For working women, this sentiment was best articulated by labor activist Rose Schneiderman in her famous "bread and roses" speech of 1911: "What the woman who labors wants is the right to live, not simply exist—the right to life as the rich woman has the right to life, and the sun and music and art." Addressing middle-class onlookers, she continued: "You have nothing that the humblest worker has not a right to have also. The worker must have bread, but she must have roses, too." Supporters of the labor movement who worked in settlement houses embraced this right to recreation through offering a range of activities to workers of all age groups. Along with basketball and gymnastics, evening programs at Hull House included adult art education and the nation's first improv theater classes.[54]

Some settlement house workers even argued that access to recreation could protect the bodies of working-class children from overstrain in the labor force. According to Addams, evening dance classes at Hull House encouraged "symmetrical muscular development" among "young people who work long hours in sedentary occupations." Another Hull House worker agreed in 1906 that dance lessons stimulated "muscular activity" to counteract "the monotonous work of modern industry" for teenage workers. The founder of Chicago Commons, social worker Graham Taylor, explained the goal of gym classes for fourteen- to eighteen-year-old girls in similar terms. He argued that exercise drills helped working-class girls build muscle to defend themselves against "confining work." Many girls in the meatpacking district benefited from this "building-up process" while employed in factories and warehouses. Chicago Commons, he summarized in 1904, offered "the exercises that their active bodies demand." Perhaps most importantly, these activities were fun.[55]

Settlement house workers asserted that a child's right to recreation could protect working-class children from bodily harm. This notion directly contradicted mainstream recommendations for working-class girls. The *Chicago Tribune* summarized the professional view on working girl recreation in 1909: "Complete relaxation is what she needs." According to leading physical educators, an evening gym class after a long day of work added too much stress to the working girl's mind and body. Vigorous exercise left her "mind wandering" and made "even the most beautiful girl absolutely ugly." The working girl needed to counteract the stress of wage earning by "relaxing every muscle" and being "lazy if she can." Child labor activists argued the opposite, particularly by the 1910s, when girls' industrial labor was on the rise. In 1912, Florence Kelley asserted that expanding physical education for all children could help the future worker care for their "growing body" and prevent "the denigrating physique of the working children." Physical culture did not overstrain working-class girls, according to Kelley. On the contrary, exercise was essential to offset "hours of utterly stupefying work."[56]

Child labor activists worried that girls who left school to perform domestic duties for their families also jeopardized their health through lack of recreation. In the 1900s, newspapers in Chicago and New York reported on the growing phenomenon of girls who worked as "little mothers" in their own homes while their parents earned wages. The press suggested that immigrant mothers robbed daughters of their right to childhood play by relying on them as unpaid caretakers. The *Chicago Tribune* published multiple features on working-class girls who cared for younger siblings at home instead of attending public school. As one journalist reported, the city's "little mothers" were "full of worry and responsibility." Another argued that the work of "little motherhood" deprived girls of "childhood's joys," remarking that the average little mother had "never known normal play." The reporter recounted an alleged conversation among a group of girls around the age of twelve who fed infants on a downtown stoop during the school day. These children did not discuss "delights and amusements of the normal little girl." Instead, the girls were consumed with concerns that belonged "in the world of their parents," like feeding schedules and the status of a nearby labor strike.[57]

These articles reflected middle-class ideals of a protected childhood. Press coverage affirmed that girlhood was a distinct life stage that should be characterized by education and play rather than caretaking and labor. The *Chicago Tribune* reported that "little motherhood" was not only socially inappropriate but physically dangerous for school-age girls. They described little mothers as "weary, repressed," and "overanxious." Their faces were "starved" and "pale." Their bodies were "pathetically wistful." The work of little motherhood was too strenuous for a young girl, who needed time for "rest and recreation." Days spent hunching over toddlers and carrying infants was bad for their physical development, making girls "sedate and elderly." This attention to girlhood bodies aligned little mothers with child workers in shops and factories. The press implied that caretaking in the home was as physically strenuous for growing American girls as the industrial workforce.[58]

Hedger investigated the health consequences of "little motherhood"

The "Little Mothers of Down Town Chicago," 1908
(*Chicago Tribune*, courtesy of ProQuest Historical Newspapers)

among second-generation immigrant girls while living at Chicago Commons settlement. "I have made an examination of many of these 'little mothers' in the stockyards," Hedger told the press in 1908. "Between 40 and 50 per cent of the children have curvature of the spine.... The little mothers carry babies which are far beyond their strength." Hedger was sympathetic to the plight of working immigrant mothers in the stockyards district and blamed systemic problems of poverty for the ruined "health and mentality" of their second-generation daughters. Their immigrant mothers had no choice but "to work for a living," she wrote. "They have to make their older children bring up the younger ones." Hedger warned that this premature burden could prevent little mothers from safely having their own children in the future: "Reproduction could cost them their life."[59]

Child labor reformers pushed state officials to criminalize immigrant parents for employing their daughters as "little mothers." Working-class parents who kept their daughters at home to care for younger siblings were also penalized for violating the child labor and attendance laws of 1903. In 1907, truant officers issued a warning to parents that they would be "brought into court and punished" for keeping girls "home as drudges." One such girl, Fannie Shapiro, moved in with her aunt and uncle when she immigrated to Chicago from Russia in 1906. "My whole hope [was] that I was coming to this country to get an education," she recalled in an oral history decades later. "It didn't work out that way." Instead, Shapiro stayed home during the school day keeping house and caring for young cousins while her uncle and aunt ran a family store. Many families relied on the oldest girl in the household to care for younger children while the parents earned wages. In 1906, truant officers in Chicago compiled a list of the most common excuses given by girls who left school without a work certificate before age sixteen. These excuses included: "Kept home to mind the baby"; "Helped mother on wash day"; or "Keeping house for father since mother died."[60]

Immigrant parents pleaded with truant officers that their daughters' domestic help did not constitute illegal child labor. Mothers argued that they had two options: send their oldest daughters to earn wages while they cared for younger children at home or keep their oldest daughter at home to watch siblings while the mother worked. Keeping their daughters at home seemed like the better option for many struggling families. State and school officials criminalized both scenarios. In one example, truant officers visited the home of a girl who left school at age eight to care for younger siblings while her widowed mother worked as a laundress. According to truant officers, the mother was "defiant" when they suggested she had violated state child labor laws by "employing" her daughter in the home. The mother argued that she needed someone to look over the other children while she was out "earning something for them to eat." Did the officers prefer that her eldest daughter earn wages at eight years old instead?[61]

State officials responded to the problem of "little motherhood" by amending the 1903 state laws to regulate girls' unpaid labor in the home. In 1908, legislators voted that girls who worked in their family homes without pay were "necessarily and lawfully employed" under the Child Labor Law of 1903. Therefore, girls could apply for work certification at age fourteen and leave school for "employment by parents without compensation." In addition, school officials added "housework" to their list of excusable absences for girls under the age of fourteen. Girls could leave school temporarily at any age for housework, personal illness, or a death in the family. School officials reported the following year that "work at home" was the second most cited excuse for missing school after personal illness.[62]

This acknowledgment of girls' unpaid domestic work in state labor and school attendance policy is significant for multiple reasons. First, these reforms offer a rare example of school policy adapting to the needs of immigrant parents. "Girls may work at home," announced the *Chicago Tribune*, "a state of affairs which, the poorer families plead, is absolutely necessary." State and school officials acknowledged that immigrant parents often relied on the support of their daughters to fulfill caretaking duties at home to keep families afloat. Furthermore, school and state officials implied that the unpaid work of girls in the home was "labor." By addressing the work of little motherhood in child labor policy, Illinois officials placed girls' unpaid household work on equal footing with wage-earning pursuits in the public workforce.[63]

This equivalence, however, also inscribed new boundaries around legal girlhood labor. The unpaid domestic work of girls in their own homes came under the supervision of state and school bureaucracies after 1908. Truant officers could hold parents responsible for violating child labor and school attendance laws if their daughters labored in their own homes without a work certificate. In 1908, one settlement house worker suggested that keeping daughters at home before the legal working age of fourteen was even more despicable than sending them into the workforce. "Here we have something worse than child labor," she argued. "We have child slavery." The 1908 amendment to the 1903 Child Labor Law expanded the definition of girlhood labor while the boundaries of boyhood labor remained the same (wage earning). In doing so, the amendment brought child labor regulations into working-class homes in the name of protecting a girl's right to "childhood's joys."[64]

Conclusion

At the turn of the twentieth century, women child labor reformers looked to the school system to oversee when white American-born girls entered the workforce. Their movement led to new legal systems that regulated childhood labor and mandated school attendance for all urban children.

Anxieties about white American-born girls sat at the center of these reforms. Illinois's Child Labor Law of 1903 enforced gendered age restrictions that suggested the protected state of girlhood extended longer than that of boyhood. The Compulsory Attendance Law of 1903 placed school officials in charge of decisions that used to fall only to families, such as how and why a child might contribute to the family income. New public school bureaucracies like the Child Study Department encouraged bodily normativity among working-class children attempting to leave school for work. In doing so, they reinforced child labor activists' assertion that the "average" white American girl was simply too weak to leave school before age sixteen.

Labor reformers like Florence Kelley advanced progressive critiques of industrial capitalism in demanding protective laws for working-class children. Kelley wanted state regulation of factories for the safety of all workers, and she believed that working-class children had a right to a protected middle-class childhood. Women in urban settlement houses were radical to suggest that physical exercise was not only healthy for growing bodies but essential to a working-class child's right to leisure. Centering girls in their movement, however, highlights how the omnipresent racial sciences of degenerative theory and eugenics touched every corner of Progressive Era reform. Settlement house workers like Dr. Caroline Hedger and Louise Montgomery suggested that the danger of work for white American-born girls was heightened by their social responsibilities as future "mothers of the race." They rendered Black child labor invisible in their writing, teaching, and reform initiatives. Instead, they implied that only one type of girl—the future mother of white American-born children—was worthy of protection from the state.

These child labor reformers promoted a new assumption that regular school attendance was an essential feature of a healthy and protected childhood. Indeed, they successfully argued that education rather than labor would become the cornerstone of a normal childhood in the twentieth century. Working-class girls filled an awkward position in this new paradigm. Child labor reformers criminalized "little motherhood" because this labor deprived girls of their childhood right to a public education. Yet this legal change coincided with women's investment in domestic education for girls. Women's groups funded evening schools for "little housekeepers" during this period and promoted courses like cooking and sewing in the public schools. Domestic work under the guidance of reformers and school officials was *education*. Domestic work in a family home to help a wage-earning mother was *labor*. At the turn of the century, this cultural tension over where and how girls conducted housework brought a new movement for "domestic science" into the urban public school.

[CHAPTER THREE]

The Bane of the Tenement

Educating Immigrant Daughters for
Scientific Housekeeping, 1890–1910

Child labor activists suggested that tenement housing was as dangerous for white American-born girls as industrial manufacturing. Chicago's West Side tenement district near Hull House was purportedly the most crowded in the world at the turn of the twentieth century. Home to immigrant families from eastern Europe, the average apartment was 300 square feet and lacked ventilation and indoor plumbing. Less than 3 percent of tenement units had bathtubs for residents, who spent their days laboring in slaughterhouses and factories. Florence Kelley argued that tenement mothers exacerbated domestic health issues due to a lack of domestic education. "The bane of the tenement is the unskilled mother," Kelley wrote in 1897. She explained that the average immigrant mother exposed her children to illness through improper cooking and "the vermin she does not know how to banish." American-born girls who grew up in these conditions would repeat their mothers' mistakes, feeding future citizens "soggy potatoes" with "beer, coffee, cucumbers, and bananas." Kelley argued that public schools had a responsibility to teach immigrant daughters proper housekeeping for the safety of themselves and their future families. If not, countless children would be "poisoned by the hopeless ignorance of their school-bred mother."[1]

School reformers like Kelley altered girls' public education in a flawed attempt to address serious domestic health issues at the turn of the twentieth century. They assumed that immigrant mothers lacked the skills to protect their families from "house diseases" like typhoid or to cook nutritious meals for their hungry children. Kelley believed that public school officials had a responsibility to teach American-born daughters the "science of housekeeping" that their own mothers never learned. Women school reformers brought sewing, cooking, housekeeping, and childcare courses into neighborhood elementary schools to improve domestic health in the tenements through girlhood education. Training girls as expert housekeepers gendered the curriculum and began a twentieth-century tradition of training boys and girls for separate work roles.²

Domestic labor took on a new scientific significance in the late nineteenth century with the advent of more modern understandings of sanitation and nutrition. In the 1880s and 1890s, college-educated "domestic scientists" argued that cooking and cleaning were serious matters of public health that required a rigorous training in chemistry, germ theory, and diet. Gender historians have highlighted how white college-educated women embraced domestic science to carve out new professional careers in hospitals and universities. Black domestic scientists also promoted the social value of women's unpaid housekeeping and used domestic science to counter racial stereotypes about Black home life. Scholarship on domestic science and its successor, home economics, overlook a primary function of this educational movement in cities like Chicago: redirecting the labor of working-class girls to solve public health crises.³

Women school reformers enforced their assumptions about gender, race, and class through domestic science instruction in the public schools. Middle-class daughters, they reasoned, could learn domestic skills from their own stay-at-home mothers. Only "girls of the busy poor" required public investment in their domestic training. School reformers argued that domestic science would help all girls excel as mothers and homemakers in the future. Only immigrant daughters had the special burden of using their domestic science training right away to protect tenement homes from "ignorant" parents. In some South Side schools, local school officials used domestic science classes to train Black girls for paid work as domestic servants. These dueling expectations for domestic science in the elementary schools conflicted with state responses to child labor. As explored in chapter 2, school officials prohibited working-class girls under the age of fourteen from leaving school to perform household labor for their families. The same officials required that working-class girls under the age of fourteen practice household labor in the classroom.

Domestic science entered Chicago public schools to equip second-generation girls with a twin vocation: educated housekeeper and public health informant. These courses emerged alongside "manual training" (shop class) for boys. Both programs reflect the interest of school officials to offer more "practical" coursework for urban children through hands-on learning. Together, domestic science and manual training segregated the school day by gender to prepare boys and girls for disparate work roles.⁴ Yet these courses were not two sides of the same coin. Women reformers promoted domestic science to address complex social issues like infant mortality and the spread of infectious disease. Domestic science teachers expected girls to bring their education home, share new knowledge with parents, and uplift the health of their families. Women's high expectations for the domestic science movement placed specific burdens on female students. Unlike shop class for boys, domestic science positioned girlhood labor as a potential substitute for public services.

Not Mere Drudgery

Epidemics like typhoid and cholera spread quickly in American cities due to overcrowding and poor sanitation in urban neighborhoods. For most of the nineteenth century, the cause of contagious illness was poorly understood. Some medical professionals argued that typhoid resulted from exposure to a chemical substance rather than infection. Others suggested that foodborne illnesses signaled the failure of weak bodies rather than the result of bacteria in rotten produce or undercooked meat. A new generation of scientists in Europe and the United States challenged these assumptions in the 1870s. They discovered that invisible microbes called "germs" could spread between organisms and cause deadly epidemics. Germ theory revolutionized Western medicine and led to new departments in hospitals and colleges dedicated to the science of public health, sanitation, and disease prevention. The discovery of germs also forever changed cultural perceptions of cleanliness and hygiene. By the late nineteenth century, being clean was no longer just a symbol of class or virtue. Being clean was a requirement for physical health and safety.[5]

College-educated women helped spread this "gospel of germs" in the late nineteenth century. Most famous among them was Ellen Swallow Richards, the first woman admitted to the Massachusetts Institute of Technology (MIT) in 1870, where she majored in chemistry. Richards worked at MIT as an unpaid professor after receiving her master of science degree. She focused her research on the application of chemistry to home sanitation and cooking techniques. Her books *The Chemistry of Cooking and Cleaning* (1882) and *Food Materials and Their Adulterations* (1885) explained to lay readers how "invisible enemies" (germs) could grow in meat, live on bathroom floors, and fester in dirty bed linens. Richards argued that the seemingly simple tasks of cooking and cleaning could have serious health ramifications if performed incorrectly. Women needed rigorous training to understand how housekeeping countered the spread of germs and nutritious cooking aided growing bodies. As Richards argued: "Sweeping and cleaning and laundry work are all processes of sanitation, not mere drudgery imposed by tradition." A basic understanding of the science of domesticity, she continued, would make American women "better housekeepers, better cooks, better wives and mothers."[6]

Richards helped pioneer the field of domestic science, which linked household skills like cooking and housekeeping to the academic study of chemistry, sanitation, and nutrition. Centering domesticity in her research legitimized women scientists who hoped to create space for themselves in male-dominated university departments and hospitals. Richards suggested that women chemists had something unique to offer science and medicine because of their gender. Their maternal perspective applied to scientific research of the home would make women better mothers and protect children. Domestic scientists like Richards believed firmly in the power of science to solve domestic health problems. They likely also knew that connecting domesticity to science would open doors for college-educated women like themselves in academic leadership.[7]

Black women promoted domestic science through urban women's clubs at the turn of the century. College-educated Black women distributed literature on home sanitation, held cooking demonstrations for neighborhood mothers, and ran free "domestic science schools" in cities like Boston and New York. Domestic science was part of Black women's "politics of respectability" in which reformers emphasized the dignity of their work, religion, and home lives to demand civic equality. Josephine St. Pierre Ruffin was a Boston-born clubwoman and civil rights reformer who edited the nation's first periodical for Black women, *The Woman's Era* (1894–97). In the newspaper's first issue, Ruffin published an article encouraging fellow clubwomen to promote "civilized homes" through domestic science education. A more scientific approach to the home would encourage social respect for Black homemakers and demonstrate their implicit rights to citizenship. As the article concluded: "The science of home-making is thus the very keystone of the political arch."[8]

The science of domesticity reached a national audience in Chicago during the World's Columbian Exposition of 1893. Members of the Chicago Woman's Club (CWC) began meetings two years prior to discuss how clubwomen could "awaken the public mind" to their work. "Domestic science is as important as medical science," declared clubwoman and social reformer Emma Cornelia Sickels at an 1891 planning meeting. In her role as president of the Women's Committee for the World's Fair, Sickels invited Richards to host a domestic science exhibition as the centerpiece of the exposition's woman-run programming. With the help of another unpaid chemistry lecturer from MIT, Mary Hinman Abel, Richards organized a kitchen exhibit to demonstrate the science of cooking and nutrition. The "Rumford Kitchen" exhibit resembled a modest New England farmhouse on the outside with a wide front porch and flower beds under each window. Inside, the Rumford Kitchen reflected the values of science and modernity exemplified by "The White City" fairgrounds. Richards and Abel served "scientific" meals for thirty-two cents a plate including baked beans with brown bread and applesauce, beef broth with gingerbread. Each meal came with nutritional menu cards listing the exact weight of each dish, measurements of ingredients, and the number of calories. An estimated ten thousand fairgoers visited the Rumford Kitchen in 1893 to learn the chemistry of cooking.[9]

The CWC organized the first national organization dedicated to "household science" after the 1893 World's Fair: the National Household Economic Association (NHEA). Founding members included Chicago clubwomen like Ellen Martin Henrotin and Emma Sickels. The NHEA also welcomed Jane Addams and other middle-class social reformers in the settlement house movement. The group hosted their first annual conference in 1894 to discuss a broad range of domestic issues such as the proper disposal of trash, residential plumbing systems, and home sanitation to stop the spread of contagious disease. The NHEA had chapters in twenty-eight states by 1897. The NHEA excluded Black clubwomen and social reformers from membership, as did its twentieth-century successor, the American Home Economics Association (AHEA).[10]

The NHEA engaged middle- and upper-class white women in a range of conversations about urban public health. They discussed how the infrastructure of industrial capitalism polluted air, water, and streets across the northern Manufacturing Belt. In an era before basic safety regulations, factories and stockyards dumped chemicals and rotten meat into nearby lakes and rivers that served local water supplies. The runaway speed of urban population growth and the corruption of urban political machines exacerbated the health dangers of living near sites of industrial production. In many cities, neighborhoods lacked basic public health services like garbage pickup or sewer systems into the twentieth century. NHEA members debated municipal issues like water treatment at their national conferences. They used the expertise of domestic science to justify "municipal housekeeping" campaigns, like lobbying for garbage pickup and water purification plants to improve neighborhood health.[11]

Domestic science legitimized middle-class expectations of cleanliness that many NHEA members already took for granted. The doctrine of "a place for everything and everything in its place" had dictated interior design and housekeeping literature since before the Civil War. Most middle- and upper-class women assumed that good homes were cleaned regularly and free from clutter. They assumed good mothers thought carefully about cooking and lovingly sewed their children's hats and mittens before the winter cold season. Domestic science appealed to urban women reformers who were concerned about domestic hygiene and the spread of "house diseases" in cities like Chicago. The movement gave credibility to their existing aesthetic choices, confirming for many NHEA members that their way of running the home was not only preferable but safer.[12]

Growing awareness of household science by the turn of the century allowed college-educated women to lobby for new departments in higher education. The University of Chicago's dean of women, Marion Talbot, established a Department of Sanitary Science in 1894 (renamed the Department of Household Administration in 1904). Talbot was a former student of Ellen Richards at MIT and echoed her mentor's view that women had a place in public health because of their gender. Talbot told a reporter in 1894 that domestic science was not "the latest fashionable distraction for young ladies." On the contrary: "It has been too much the fashion to leave sanitary science to men."[13] Black educators also founded domestic science departments to teach "practical housewifery" at the turn of the century. Margaret Murray Washington, wife of educator Booker T. Washington, established a domestic science department at Tuskegee University in Alabama while serving as the university's dean of women. The Washingtons were among an elite college-educated contingent of Black southerners who hoped to improve the social status of African Americans in the New South through respectable education and employment. Murray Washington hoped the department would train a new generation of Black women teachers and social workers ready to assert their scientific expertise.[14]

Domestic scientists who worked in urban colleges and hospitals conducted outreach work to teach working-class mothers the importance of keeping a sanitary home. Students in Talbot's department worked as "agents of tenements" to dispense domestic science literature specifically to immigrant mothers. Talbot's students also organized housekeeping courses for mothers at the university's social settlement house. For a tuition of twenty-five cents, tenement women could enroll in a ten-week "domestic science and economy" course that including cooking, sewing, and first-aid classes. Black domestic scientists and "social service nurses" from Provident Hospital, the first Black-run hospital in America, made similar investments in educating working Black mothers in Chicago. In the 1910s, Black nurses went door-to-door with health information and gave demonstrations on correct medical treatment of sick babies to local mothers.[15]

Many domestic science principles were unrealistic for working-class families living in crowded urban apartment complexes. Working-class women provided for their families by working outside the home. Grueling days laboring as domestic servants, packers, or factory hands left little time to clean, cook, or mend children's clothing at home. Working mothers who found time to keep house lacked basic resources to do so in the manner of the middle-class framework. Indoor plumbing was virtually nonexistent in tenement districts occupied by recent immigrants. Assuming they had the time to do so, working mothers had to haul their laundry to public washhouses, which also offered showers for personal bathing and sinks for hand washing. These services were not free in many cities. The public bath and washhouses of Philadelphia charged five or ten cents per shower and limited individual water use to twenty minutes. Personal and household hygiene was a basic requirement of domestic science. Yet these were luxuries for many working-class families.[16]

Immigrant households experienced higher rates of domestic pollution due to women's participation in the "sweating system" of outsourced labor. The growing demand for "ready-made" clothing in the late nineteenth century brought garment work out of the factory and into tenement apartments. Working-class immigrant mothers sewed garments at home to supplement factory production. According to Florence Kelley, sweatshop workers brought dangerous industrial pollutants into the home that were "infected with the most fatal maladies of childhood." She described home sweatshops as "the natural abodes of disease and the breeding places of infection and epidemics." Along with health concerns about contaminants, reformers criticized the sweating system for eroding the middle-class doctrine of separate spheres. As the "woman's sphere," the home should be shielded from the public realm of industrialism. A mother's choice to earn income at home through sweating disrupted the middle-class mother-daughter relationship and the expected tranquility of the domestic sphere. In the words of middle-class reformer and labor activist Margaret Dreier Robins, bringing manufacturing into the domestic space was "home-destroying."[17]

Domestic scientists hoped to establish themselves in male-dominated fields of science, achieve greater social equality, and improve the domestic lives of busy working mothers. Urban clubwomen, college students, and NHEA members had faith that domestic science could uplift urban families and protect public health. Spreading this gospel was important work that advanced popular understandings of contagious disease and malnutrition. At the same time, urban domestic scientists suggested that at least some of the burden for good domestic health fell on busy working-class women in under-resourced communities. Centering education meant that good health and domestic safety were a woman's personal responsibility, which she could tackle only through training and expertise.[18]

Sewing for Girls of the Busy Poor

Urban reformers judged the physical appearance of urban children as evidence of their mothers' poor domestic skills. In the late nineteenth century, Chicago students often came to school in dirty and tattered clothes. They walked in broken shoes and lacked hats and mittens for the harsh Chicago winters. The physical appearance of these children challenged middle-class assumptions that a good mother ensured every aspect of her child's physical comfort before sending them to school. Lack of sufficient attire for students fueled xenophobic assumptions among many white reformers that ignorant immigrant mothers threatened the health of their own American-born children. These assumptions justified the introduction of sewing classes in Chicago public schools in 1893.[19]

Some reformers argued that immigrant mothers lacked "average intelligence" about the health consequences of poor clothing. An 1892 article in *Harper's Bazaar* relayed the experience of one social reformer who visited a tenement home and watched an immigrant mother throw her children's torn clothing in the fire. The reformer was "aghast" at the wastefulness of this "poor creature" who did not know how to sew patches or mend holes. After some "urgency," the reformer convinced the woman to attend sewing classes to mend her children's winter clothing and save her money. Immigrant mothers who had sewing skills from working in the garment industry were also criticized for choosing unhealthy clothing options. An 1890 article in the *Ladies' Home Journal* described mothers who let their children out in "bare arms and low neck fashions" as "cruel and barbarous." Delicate arms needed coverage to ward off "bronchitis" and preserve a child's "nerve force." Other social reformers argued that a lack of free time among "overworked mothers" was no excuse for not investing in their children's physical well-being. Temperance activist Eleanor Kirk argued in 1891 that "poverty-stricken conditions" did not excuse "the overworked mother . . . from her share of responsibility."[20]

Protestant women's groups opened free sewing schools in Chicago churches for immigrant children in the 1880s. Their goal was to teach girls specifically to make and mend their own clothing, hats, and mittens. According to one sewing school organizer, children in the tenement districts could not rely on "the overworked mother" to preserve their health. Girls in these communities needed to take on this maternal labor for themselves. In the 1890s, public school officials encouraged girls to attend the free sewing schools to address what they saw as serious signs of physical neglect among schoolchildren. As one Chicago teacher wrote, teaching children to sew mittens would mean fewer "frozen fingers" among "little foreigners."[21]

Boys attended some sewing schools in small numbers, and some catered exclusively to girls. One of the city's largest sewing schools at Moody's Evangelical Church taught over two hundred girls and about twenty boys each week how to hold a thimble, work a needle, and stitch a canvas patch. The Sewing School Association ran multiple evening programs expressly for "girls of the busy poor" with working mothers in immigrant neighborhoods. Led by Protestant society women, the Sewing School Association also taught middle-class cultural values like the importance of a tidy appearance. Their goal was to teach second-generation girls both sewing skills and "good manners." According to the *Chicago Tribune*, women's groups ran at least twenty-five free sewing schools in Chicago by 1895 attended by nearly 10,000 girls each week.[22]

The CWC advocated for sewing instruction in the primary grades when members joined the Chicago Board of Education (BOE) in 1888. Clubwomen wanted sewing in the primary grades to reach girls before they left the school system in their teens. CWC member Lucy Flower joined the BOE in 1891. Flower was married to a wealthy banker and was well-known in reform circles for helping open the first state-funded carceral school for Illinois boys during the 1880s (Glenwood Manual Training School). Flower's first initiative as a school board member was creating a required sewing course for girls in grades six through eight. She pointed to the success of the free sewing schools run by the Sewing School Association as a worthy investment in the physical health and appearance of working-class children. Learning to sew could "raise the condition of the poor" and "transform a child from rags into respectability," she announced in 1891.[23]

Flower also assumed this education was specifically relevant to the daughters of immigrant mothers. The BOE voted to approve Flower's "sewing experiment" in 1892 and launched the first girls-only course in Chicago public schools. For an hour each week, girls in grades six through eight learned to work a needle, hold a thimble, and mend their own clothing. Girls made new hats, dresses, and mittens in some schools and could take garments home if deemed acceptable by their teachers. Flower held a press conference explaining the purpose of the girls-only course in 1892. She argued that industrial capitalism disrupted the traditional mother-daughter relationship of "home education" in many working-class families. "Children aren't taught to sew at home because their mothers haven't the time to devote to them," she explained to reporters. Instead, teachers in the public schools needed to fill this maternal role to ensure that daughters from working-class families learned an essential domestic skill.[24]

Flower's "sewing experiment" faced immediate backlash from the press. Between 1892 and 1893, editors at the *Chicago Tribune* published over a dozen articles accusing "fad subjects" like sewing of "crowding out writing" and other core subjects in the school curriculum. *Tribune* editors argued that the BOE was under the thumb of "sewing faddists" like Flower who wasted "time, energy, and money." They also accused women sewing teachers of making the highest salaries in the school system. They alleged that sewing took up more time in the school day than any other subject (neither accusation was true). *Tribune* editors criticized other new additions to the curriculum, like drawing and music, as "fads" that wasted taxpayer dollars. Yet none of these new electives faced the same derision as the all-girls sewing classes.[25]

Negative coverage of the sewing course revealed a wider resistance to women in school leadership. Critics alleged that the appointment of women like Flower to the Chicago BOE would result in sentimental "fads and frills" that distracted from serious academic pursuits. Women's support for a girls-only course stoked concerns that public schools were already too feminized. Girls far outnumbered boys in the public high schools to pursue teaching careers, and women were surpassing men in the ranks of public school teachers during the 1890s. When criticizing "the sewing fad," the *Tribune* suggested that boys would be further neglected in classrooms overrun by women and girls. In one article, a *Tribune* editor offered an unfortunate scenario: "While the distracted teacher is showing Mary how to hold her needle, Nettie how to hem, and some one else how to unravel a succession of knots and tangles, poor John and Henry will probably condole with each other by whispering, talking, or laughing at the attempts of the girls." The author concluded: "If the girls must sew, let their mothers teach them as girls were taught in our day—at home."[26]

The BOE introduced another "fad" subject alongside sewing that escaped the *Tribune*'s criticism altogether: manual training for boys. Manual training classes included basic woodworking, drafting, and sometimes stonecutting exercises for male students in grades six through eight. The wealthy owner of a brass piping empire, Richard T. Crane, donated the funds to outfit the first shop rooms in Chicago elementary schools. BOE members encouraged other philanthropists including Cyrus H. McCormick Jr. to finance additional manual training shop rooms for boys. McCormick—whose father invented the mechanical reaper—provided public school equipment for weekly instruction with screw-cutting engine lathes and work benches for carpentry lessons. Boys in the upper-elementary grades (six through eight) took manual training classes weekly while girls engaged in sewing lessons. In schools without manual training equipment, boys traveled to the nearest elementary school with a "manual training center" (shop room) for their hourly instruction.[27]

Like the physical culture movement, support for manual training reflected popular gender anxieties about the future of masculinity in industrialized cities. Male school officials argued that boys required more physical outlets during the school day than girls. While girls were easily engaged in silent reading and studying, boys were natural extroverts who needed to release their masculine energies. As one school official reported, the city's manual training centers improved "self-confidence and dignity among boys" by fulfilling their natural desire for hands-on work. *Tribune* editors celebrated the expansion of manual training centers in neighborhood schools for this reason. Shop class interrupted the sedentary school day with physical exertion to strengthen male bodies. In doing so, manual training prepared a new generation of "healthy, robust men who earn their living by the sweat of their brow."[28]

The Chicago BOE met to discuss the future of Flower's "sewing experiment" under the barrage of negative press in 1893. Her fellow board members voted unanimously to discontinue sewing classes by the end of the year. Flower was livid. She demanded: "Can you justly call anything a 'fad' which is an absolute essential to the decent maintenance of life for every man, woman, and child?" In a series of letters to the *Tribune* editors, Flower reiterated that working-class girls could not learn sewing at home because their mothers were too busy. "Those who live in a good locality, where children are carefully watched and trained at home, think sewing a useless waste of time," she argued. Only those "who live in a poor neighborhood or who study the needs of such" understood the necessity of sewing instruction for working-class daughters. Meanwhile, the BOE expanded manual training for boys in additional neighborhood schools. Over the next five years, school officials outfitted thirty-four public schools with shop room equipment.[29]

In this controversy over "the sewing fad," Flower prompted a significant assumption about the public school system's responsibility to girls with working-class mothers. The *Tribune* editors did not argue that sewing classes were a waste of public school resources because sewing was unimportant. Rather, they believed that sewing classes were a waste of school resources because girls should learn to sew at home. In a middle-class framework, teaching daughters to sew was the private responsibility of homemaking mothers. But Flower argued that teaching daughters to sew was a public responsibility in a working-class context. In crowded tenement districts where both parents worked, the state needed to step in and teach girls to sew to protect their physical health.

Beefsteakology in the Public Schools

Women's groups also lobbied for cooking and cleaning courses as a public health initiative in the 1890s. Social workers argued that these were important skills to address high rates of malnutrition and infectious disease in immigrant neighborhoods. Florence Kelley highlighted the impact of vitamin deficiency among immigrant children in her work as a labor reformer. She argued that immigrant mothers were ignorant of the science of nutrition, which led them to feed their children "bananas, bologna, beer, and coffee." Kelley feared that their daughters would grow up to do the same to the detriment of future "native-born citizens." Kelley argued that public schools had a responsibility to protect children from malnutrition by teaching immigrant daughters to cook effectively. In 1897, she criticized the "stupid curriculum" of New York City public schools for not meeting the domestic needs of immigrant communities. Girls growing up in the city's "Italian colonies" needed less "words and numbers" and more domestic science.[30]

Urban settlement houses offered cooking and cleaning classes to girls before this education entered the public schools. Jane Addams introduced an evening domestic science class at Hull House for girls under sixteen years old in 1897. Her investment in domestic science education expanded over the next decade, culminating in the creation of the Hull House Practical Housekeeping Center in 1909. The center occupied a four-room model apartment across the street from Hull House that Addams outfitted "for an average tenement family." Social workers trained in domestic science offered cooking classes for teenage girls three nights a week. Girls also learned to care for the model apartment by decorating and sweeping. As one Hull House worker explained, the center helped girls "make their homes as attractive and healthy as possible in the surroundings in which they live."[31]

Women in school governance brought cooking out of the settlement house and into the public school at the turn of the century. In 1898, a group of women school officials (most CWC members) and assistant superintendents organized a Committee on Domestic Science to educate their male colleagues. On behalf of the committee, Ella Flagg Young traveled to the East Coast to report on the successful integration of cooking classes in Boston public schools. Young first joined the school system as a seventeen-year-old teacher and worked her way up to the position of assistant superintendent. She argued that regular cooking instruction in the public schools addressed serious health issues impacting public school children like typhoid and anemia. Young argued that Chicago schools needed to introduce

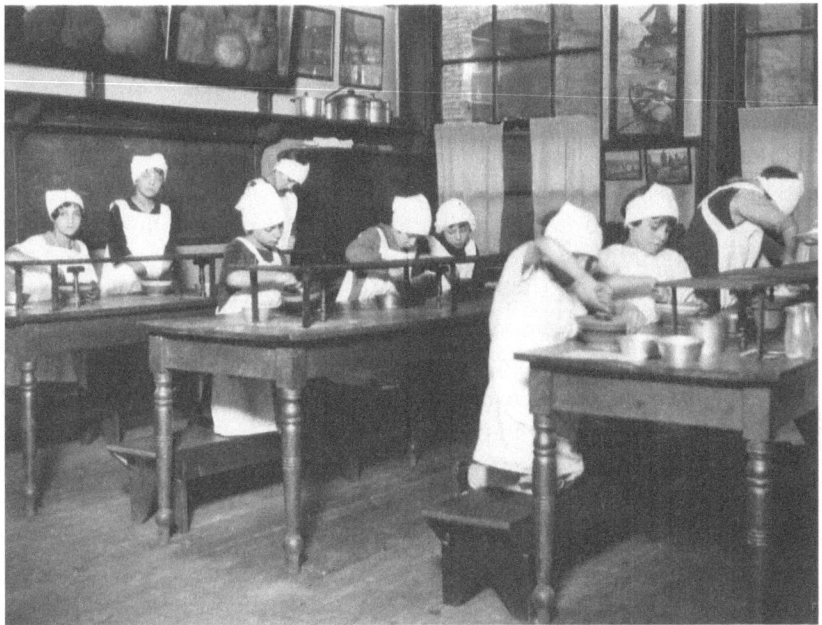

A Hull House cooking class for girls, c. 1925 (Hull-House Photograph Collection, Special Collections and University Archives, University of Illinois Chicago)

"cooking laboratories" where girls donned lab coats and white hats to learn the chemistry of cooking in lab-like classrooms lined with gas stovetops.[32]

The Chicago BOE voted to approve Young's proposal for cooking classes on one condition: the courses were funded entirely by the CWC and cost the school board nothing. Clubwomen outfitted two elementary schools with "domestic science centers" on "an experimental basis" in 1898. Girls learned cooking and kitchen sanitation in classrooms outfitted like Boston's cooking labs. Nancy "Nettie" McCormick—daughter-in-law to the inventor of the mechanical reaper—paid to equip a South Side classroom with sinks lined against one wall and ranges against the other. An adjoining classroom resembled a dining room where girls practiced serving and table setting. Elizabeth Stickney—whose late husband served as president of the Stock Yards National Bank—funded the second domestic science center at Kozminski Elementary School in Hyde Park. School officials used donations from clubwomen to hire a full-time teacher who traveled between the two schools lugging bags of fresh groceries for cooking instruction. Hundreds of girls in grades six through eight commuted to the centers weekly from nearby neighborhood schools.[33]

The two CWC-funded domestic science centers, however, did not educate working-class girls with busy immigrant mothers. Clubwoman Evelyn Allen Frake reported on the work of the centers to the BOE. Both domestic science centers were in Hyde Park, the posh neighborhood surrounding the University of Chicago, and catered to mostly middle-class students with white American-born parents. Local school officials noted that the cooking classes had improved the manners and temperament of girls who were more "careful and methodical." But they suggested the centers should relocate closer to the tenement districts. As one school official complained, Hyde Park girls were "from comfortable homes" and would not earn wages after elementary school. Many of these girls would likely employ domestic servants as adults and would "never have very much cooking to do." These girls also did not have working mothers. Their mothers could presumably pass down cooking skills themselves and did not need public school officials to fill this maternal role in their absence.[34]

On Frake's suggestion, the Chicago BOE voted to expand domestic science in additional elementary schools to reach working-class girls the following year. School officials hoped that relocating the centers would be "beneficial to the State" by addressing public health issues caused by "the centralization of population in cities." The BOE was nearly unanimous in their vote to assume financial responsibility for an expansion of cooking instruction into immigrant neighborhoods. Their support signaled the success of women's lobbying efforts for greater investment in girls' domestic education. Even the skeptical editors of the *Chicago Tribune* conceded in a 1905 headline: "Fads Are Here to Stay."[35]

The Chicago BOE approved ten additional domestic science centers in 1899 that opened over the next five years. Each featured a "cooking lab" equipped with sinks and stovetops. Some had adjoining classrooms for lessons on meal serving and nutrition. Unlike the first two centers funded by clubwomen, school officials established these centers in the city's most crowded elementary schools in immigrant communities. Five opened in predominantly Greek and "Bohemian" neighborhoods on the city's West Side. Three were in working-class Irish and German communities near the stockyards and railyards of southwest Chicago. These schools catered to the children of mothers who worked and girls who would likely spend their teen years working in factories, warehouses, and downtown shops.[36]

School officials expanded manual training centers for boys more evenly throughout the elementary schools. The BOE opened thirty-eight domestic science centers in public elementary schools by 1909 (13 percent of all elementary schools). The number of manual training centers for boys mushroomed to 157 by 1909 (55 percent of all elementary schools). Cultural assumptions about gender and class help explain why school officials invested in more shop rooms for boys in the primary grades. The Chicago BOE considered manual training valuable for all schoolboys regardless of class or ethnicity. School officials and business leaders promoted woodworking as an important physical outlet for the boy who was a "creature of action" and happiest "when he can make something." In contrast, women reformers promoted domestic science classes as appropriate education specifically for working-class girls living in immigrant communities with laboring parents.[37]

Domestic science requirements disrupted the school lives of immigrant daughters in working-class neighborhoods. At the turn of the century, girls in grades six through eight who did not have a domestic science center at their own schoolhouse traveled to their closest "center" once a week. By 1903, over 5,000 girls from 145 schools traveled to the ten domestic science centers. Some of these commutes were up to an hour long, according to school officials. They required girls to pass through industrialized neighborhoods and across train lines with their teachers for weekly instruction. Teachers and local school officials complained to the board about the waste of time taken to transport girls to domestic science rooms for their weekly cooking instruction. Domestic science classes in some neighborhoods were shortened to accommodate the longer commutes.[38]

The design of domestic science centers reflected middle-class standards of cleanliness championed by the domestic science movement. School officials complained that renovating classrooms as cooking labs posed greater difficulty than shop rooms due to the importance of sanitation. Cooking labs needed proper drainage, ventilation, and access to gas for baking and boiling. Domestic centers could not be on the first floor of a schoolhouse because dust and dirt from the nearby street might come through the windows and contaminate food and textiles. Basements had also proven to be poor environments for cooking classes due to ventilation issues. Manual training centers—like factories and workshops—were acceptable environments for dust, dirt, and smoke. But like the scientifically-run home, domestic science centers needed to be spotless. This obsession with a spotless learning environments did not, of course, reflect the realities of students' domestic lives. How were girls expected to replicate these conditions in tenement districts?[39]

School officials reintroduced sewing and mending lessons as part of the domestic science curriculum. Sixth-grade girls spent at least an hour a week learning to mend, patch, and make household items like mittens in domestic science centers. Girls in grades seven and eight practiced more advanced needle skills like embroidery and dressmaking. School officials argued that sewing was a science that supported the public health goals of cooking and cleaning instruction. Prospective teachers at the Normal School not only needed sewing skills; they had to pass an exam that proved they understood "the relative heat absorption of wool and cotton." Like cooking, sewing instruction also promoted a middle-class understanding of respectability. Girls learned to make respectable clothing. Embroidery and lacework lessons taught girls to add special touches to their homes, adding beauty to their domestic spaces.[40]

School officials argued that domestic science successfully trained girls to uplift their immigrant households. "Many schoolgirls of 15 years know more about the care and economies of the home than their mothers," declared one district superintendent in 1903. He told the press about one girl attending a North Side domestic science center who took "control of the home" for a month and saved her parents twenty-three dollars. After this successful experience, the girl was now "teaching her mother how to manage the home." Five years later, school officials required 15,000 girls to go home and demonstrate their domestic science training for their parents. School officials reported receiving letters from parents thanking them for the introduction of "beefsteakology" and "breadometry" in their households. "The public school girl," the *Tribune* reported, "has gone home from the public school and warned her parents against the overcrowding of sleeping rooms, she has preached to them the gospel of fresh air, of house sanitation, of cleanliness." According to the *Tribune*, domestic science transformed eighth-grade girls into effective public health educators.[41]

By establishing domestic science centers in select neighborhoods, school officials harnessed the domestic labor of immigrant daughters as a tool for public health. Doing so cemented class assumptions about girlhood into the geography of Chicago's neighborhood school system. Chicago school officials did not introduce domestic science into the curriculum to teach *all* girls the new science of housekeeping. Rather, they used the education of working-class immigrant daughters to bring middle-class standards of domesticity into the tenement districts and to teach these girls to dress themselves "respectably."

Domestic Science or Domestic Service?

The domestic science movement created confusion about the purpose of household training for girls: service for wages or housekeeping for public health. Among the NHEA's founding goals was to professionalize domestic service through domestic science. The NHEA pledged to "systematize domestic service" and secure "skilled labor in every department in our home." Some NHEA members funded private schools of housekeeping in East Coast cities at the turn of the century. The Chicago branch had a Committee on Industrial Schools that kept carceral school administrators informed on the latest domestic science pedagogy. These women suggested that a lack of scientific knowledge among working-class servants put middle-class families in danger. Domestic scientists needed to teach girls to wash their hands and sanitize cooking utensils to protect their employers from "house diseases" like typhoid. Like other efforts to professionalize domestic service, however, NHEA programs were poorly attended due to the unpopularity of service work among their target demographic of white working-class women.[42]

Black clubwomen also hoped to destigmatize domestic service through domestic science education at the turn of the twentieth century. Fannie Barrier Williams was born free in antebellum Pennsylvania and was the first Black woman to gain membership to the CWC in 1894. Williams argued that domestic science could bring "a new dignity" to a profession that employed 70 percent of Black working women in Illinois. "Our girls," she wrote in 1903, "must be made to feel that there is no stepping down when they become professional housekeepers." Yet Williams was suspicious of her colleagues in the CWC who were uninterested in collaborating with Black women in groups like the NHEA. She worried that the domestic service initiatives of the NHEA could create a new class of elite white servants while Black women were "relegated to the positions of scrub women and dishwashers." Williams's fears were well-founded. The short-lived domestic service schools run by NHEA members catered almost exclusively to white American-born girls.[43]

Members of the NHEA professionalized the work of white women's unpaid homemaking in opposition to the drudgery of paid domestic labor. Members argued that rapid industrialism and urbanization made women's housekeeping responsibilities more difficult and dangerous. The "new homemakers" of American cities, as one member called them, needed to understand the threat of dust, bacteria, and vermin and assume a more scientific role within their homes. The Chicago NHEA chapter ran a correspondence school that shared lesson plans and reading material on applying "the resources of modern science" to urban homemaking. The program was overseen by a board of clubwomen, including Ellen Martin Henrotin, and headquartered at the Armour Institute of Chicago. "Rapid industrial changes have taken place during the last generation," wrote CWC member and dean of the school, Maurice Le Basquet. "Present day home making must necessarily be a *new* profession." Women in the domestic science movement used the terms "profession" and "professional" to describe their own unpaid homemaking duties. Doing so did not suggest an interest in challenging the breadwinner model by paying homemakers for their socially essential caretaking labor. Professionalism was about education and expertise, not money. NHEA members called their own unpaid homemaking a profession at the same time that live-in domestic professionals were exiting their homes.[44]

Women school reformers argued that public school domestic science centers were not for future domestic servants. The Chicago BOE appointed Ella Flagg Young as director of domestic science in 1898 and tasked her with hiring teachers to staff domestic science classrooms. The Chicago Normal School established a domestic science department to standardize the training of teachers by 1903. Young told the press that trained teachers could not only cook, but understood "the chemical symbols for water and carbon dioxide" to run scientific cooking labs. She insisted that the white hats and aprons donned by girls in cooking class were modeled after scientists in a laboratory rather than the white uniforms of domestic servants. Lesson plans from the early twentieth century suggest that teachers used their training to promote an American diet and middle-class standards of healthful eating. Girls learned to boil potatoes, bake biscuits, and make beef broth. They learned the importance of giving warm milk to infants and cleaning their fingernails before entering the kitchen.[45]

Young hoped to expand domestic science education throughout the elementary schools to reach all urban girls regardless of class and ethnicity. Young briefly left school governance at the turn of the century to earn her PhD with famed pedagogue John Dewey at the University of Chicago. Young worked in what she dubbed Dewey's "Laboratory School," an experimental elementary school where graduate students put their abstract philosophy of education into practice on real children. In her 1901 dissertation, "Isolation in the School," Young argued that public education should always evolve to meet changing community needs. Domestic science met the modern challenges of public health that girls needed in all urban neighborhoods, not just tenements. Furthermore, Young considered public education a cornerstone of American democracy that should be equally accessible to all students. She was often praised by the Black press for supporting racial integration and for chastising local school officials who tried to segregate school activities.[46]

Young brought domestic science centers out of immigrant neighborhoods and into the regular schooling of all elementary school girls in the 1910s. After earning her doctorate, Dr. Young returned to the school system in 1909 as Chicago's first female superintendent of schools and the first woman to oversee a major school system in America. At sixty-four years

Ella Flagg Young (1845–1918), c. 1910 (DN-0007581, Chicago Daily News collection, Chicago History Museum)

old, she was arguably the most powerful woman in urban politics and the highest-paid woman in the country, with a salary of $10,000. Young was heralded by the press as "the Champion of Girl Pupils" after announcing her plan to devote more resources to the girls' curriculum. At a press conference in 1909, Young criticized school officials for allowing domestic science to lag behind manual training in neighborhood public schools. "When the two departments were established it was the order to install them together," she explained. "Every school should have its room for the teaching of domestic science."[47]

Young worked with school architect Dwight Perkins toward her ambitious goal of establishing a domestic science center in each of Chicago's 233 neighborhood schools. In her first two years as superintendent, the number of domestic science centers increased from 38 to 109. By the end of her superintendency in 1915, domestic science equipment was installed in 199 schoolhouses across the city and nearly all public high schools. Many of the new cooking laboratories had adjoining rooms filled with dining tables and chairs constructed by boys in manual training classes. By 1912, only eighteen schools on the Far West and South Sides of the city lacked facilities for cooking and were too isolated for girls to easily walk elsewhere for weekly instruction.[48]

Young expanded the power of professional domestic scientists in the school system, many of whom were members of the NHEA. Domestic science teachers became regular members of the elementary school teaching staff and were paid accordingly.[49] Young hired a new director of domestic science in 1910, Mary Snow, to oversee girls' training for "personal, household, or community usefulness." At age fifty-one, Snow was also a lifelong educator who, like Young, made history as the first female superintendent of schools in her home state of Maine before serving as director of the Pratt Institute in New York. An NHEA member, Snow believed that girls required specialized training to increase their "industrial and social efficiency" as informed mothers and homemakers. "The home of the future," she wrote in 1910, "will reap the larger benefit through this early training in the duties of motherhood."[50]

Middle-class parents protested Young's expansion of domestic science centers because they associated cooking classes with the racialized work of domestic service. According to the BOE, parents fought to close the first domestic science centers in Hyde Park because they "didn't want their daughters trained as cooks." East Coast school districts faced similar pushback from white American-born parents in the early twentieth century. "I shouldn't want Margaret to waste her time on cooking at school," one mother wrote of domestic science classes in New York. "I can teach her that at home." The mother of another fourteen-year-old student in New York explained why her daughter did not need cooking classes: "Emma will never have any cooking to do, she will always have servants," she reasoned. The mother suggested that domestic science training was inappropriate for her daughters' future as a middle-class housewife. "I'd rather she would spend her time on music and art," she explained. These mothers implied that domestic science was inappropriate for their daughters because of their race and class status. In Chicago, Young attempted to avoid this confusion between domestic *science* and domestic *service* by renaming the classes "household arts."[51]

Black parents seemed less concerned that Young was training their children for service work. Chicago's Black reform community generally embraced domestic science as respectable education for girls. The nation's most influential Black daily, the *Chicago Defender*, praised Young as "the worthy school head" for her curricular reforms and published a regular column sharing domestic science tips. In 1910, parents complained that white teachers were "attempting to draw the color line" at Raymond Elementary School by excluding their children from social activities and making them use inferior school resources. The *Defender* encouraged parents to protest the Raymond School for having "children shoved out" and giving girls "the old stoves used by the whites." Black parents wanted their daughters to have equal access to all public school resources, including domestic science centers.⁵²

Local school officials, however, *did* use some domestic science centers to train girls for domestic service after Young left the school system. In 1915, the BOE outlined an "industrial course in household arts" that emphasized skills for paid labor including laundry work, waitressing, and live-in service. The BOE encouraged local principals to use their household arts center for the vocational course "where conditions make it appear advisable." The board was not specific in what "advisable" conditions warranted the industrial course for girls in grades six through eight. But in the context of the Great Migration, their language created space for school officials in increasingly Black districts to use domestic science centers for domestic service instruction. School officials piloted this "industrial course" for girls two years after introducing an "industrial division" for truant boys at the Doolittle School, where Black children made up 97 percent of the student body by 1918.⁵³

Race and class distinctions shaped how parents understood the purpose of domestic science in the elementary schools. Despite conflicting views, Young's expansion of "household arts" normalized domestic education as a twentieth-century feature of a girl's public education. Household arts requirements for girls in grades six through eight gendered the elementary school curriculum and confirmed the assertion of women's groups that schools had a responsibility to invest in better homes and healthier families. The value of girls' domestic labor in these courses was not treated as equal. Undergirding the movement were assumptions that middle-class girls needed domestic skills for their future womanly duties as full-time homemakers with professional expertise. Local school officials still expected working-class girls to fill heavier labor burdens in girlhood as domestic servants or public health crusaders within their own homes.

Certified Little Mothers

The domestic science movement highlights a central irony about gender, child labor, and education for girls in Progressive Era public schools. As explored in chapter 2, school officials chastised parents who kept girls home from school to perform housekeeping duties on behalf of working mothers. The state criminalized parents for keeping daughters "home as drudges" without work certificates after 1908. Investments in domestic science coincided with these state restrictions on girls' paid and unpaid labor. School officials required girls in the upper-elementary grades to engage in the labor of sewing, cooking, and cleaning in school while criminalizing mothers for engaging their own daughters in the same work at home. The "industrial course" for domestic service is the most obvious example of this hypocrisy. The state could charge parents and employers for violating child labor laws if they employed girls as paid domestic servants before the legal working age of fourteen. Yet girls as young as eleven practiced the role of child laborer at least once a week in neighborhood public schools.

Women school officials also introduced courses on the science of infant care that contradicted concern for the girlhood labor of "little motherhood." In 1910, health educator Dr. Caroline Hedger worked with Young to bring a ten-week course for "little mothers" into the public elementary schools. According to the course syllabus, their objective was to teach girls how to care for younger siblings without "risk to themselves or their charges" during "the absence of the employed mother." The Chicago Department of Health funded the courses, which taught basic infant care to girls under fourteen years old (the legal working age). Health officials gave each girl a lifelike doll the size of a two-year-old child on which they practiced feeding, cleaning, and dressing. Girls took their doll's temperature and learned to cradle the doll's neck without straining their own backs. They studied principles of the domestic science movement like the importance of fresh air in the home and dusting to remove household allergens. School officials stressed the importance of physical appearance in little mothers' courses across the industrial North. A sample syllabus prepared by the Child Federation of Philadelphia recommended school officials give girls doll-size mittens, hats, diapers, undershirts, binders, cloaks, hoods, dresses, stockings, socks, and shoes to clothe their practice babies.[54]

Health experts like Hedger argued that the work of little motherhood deprived girls of their right to a normal childhood. She taught health classes in the public schools that emphasized how little mothers strained their bodies and destroyed their reproductive health. In creating dedicating coursework for "little mothers," Hedger and Young seemed to acknowledge the importance of these girlhood responsibilities. Indeed, middle-class observers suggested that girl caregivers in tenement districts were both tragic and heroic. The press commented on the joy of little mothers and the sweetness expressed toward their younger siblings. Physically exhausted, the little mother was nevertheless "seldom sad" because she possessed "mother passion implanted by mother nature." The press suggested this maternal labor was unfortunate but, ultimately, noble and necessary for daughters of busy working mothers who had to neglect childcare duties. According to one *Chicago Tribune* reporter, the city's "women children" were "unconscious heroines and martyrs."[55]

Little mothers' courses supported the broader goals of women in the domestic science movement to improve the health of urban homes through education reform. Infant mortality was a real public health crisis in industrial cities like Chicago. An estimated 15 percent of babies in Chicago died before their first birthdays in 1897. Twelve-year-old girls surely suffered from physical and emotional strain while caretaking for working mothers, who lacked access to childcare resources. But like domestic science, little mothers' courses placed the burden of addressing these valid public health concerns onto girls. In 1912, school officials argued that "legislative enactment" or the work of "protective agencies" could not solve "the problem of child saving" alone. Public schools also needed to raise the "intelligence" of girls so they could save younger siblings through "motherly care."[56]

Little mothers' courses in the public schools regulated the household contributions of girls to their own families. Urban school officials often gave girls diplomas, certificates, or badges at the end of the courses to verify girls' status as "certified little mothers." This certification confirmed that the public schools had prepared schoolgirls to perform caretaking duties at home by age fourteen. Issuing diplomas supported the goals of the domestic science movement that women's work in the home was a serious and "professional" vocation rooted in dedicated training. In Chicago, this certification process further policed when and where girls labored. School records do not indicate what girls were expected to do with their "little mother certificates." School officials may have required them for girls to gain work certification to support their mothers at home under the 1908 amendment to the state's child labor law. At the very least, the program implied that only "certified little mothers" educated by school and city officials had the expertise to care for younger siblings at home.

School and health officials designed these courses to protect the American-born children of immigrants only. Young and Hedger introduced little mothers' courses in the most crowded immigrant neighborhoods. According to Hedger, the class was designed for school districts with the highest rates of "proxy motherhood" near stockyards and factories. Forty-eight elementary schools on the West and Southwest Sides of the city offered the course in 1910. By 1915, roughly 2,000 girls enrolled in the little mothers' course each year. School and health officials collaborated to open "Little Mothers' Leagues" in immigrant neighborhoods across the Manufacturing Belt from Boston to New York to Madison, Wisconsin. Local school leaders in these cities were often explicit that the daughters of "foreign-born people" needed training to protect younger siblings from mothers who were "fixed in their ignorance." The courses therefore reflect the wider assumption of white "child-saving" reformers that the state needed to protect white American-born children through educating immigrant girls.[57]

A "Little Mothers Class" at Washburne Elementary School, West Fourteenth Street and Union Avenue, 1908 (DN-0009517, Chicago Daily News collection, Chicago History Museum)

Black educators and social reformers were less invested in the "little mothers' movement." Instead, they brought this education to actual mothers by organizing courses for adults on infant care and cooking in urban settlement houses. One notable exception was the Armstrong Association in Philadelphia, a Black social service organization that offered free little mother classes to Black girls between the ages of twelve and fifteen. Unlike white school officials, however, the Black press emphasized the value of this education for girls' future work as women when they became mothers. The NAACP's monthly magazine *The Crisis* covered a Little Mothers' League in a Cincinnati public school in 1917. The article praised the value of this education for Black girls to help "the colored mothers of tomorrow . . . conserve the infant for the race." According to *The Crisis*, the primary goal was to look forward to future race mothers rather than enlist girlhood labor in the present.[58]

School officials expected only white American-born girls to use little motherhood training in their girlhoods and teach their immigrant mothers to better care for children. In 1912, the BOE explained that "useful and healthful suggestions" should be "carried from these classes to the homes." The Department of Health gave girls printed handouts and "healthgrams" with information on nursing and diarrhea to bring home to their mothers.

Reformers argued that daughters were better teachers because many of their mothers "do not speak English" or were too busy to attend domestic science classes themselves. The course was another means of saddling young immigrant girls with the dual vocation of educated caretaker and public health informant in the era of child labor restriction.[59]

Conclusion

Women in the domestic science movement argued that public schools had a responsibility to address domestic health issues through education reform. White clubwomen and social reformers relied on disparaging assessments of immigrant women's housekeeping to bring this training into the public schools. They argued that busy immigrant mothers lacked the knowledge or, at the very least, the time to invest in the well-being of their homes and children. Public education needed to adapt to address this neglect. Domestic scientists had faith in the power of education to solve modern social issues impacting women and children in industrial cities. But the logic underlying their public school programs was flawed. Immigrant families did not need daughters with housekeeping skills; they needed better housing. Immigrant mothers did not need childcare training for their daughters; they needed childcare services, higher wages, and shorter workdays.

The domestic science movement legitimized the work of many Black and white women in the first generation of female college graduates who created careers for themselves in colleges and hospitals spreading "the gospel of germs." Members of the NHEA embraced the movement to professionalize their own unpaid work as homemakers and uplift the social importance of white middle-class womanhood. They used domestic science to remake working-class girlhood in the process. School officials pushed the expectations of scientific housekeeping onto girls from immigrant and working-class families. They harnessed their labor to spread public health information into tenement districts. These goals stood in sharp relief to the introduction of manual training for boys in the 1890s. School officials did not expect boys to take their shop class education home to their fathers. They did not argue that woodworking skills would create healthier families and safer homes. The burden of these educational expectations was placed solely on girls.

Domestic science and manual training gendered the public school curriculum in new ways at the turn of the twentieth century. These programs began a near century-long tradition of segregating students by sex in American public schools to prepare them for gendered labor roles. Shop class taught the virtues of strenuous manhood and hard work for productive breadwinning. Domestic science equipped girls with homemaking expertise for scientific motherhood. Chicago children in grades six through eight could not opt out of these courses. Gendered education for labor was a requirement of their public education. In the 1910s, school reformers introduced new vocational electives in the high schools that built on this elementary school foundation. Vocational programs at the high school level also catered to the American-born children of working-class immigrants. But unlike domestic science in the primary grades, girls at the high school level could elect to ignore them.

[CHAPTER FOUR]

A School Built Around the Girl

Education for Paid and Unpaid Labor in
Chicago High Schools, 1900–1915

In 1914, Agnes Nestor of the Chicago Women's Trade Union League (WTUL) went to the offices of the Chicago Board of Education (BOE) with a resolution in hand. Nestor, a twenty-three-year-old glove maker and labor activist, hoped to convince school officials to offer a course on collective bargaining for students enrolled in vocational programs in public high schools. She argued that working-age girls (over fourteen) needed to learn their labor rights to avoid dangerous and poorly paid positions in the industrial economy. Nestor was surprised when Superintendent Ella Flagg Young agreed to a meeting. Young and Nestor did not always get along. Young was a supporter of household arts education and had ignored previous requests of labor women to introduce "industrial arts" into the girls' high school curriculum. Nestor was shocked when Young expressed enthusiasm for a collective bargaining course and agreed to bring Nestor's resolution to the school board. Unfortunately, Young thought Nestor had suggested a course for girls on how to *buy*—a concept affiliated with the home economics movement—rather than how to *bargain*. "Evidently our terms were not familiar to her," Nestor later lamented, "as she had no previous familiarity with [organized] labor."[1]

The misunderstanding between Nestor and Young highlights competing views on the purpose of vocational education for girls in secondary education. Across the industrial North, women labor activists urged school officials to introduce needle trade programs at the high school level so girls of legal working age could train for dressmaking and millinery jobs. They wanted vocational programs to teach both labor skills and labor values to help working girls assert their rights in the female economy. Women school officials, social workers, and club members argued that girls of legal working age also needed domestic training for the safety of their future families. Chicago women who invested in reforming the girl's high school curriculum ultimately agreed to compromise their visions to achieve a shared goal of improving both the home and labor lives of working-class teens. Together, they gendered the high school curriculum by promoting a narrow vision of "respectable" labor for the white working girl.[2]

This chapter places women and girls at the center of the "vocational education movement" that transformed urban high schools between 1900 and 1915. One percent of Chicago children graduated from a four-year high school in 1910. Less than 10 percent of children graduated from high school nationally by World War I. This small minority of urban students were mostly the children of middle-class parents who planned to attend college or pursue teaching careers with their high school diplomas. In the era of anti–child labor activism, urban school reformers hoped to extend the school lives of working-class children and help them avoid dead-end jobs by making the high school curriculum more relevant to their future employment. Histories of this reform movement typically focus on male-led initiatives that targeted boys with high school shop classes for future builders, engineers, and mechanics. Women school reformers were also active in promoting vocationalism for girls and introducing new work-oriented programs in secondary education. Labor women, settlement house workers, and clubwomen altered the form and function of a high school education by demanding gender segregation through girls-only public schools.[3]

Women's vocational school reform was out of step with the educational and employment interests of actual high school students before World War I. Unlike shop classes for boys, Chicago girls were largely uninterested in new vocational electives for needle trades. Many first- and second-generation immigrants continued to leave school for work before high school and ignored vocational school reform altogether. Those who pursued two- or four-year high school degrees hoped to strengthen English and typing skills for work in downtown offices rather than the needle trade programs privileged by labor women like Nestor. Black high school students were the least interested in successful women-led school reforms. Black girls focused on academic subjects to pursue teaching careers and excel in college. Women school reformers hoped to advance their social agenda of preserving the respectable "female economy" of women-run garment shops and improving working-class homes through vocational education. Using school reform as social reform, these women failed to consider what girls actually wanted from a high school education.[4]

Chicago girls often challenged the work of women school reformers by navigating new vocational programs to serve their own interests. Joint activism by the Chicago Woman's Club (CWC) and Chicago WTUL led school officials to establish the city's only public trade school for girls in 1911: the Lucy Flower Technical School for Girls (Flower Tech). But many students did not enroll in "the school built around the girl" for its needle trade or household arts classes designed by school reformers. Black girls reimagined Flower Tech as "the poor man's Vassar" by promoting the school as a prestigious institution for respectable girls with college ambitions. Black girls followed Flower Tech to the Garfield Park neighborhood when officials relocated the school far from the South Side's Black Metropolis in 1927. Groups like the CWC and Chicago WTUL successfully reformed the girls' high school curriculum and lobbied for a girls-only public institution in the 1910s. But the local history of Flower Tech reveals the limitations of these groups' attempts to direct the labor lives of working-class girls through school reform.

The Fourteen-to-Sixteen Problem

The urban high school underwent a radical transformation at the turn of the century to appeal to children of legal working age. School officials argued that high schools needed more "practical" education to prevent working-class children from leaving school for jobs with their work certificates at age fourteen. In Chicago, the BOE outfitted high school classrooms with shop room equipment that advanced the work of "manual training" in the elementary schools. School districts across the urban North also established a new type of public institution—the "trade" or "technical" high school—to appeal to the working-class boy. These vocational schools had dedicated shop rooms for boys to study carpentry, foundry, engineering, and machine shop before exiting the school system for apprenticeships in these fields. Reformers hoped to integrate the public high school into the urban economy by building connections between schools and employers. In doing so, vocational school reform promoted a new assumption that the primary role of a secondary education was preparation for work.[5]

The Massachusetts Commission on Industrial and Technical Education, popularly known as the Douglas Commission, encouraged urban school officials to introduce vocational programs in 1906. The Douglas Commission issued a widely read report on the condition of thousands of children in Massachusetts (mostly the children of immigrants) who left school for work at the legal age of fourteen. Social reformer Susan M. Kingsbury, who investigated child labor for the commission, reported that few fourteen-year-old workers found stable or safe employment in cities. Most teenage workers had dead-end jobs as factory hands where they had no prospects of advancing to better-paid positions. While children could join the workforce at age fourteen, most employers preferred to invest in workers who were at least sixteen years old. This "fourteen-to-sixteen problem" meant that children often floated from job to job for two years after leaving the school system and with bouts of idleness in between. The Douglas Commission's report promoted vocational education in urban high schools as a solution to the fourteen-to-sixteen problem. They recommended two-year vocational programs to encourage high school attendance and improve the child worker's employment prospects by age sixteen. Two-year vocational programs could also curb child labor by giving students a reason to extend their school lives on the promise of higher wages.[6]

A group of influential male educators, social scientists, and businessmen founded the National Society for the Promotion of Industrial Education (NSPIE) in 1906 to lobby for vocational education (or "industrial education") in urban high schools.[7] The NSPIE promoted the Douglas Commission's recommendation for two- and four-year vocational programs in industrial trades. Members were particularly concerned that the United States would fall behind their industrial competitors, especially Germany, if local governments did not devote more resources to training skilled workers in the manufacturing sector. In a 1908 study, the NSPIE reported that 55 percent of male students in Berlin between the ages of fourteen and sixteen enrolled in trade programs to become "real craftsmen." But in the manufacturing center of Chicago, less than 1 percent of male students received dedicated trade training according to their findings. "In the long run," a NSPIE representative announced, "American industry will pay the penalty of this unpreparedness." Even President Theodore Roosevelt supported the NSPIE's mission, arguing in 1908 that vocational training was "vital to our future progress" to compete "for the markets of the world."[8]

Jane Addams joined the NSPIE the following year to promote vocational education for girls in their national lobbying efforts. Addams viewed vocationalism as an important public investment to better the labor lives of all working-class children. In 1907, Addams argued that high schools failed to prepare urban students for productive careers in industry. High school teachers were trapped in "the caves of classic learning," which only benefited middle-class students bound for college or teaching careers. Addams feared that high schools would become obsolete if school officials did not reform the curricula with the working child in mind. High schools needed hands-on trade courses and vocational guidance. Teachers needed to offer new classes on subjects like the history of American manufacturing. She warned that "education grows meaningless" when school officials "separate educational interests from contemporary life."[9]

Addams was one of the few NSPIE members who advocated for girls' vocational education. Addams and Mary Morton Kehew, a social reformer in

Boston, were the only women on the society's board of managers. Addams and Kehew organized a Women's Sub-Committee of the NSPIE in 1907 to investigate the vocational needs of girls who left school for industrial work in American cities. They reported in 1908 that the average girl worker under the age of twenty made six to eight dollars a week, usually as a factory hand, if she lacked vocational training. Women and girls who studied a trade like dressmaking or millinery made an average of fifteen to twenty dollars per week. Addams and Kehew concluded that girls needed vocational training as much if not more than boys "for the industrial civilization in which they are to live" if the United States hoped "to maintain her rank as a great industrial Nation."[10]

Addams and Kehew both supported the women's labor movement and helped organize the National WTUL in 1903. The National WTUL was a cross-class coalition of women dedicated to organizing female workers in labor unions, spreading awareness of women's working conditions, and advocating for protective labor legislation for women. Local chapters of the WTUL were often governed by middle-class and college-educated reformers like Addams and Kehew and represented by a rank and file of trade union women. Members argued that a lack of union representation further marginalized working women by limiting their access to vocational training and apprenticeships. The National WTUL's constitution declared their commitment to public vocational schools that could help women and girls "increase their economic value" through learning skilled trades like dressmaking. By the 1910s, the National WTUL encouraged members to pursue seats on local school boards to oversee "exactly what education the girls are getting." One of the WTUL's most active local chapters was in Chicago, where Addams had built ties between her fellow middle-class reformers and the labor community.[11]

WTUL members had different goals for the vocational education movement than most members of the NSPIE. One of the WTUL's most vocal advocates of vocational education in public high schools was Agnes Nestor. Nestor was the American-born daughter of Irish immigrants who had worked as a glove maker in Chicago since the age of fourteen. In 1903, she helped organize the International Ladies' Glove Workers Union and lobbied for protective labor laws for women workers in Illinois. Nestor argued that Chicago needed public trade schools to teach girls dressmaking, millinery, and garment design. She also wanted vocational education for both male and female students to teach the values of and rights secured by the labor movement. During an American Federation of Labor (AFL) convention in 1909, Nestor suggested that vocational programs should teach students the history of capitalism and the philosophy of collective bargaining. She

Agnes Nestor (1880–1948), 1914 (George Grantham Bain Collection, Library of Congress, Prints & Photographs Division)

believed school officials should require students to learn their local labor laws before leaving school for positions in shops and factories.[12]

Local WTUL members hoped to use vocational education to improve the future working lives of blue-collar women in the needle trades and protect the working girl from industrial oppression. Margaret Dreier Robins, a college-educated social reformer and president of the Chicago WTUL from 1907 to 1914, argued that women would remain on the lowest rungs of the garment industry without training in both labor skills and values. She asserted that a vocational program for future dressmakers should include the study of current labor laws, textile production methods, and the knowledge of how to supervise a shop room. At an NSPIE conference in 1910, Robins described this as the difference between teaching a girl to labor and teaching a girl "the value of her labor power." Robins espoused a different vision of vocational training than the NSPIE leadership. According to its constitution, NSPIE was founded to help students became more "effective economic units" through trade education. The New York hat-stitcher and union organizer Rose Schneiderman argued that the WTUL had different goals for vocational school reform. "The Women's Trade Union League is not interested merely in making more efficient machines out of our people," wrote Schneiderman. "We want to make better human beings."[13]

Men's labor unions were more suspicious of the vocational education movement and hesitant to join groups like the NSPIE in its early years. In Chicago, male labor leaders feared that public schools would train strikebreakers or destabilize the union apprenticeship tradition. Early financial support for vocational schools came from wealthy business leaders, which deepened antipathy among male trade unions. The AFL eventually joined the NSPIE in 1910 to work with, rather than against, middle-class education reformers on vocational programming in urban high schools. The National WTUL supported vocational education much sooner than male labor groups because women union leaders like Nestor had virtually no power for business leaders to threaten. Instead, labor women hoped to forge alliances with school officials as early as 1903 to train working-class girls for the female-dominated needle trades.[14]

The School of the Future

Chicago's superintendent of schools from 1900 to 1909, Edwin G. Cooley, embraced the Douglas Commission's recommendations to reform the public high school through vocationalism. Cooley was a former blacksmith turned progressive pedagogue who wanted the BOE to consider the future employment opportunities of working-class boys. Chicago school officials had designed the high school curriculum with the children of middle-class parents in mind. Most high school students—nearly seven out of ten at the turn of the century—were middle-class girls preparing for teaching careers. In the 1890s, the Chicago BOE introduced "commercial" classes (accounting and typing) to correct the gender imbalance by appealing to middle-class boys bound for professional careers. As one school official explained, white-collar courses prepared future "captains of commerce" to help the United States win "the global struggle for commercial supremacy." Cooley argued that commercial education neglected the working classes. "It has taken us a long time to wake up to the fact that we should also help the mechanic, the clerk, and the farmer," Cooley wrote in 1908. "They make up the body of our citizenship and they have been discriminated against."[15]

Under Cooley's leadership, school officials equipped nearly half of Chicago's public high schools with factory-style workrooms for boys to learn carpentry, foundry, machine repair, pipefitting, construction drawing, and electric work. Chicago school officials also constructed two new high schools dedicated to the industrial training of high school boys: the Richard T. Crane Technical High School for Boys (est. 1903) and the Albert Grannis Lane Technical High School for Boys (est. 1909).[16] School officials designed both "Crane Tech" and "Lane Tech" with expensive shop room machinery for foundry, wood turning, electric construction, carpentry, bookbinding, and mechanical drawing. Lane Tech was the city's largest school, built to accommodate 2,500 male students. Each shop room had an adjoining lecture hall where pupils received instruction in trade technique and method. Chicago's technical high schools also offered a standard high school curriculum but did not include commercial classes for white-collar work like typing or accounting. Cooley argued that vocational education should focus on industrial labor rather than white-collar jobs. "The school of the future will in all grades be industrial," he announced in 1909.[17]

Cooley and his supporters hoped that trade education would imbue the high school curriculum with virtues of strenuous manhood like action, energy, and hard work. Along with manual training for younger boys, school officials argued that trade education would appeal to older boys' "natural" proclivity for physical exertion. Gender anxieties help explain why male reformers like Cooley emphasized industrial education for trades rather than commercial education for white-collar work. Office culture also threatened expectations of strenuous American manhood. Turn-of-the-century observers described the sedentary office worker or salaried middle manager as effeminate and "overcivilized." President Theodore Roosevelt—who embodied the "strenuous man" ideal—wrote in 1907 that professional college-educated men were often "too fastidious and too sensitive to take part in the rough hurly-burly of the actual work of the world."[18]

At the height of the vocational education movement, Chicago officials mocked East Coast school districts that prioritized commercial education over industrial training for boys. The school systems of Boston and Philadelphia emphasized vocational training for future managers and business leaders by expanding commercial programs for their mostly middle-class high school students. Cooley and his colleagues argued that these East Coast high schools made boys sheepish. Chicago's technical schools turned boys into masculine tradesmen. In 1908, the principal of Lane Tech argued that Boston boys lacked "the strength and virility and rough and ready manners of our Chicago youth" due to the city's focus on white-collar coursework. After spending a day among Boston's male students who were "so good that they would not even whisper," he longed for "the brain and brawn of our red-corpuscled Chicago boys."[19]

Chicago school officials reformed high school programs with the American-born sons of European immigrants in mind. Both Crane Tech and Lane Tech were geographically removed from Chicago's South Side Black Metropolis. At Crane Tech, only three out of ninety graduating students were Black in 1913, and Lane Tech's class was all white. Chicago's Black reform community encouraged boys to pursue two-year vocational programs introduced in many neighborhood high schools. The *Chicago Defender* frequently published articles encouraging Black students to take full advance of "the splendid unrestricted system of learning in the northern cities." They complained that too many teenage boys loitered on the streets during school days and posed an embarrassment to their parents during a critical era of social uplift. Middle-class Black reformers hoped that access to trade education could increase the future employment prospects of Black boys in a racist labor system.[20]

Addams argued that Cooley's "schools of the future" should support the future labor lives of working-class girls. The mayor of Chicago appointed Addams to the Chicago BOE during Cooley's leadership. She tried to convince her fellow board members to establish vocational high schools for girls like Crane Tech and Lane Tech for boys. Addams and her colleagues in the Chicago WTUL also wanted high schools to emphasize industrial trades for girls rather than commercial training for white-collar jobs. Their support of trade education stemmed from a different set of gender anxieties. The needle trades represented a female-dominated industry in which women could excel to run their own dressmaking or millinery shops in the company of other female workers. As Addams argued, young dressmakers offered each other sisterly "companionship" and labored under the direction of other women, who could serve as maternal guides. Women-run dress and hat shops thus provided moral protection for girl workers by keeping them away from men.[21]

This cultural interest in the garment trades ignored twentieth-century realities in the female labor force. Large-scale garment manufacturing and the piecework system replaced the woman-run shop tradition in cities like Chicago and New York by the 1910s. Millinery was a shrinking industry that employed less than 2 percent of working women in American cities by World War I. Labor women in the WTUL perhaps hoped to reinvigorate this "female economy" through vocational school reform. But only white working girls figured into their romanticized vision of female shop work. Racist hiring practices had long excluded Black women and girls from the needle trades, leading Black seamstresses to establish their own shops in Black commercial districts. Including Black-run shops, Black women and girls accounted for less than 20 percent of seamstresses and dressmakers nationwide in the early twentieth century.[22]

By looking backward, WTUL members like Addams neglected the new popularity of office work for the daughters of European immigrants. American companies increasingly relied on a vast network of office workers to manage corporate records and oversee payroll after 1900. Inventions like the calculator and typewriter mechanized these tasks and created new opportunities for young women and girls with basic typing, math, and English language skills. While labor activists worried about the morality of mixed-sex office culture, young working girls eagerly pursued this new line of work. Office jobs provided the structured hours that working-class girls desired for evening leisure and weekend excursions. A 1913 study found that over 80 percent of Chicago's female clerical employees worked less than nine hours a day and never more than six days a week. Entry-level stenography jobs did not pay well. But office work was more reliable than many sewing jobs that ebbed with the flow of fashion markets and seasonal shopping.[23]

Labor activists in the WTUL also ignored commercial education for girls because offices challenged assumptions about women's "skilled" labor. Unlike the commercial sector, jobs in the manufacturing sector were delineated by gender at the turn of the century. Women and girls performed "light" manufacturing work associated with the feminine textile and artistic trades. These trades were a source of pride for union women like Nestor. Downtown offices threatened how working-class men and women defined their gender identities in terms of work and skill because office workers performed the same tasks regardless of gender. Typing and filing were not yet feminized or considered gendered skills. This gender neutrality created cultural anxieties about the breakdown of manhood and womanhood in corporate environments. Furthermore, many labor women in the WTUL also viewed offices as morally and socially dangerous for girls. Offices were filled with men and women who were not related to each other—some married, some single—and presented obvious opportunities for social and sexual interaction. In 1900, more than 70 percent of Chicago's office workers were men and boys. Women were still the minority workers in offices. The prospect of young single girls working under men therefore created power dynamics that worried women reformers across class lines in the WTUL.[24]

A different set of turn-of-the-century gender anxieties led men and women in the vocational education movement to promote trade education in urban high schools rather than commercial education for white-collar work. Men embraced shop classes to encourage strenuous manhood and maintain economic supremacy over industrial competitors like Germany. Labor activists in the WTUL, in contrast, uplifted trade education for girls to support the political goals of the women's labor movement. They wanted girls of legal working age to train for leadership roles in women-run garment shops where they could support fellow working women in the dignified needle arts. Their fixation on needle trades ignored the skills many high school-age girls wanted by the 1910s: typing, math, and English proficiency for office work.

A Great Deal of Confusion

The Chicago WTUL worked with their allies in the CWC to promote trade education for girls in secondary education. The CWC sent multiple petitions to the BOE between 1906 and 1909 requesting two reforms to the high school curriculum. First, their petition demanded that neighborhood high schools offer a two-year "industrial arts" program for girls like the two-year programs for boys instituted by Cooley. And second, they proposed at least two new public trade schools for girls that would serve as sister institutions of Crane Tech and Lane Tech. The CWC defined "industrial arts" for girls as instruction in the female-dominated needle trades ("industrial") as well as feminine domestic trades like home sewing and decorating ("arts"). The Chicago WTUL and representatives of local women's unions endorsed the petition along with a dozen other women's groups. Together, petitioners represented some 20,000 women across the state of Illinois.[25]

Members of the CWC wanted the proposed technical schools for girls to resemble two pioneering East Coast institutions: the Manhattan Trade School for Girls (est. 1902) and the Boston Trade School for Girls (est. 1904). Women's groups helped found and financially support both schools until they were absorbed by their respective public school systems in 1908. The trade schools of Boston and New York prepared female students between the ages of fourteen and seventeen for work in the female-dominated needle trades. Students at the Manhattan Trade School learned to make swimsuits, shirts, aprons, and dresses in factory-style workrooms outfitted with rows of foot-powered sewing machines. The Boston Trade School had a program for "fancy work" skills like embroidery and lace, which girls used to make garments, gloves, and lampshades. Experienced tradeswomen in New York and Boston, some of whom were local WTUL members, taught many of the trade programs.[26]

Girls also enrolled in domestic science classes that included cooking, home sewing and mending, sanitation, and personal hygiene at the public trade schools of Boston and New York. Women in the domestic science movement had leadership roles in East Coast trade schools for girls. One of the first domestic science professors at Columbia University's Teachers College, Mary Schenck Woolman, directed the Manhattan Trade School for Girls in its opening decade. One of the founders of the Boston Trade School, middle-class social reformer Florence Marshall, argued that domestic science prepared working girls to run their homes safely when they exited the workforce for marriage. In a 1909 article, Marshall reasoned that working-class girls needed vocational training for both phases of work life so they could excel to "a better class of industry" and understand "intelligent care of the home." Domestic training also improved a working girl's character according to Marshall, making her "more responsible, more reliable, and more womanly."[27]

The Boston and Manhattan Trade Schools for Girls reflect middle- and upper-class women's shifting views on working-class girlhood in the early twentieth century. The college-educated domestic scientists and social reformers who founded these schools accepted that working-class girls needed to earn wages outside the home. They supported the goals of the women's labor movement in defending the working girl's right to better her odds in the female economy through vocational training. But these women assumed wage earning was a temporary condition of premarital girlhood. Before World War I, less than a quarter of working women in America were married. The average working women earned wages for only seven years. College-educated reformers reasoned that the working girl needed education for her transition into homemaking womanhood. They designed vocational programs to address what they saw as two phases of modern feminine labor: temporary wage earning (girlhood) followed by lifelong homemaking (womanhood).[28]

Most supporters of a girls' trade school took for granted that vocational programs would place equal if not additional weight on domestic science for girls. Social reformer Sophonisba Breckinridge, who helped found the School of Civics and Philanthropy at the University of Chicago, endorsed the CWC's proposal for a girls' technical high school in 1906. She argued that education for her working-class "sisters" should emphasize household instruction for the future safety of working-class families. "Being girls, they expect to marry," she explained to the *Chicago Tribune*. "The working girl does not assume that she will work, always. She hasn't the professional point of view.... It would hardly be natural to expect her to." Social reformers like Breckinridge were sympathetic to the financial needs of working-class girls and wanted schools to invest in their wage-earning potential. Yet they also hoped the vocational movement would funnel resources toward the socially essential work of caretakers and homemakers. This activism aligned with the larger reform goals of Breckinridge and her colleagues in the settlement house movement who wanted government officials to make greater investments in the welfare of mothers and children.[29]

Members of the WTUL also emphasized the social significance of working-class women's unpaid labor in the home. Union leaders like Nestor argued that safer and better-paid positions in the manufacturing sector would make urban women better mothers. In 1909, Nestor successfully lobbied for a ten-hour workday restriction for Illinois women on behalf of the Chicago WTUL. She argued that shorter work hours would protect women's physical stamina and allow women to devote more time and energy to homemaking and child-rearing. The assertation that improved working conditions would benefit urban households was reflected in the National WTUL's slogan: "The Eight Hour Day—A Living Wage—To Guard the Home."[30]

Labor women in the WTUL did not, however, consider vocational education the appropriate tool for supporting working-class motherhood. On the contrary, local members argued that vocational courses should prepare girls strictly for wage-earning pursuits. Leonora O'Reilly was a thirty-four-year-old seamstress and member of the New York WTUL who taught shirt making at the Manhattan Trade School for Girls. In 1914, O'Reilly responded to a question on whether "vocational education" for girls should include domestic science. She argued that the goal of vocational education was to increase wage-earning potential. Women who earned higher wages and worked fewer hours, she reasoned, had more time and physical strength to cultivate happy home lives. Better working conditions—not domestic education—would make better mothers. "I do not think that 70 per cent of children die because the mother does not know how to take care of them," O'Reilly argued. She offered another explanation: "The mother may have been so overworked in the factory or mill that she never should have brought a child into the world."[31]

In Chicago, local WTUL members worried that including domestic training in their proposal for a girls' trade school would confuse the larger goals of the vocational education movement. At an NSPIE conference in 1909, Margaret Dreier Robins argued that efforts to educate girls for their "double part" as wage earner and homemaker had created "a great deal of confusion" over the purpose of vocational education in urban high schools. "I am not saying that cooking and sewing are not necessary," Robins explained in her speech. "But when we cheat a girl out of the training she ought to have for her breadwinning capacity . . . then we make a great and grave mistake." For Robins, the purpose of vocational training was distinct from the goals of the domestic science movement. She suggested that if that domestic instruction must be offered, reformers should clarify that these classes would supplement trade training but never replace it.[32]

A coalition of labor reformers and clubwomen demanded school investments in the vocational training of working-age girls. Women's groups agreed to lobby for gender segregation in public high schools, arguing that working-class girls needed their own schools and special courses under the leadership of women. Their differing class contexts created debate over the degree to which domestic science should factor in the girls' vocational curriculum. Labor women like Nestor ultimately agreed to endorse the CWC's proposal that included both industrial education for wage earning and domestic science for the home. As labor activists feared, this uneasy alliance had long-term consequences for how school officials defined "vocational education" for girls well into the twentieth century.

The Comprehensive High School

These school reformers hoped that Ella Flagg Young would support their petition when she assumed the superintendency in 1909. Edwin Cooley was resistant to integrating trade education for girls into the neighborhood high schools. Like other men in school governance, he argued that the high school curriculum already catered too heavily to female students who crowded classrooms on their path to teacher certification. In 1902, Cooley argued that two-year trade classes could correct the gender imbalance by encouraging more fourteen- to sixteen-year-old boys to pursue secondary education. Without trade education for boys, he worried that the city's high schools would simply become "girls' schools." But the Chicago WTUL wanted curricular reform for the working-class girl. The daughters of middle-class American parents—not working-class immigrants—filled high school classrooms preparing for teaching careers. Furthermore, women's groups pointed to the gender injustice of investing substantial school resources into state-of-the-art technical schools that trained future working boys for manufacturing. They argued that the future working girl was also entitled to a dedicated trade education.[33]

Young announced her support for girls' vocational education when she began her tenure as superintendent of schools. "Since becoming superintendent I have heard nothing but boy, boy, boy," she announced at a press conference about trade education. "I think it's time we heard something about girl, girl, girl." Yet Young was skeptical of the proposal for girls-only trade schools due to her allegiance to the American tradition of coeducation. Coeducation made public schooling in the United States distinct from European countries at the turn of the century, and progressive educators like Young viewed coeducation as a symbol of the nation's democratic principles. Young was ideologically opposed to an educational system that isolated boys and girls in separate schoolhouses. Writing against the CWC's petition in 1908, Young argued: "There is no difference between the mind of a girl and the mind of a boy. You make them different when you educate them differently."[34]

Addams invited Young to a meeting of women's groups at Hull House to explain their proposal for a girls-only trade school. Young remained skeptical after Addams's presentation. "I don't agree with Miss Addams on separate high schools for boys and girls," Young reiterated. "I am a decided coeducationist... boys and girls are educated better together." Young argued that students also gained important social skills in coeducational environments because girls had a civilizing effect on their male classmates. Young wanted Chicago's high schools to provide a "comprehensive education" that combined vocational training, academic instruction, and character development opportunities for all students under one roof. Students who wanted to become dressmakers, Young suggested, should do so on their own time. "We do not need industrial training for girls," she concluded.

Addams suggested that Young's commitment to coeducation was impractical given the current imbalance of vocational programs in Chicago high schools. "I am not such a poor coeducationist," Addams quipped after Young's remarks. Ideally, Addams explained, "we could add large wings for girls to Lane and Crane" and thus create coeducation in the city's current technical high schools. But doing so was logistically impractical. Furthermore, these schools were already under the leadership of men who were not familiar with the needs of the city's working girls. Addams argued that finding "the right men to take charge of such a school" would be impossible. The better option was to create new public schools for girls run by women who could serve as maternal guides.[35]

Young also suggested that the trade school model was fundamentally classist. While she supported vocational programs in neighborhood high schools, she was critical of the dedicated trade schools for boys established during Cooley's leadership. Young argued that segregating boys and girls "who intend to earn a living" from those who were "supported by their families" would lead to resentment and "snobbishness" between students. She worried that working-class children who needed to prepare for immediate employment would be robbed of a general education and the joys of intellectual exploration. She did not believe "the American workman" should forfeit his right "to the stimulus that comes through the humanities" for the sake of job preparation. Addams and her colleagues argued that trade schools were not classist but class-conscious. The demands of industrial labor required school officials to devote greater resources to the city's working-class children.[36]

Young ultimately agreed that neighborhood high schools should offer elective vocational programs for girls who desired practical training for the workforce. In 1910, Young introduced a dozen two-year vocational programs mostly aimed at appealing to fourteen- to sixteen-year-old boys who were most likely to leave school for work at these ages. Male students could enroll in two-year programs in most Chicago high schools by 1911, including mechanical drawing, electricity, carpentry, machine shop, accounting, and stenography. She introduced one two-year vocational program specifically for girls: household arts. Young suggested that the two-year household arts program addressed the CWC's petition for a course on industrial arts. Her household arts program taught some needle trade skills like dressmaking along with domestic science skills like cooking and infant care. Young argued that girls of working age who completed the two-year household arts program were prepared to earn wages in "the textile trades" and become "efficient homemakers." All but two of Chicago's public high schools offered the two-year household arts program by 1912.[37]

These two-year programs were part of Young's larger effort to make the high school curriculum more "comprehensive." Opposed to the trade school model, the comprehensive high school model incorporated academic and vocational courses in one curriculum. Students all received a standard "English education" in reading, writing, math, and science. They all took physical culture and could pick a humanistic elective like art or a foreign language. Students could also choose a two-year vocational elective like household arts or carpentry. Young argued that comprehensive high schools embraced diversity and fostered harmony between students of different cultural and class backgrounds. These schools were therefore "the greatest service that a democratic nation can demand." The comprehensive high school, however, gendered students' high school experience in new ways. Male students were the assumed pupils of all but one of the two-year vocational programs expanded under Young's leadership (household arts). Despite her ideological commitments to coeducation, Young's high school curriculum increased the number of school activities segregated by gender and maintained disproportionate funding for male students.[38]

Furthermore, naming the two-year vocational program "household arts" instead of "industrial arts" reflected Young's commitment to domestic instruction for urban girls. The high school program was essentially an extension of domestic science in the elementary schools. School officials equipped high schools with "cooking laboratories" in the 1910s for girls to learn the science of baking and sanitation. Many cooking labs had adjoining classrooms filled with dining room furniture assembled by male carpentry students, with which girls practiced meal serving and place setting. Girls learned needle trades in most programs, but school records suggest that sewing classes emphasized making and mending household items. Girls learned to design clothing for children and sew curtains, using textbooks with titles like *Household Textiles* and *Shelter and Clothing*. As local WTUL members feared, vocational programs for the "double part" of working girl and homemaking woman resulted in milquetoast household arts classes that de-emphasized the trade skills needed to earn wages in the female economy.[39]

The two-year household arts program was unpopular among girls throughout Chicago's neighborhood high schools. Less than 2 percent of female students enrolled in household arts classes citywide in 1913. In contrast, over 50 percent of male students elected vocational coursework that year. Female students who had the luxury to pursue a secondary education—still a small minority before World War I—were uninterested in spending their school days learning to cook and sew. One Chicago student in the 1910s recalled decades later that household arts "was the last thing I wanted to major in!" Most parents who could support a secondary education for their daughters were American born and middle class. They expected their daughters to use a four-year high school diploma toward a teaching career or college. Girls who excelled in the city's public high schools before World War I continued to focus on academic studies and ignored the vocational education movement all together. Their lack of interest frustrated school officials. As one BOE member complained in 1913: "The cooking classes seem not so popular, nor the girls so enthusiastic."[40]

Black students were particularly uninterested in household arts at the high school level. Black girls pursued a four-year high school diploma to continue to college and professional careers. Many hoped to transfer to the Chicago Normal School to become teachers. Their lack of interest in household arts confused white school administrators who assumed Black girls would embrace domestic education to prepare for service work. "Negros want to know nothing about industrial training," complained one Chicago school official in 1919. "The girls don't care for sewing and cooking."

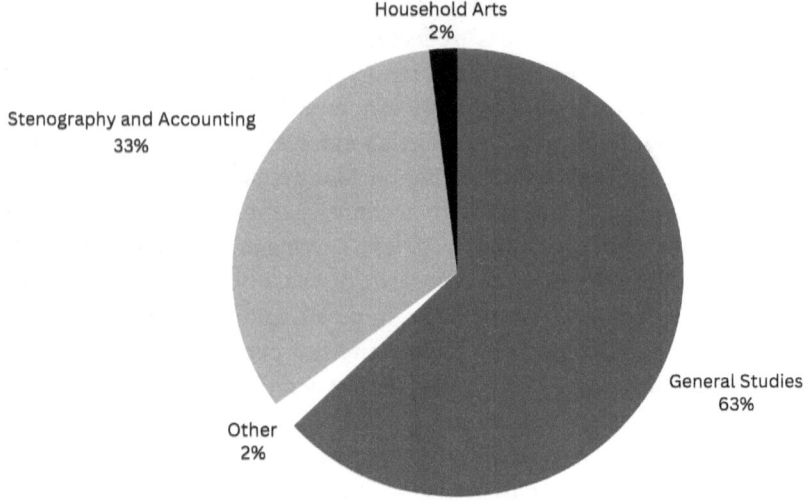

Female Student Choice of Study in Chicago High Schools, 1913

Data from the *Fifty-Ninth Annual Report of the Chicago Board of Education, 1913* (Chicago Board of Education Archives)

Some local teachers and administrators attempted to steer Black girls into household arts programs based on their racialized vision of Black women's work. Presumptuous school officials ignored the class context of Black high school students. Middle-class girls with high school diplomas did not work as servants.[41]

Stenography was the only two-year vocational elective that appealed to girls in Young's comprehensive curriculum. A third of Chicago's female high school students enrolled in stenography during the 1910s. These students overwhelmingly had white American-born or European immigrant parents. They hoped to fill new positions in the downtown clerical sector that were newly open to white English-speaking women. Men still dominated clerical jobs before World War I despite the growing need for entry-level stenographers in the corporate sector. In 1912, over 90 percent of office workers in Chicago were men and teenage boys. But girls represented 47 percent of stenography students and 30 percent of bookkeeping students in Chicago public schools that year. Office work did not simply open to white American women in the 1910s; these enrollment choices suggest that second-generation girls also pushed their way in.[42]

Girls' pursuit of teaching careers and office work was out of step with the WTUL's reform goals for vocational education. Working-class activists like

Agnes Nestor wanted to empower blue-collar girls through trade education, not pull girls out of the blue-collar field. Middle-class school reformers agreed that girls of legal working age deserved dedicated training for both paid and unpaid labor under the leadership of women. These reform goals were somewhat irrelevant to female students who prepared for college, teaching, and white-collar work in neighborhood high schools. Young's two-year vocational programs were entirely irrelevant to the masses of working-class girls who still left school for work by age fourteen with or without legal working papers.

A Technical School for Girls

Members of the Chicago WTUL remained steadfast in their belief that the city needed a dedicated technical school for the working-class girl. Their pressure to open a public trade school for girls mounted during a wave of garment workers' strikes in Chicago and New York in the winter of 1910. Outrage over oppressive labor conditions led to months-long demonstrations of garment workers on the streets of Chicago, many of whom were teenage girls from eastern and southern Europe. More than 40,000 Chicago garment workers participated in demonstrations for higher wages and safer working conditions between September 1910 and February 1911. The Chicago garment workers strike was part of a broader movement of women's labor organizing in the industrial North. The previous winter, Jewish garment workers in New York City organized the largest strike of women workers in American history—dubbed the "Uprising of 20,000"—in demand of union recognition. The International Ladies' Garment Workers Union (ILGWU) represented 85 percent of women workers in the shirtwaist industry by the end of the strike. Indeed, the beginning of the 1910s marked a major high point of union organizing among working-class girls and women.[43]

Women in the vocational education movement were deeply involved with the strikes and used this context to lobby for girls' trade education in Chicago. The Chicago WTUL supported the strikers' organization of a new chapter of the United Garment Workers (UGW). Middle- and upper-class reformers like Jane Addams supported striking women and girls by arranging legal services for them. Members of the CWC used their resources to bail picketers out of jail, testified on their behalf in court, and collected donations to make up for lost wages. The strikes confirmed reformers' assertions that the city had a responsibility to invest in the future labor lives of working-class girls. During the Chicago strikes, Ellen Martin Henrotin suggested that clubwomen establish their own private trade school for girls if the BOE refused to address this need. She argued that clubwomen could fund a "national trade school for girls" using their remaining revenue from the Woman's Building of the Chicago World's Columbian Exposition (World's Fair) of 1893.[44]

The garment strikes seemed to convince Ella Flagg Young that the city needed a public trade school for girls under women's leadership. In the winter of 1911, she announced that school officials must meet the "long felt want" for girls' industrial training. Her timely announcement came one month after the notorious Triangle Shirtwaist Factory fire in New York City, which resulted in the deaths of over one hundred girl workers in their teens due to the factory's lack of basic safety regulations. In the wake of this tragedy, Young argued that it was "the duty of the City" to protect young female workers from entering the most dangerous and "most poorly paid parts" of the industrial workforce. Young also conceded that girls should receive vocational training in a dedicated facility run by women, even though "co-education is preferable in ethical practice." She suggested the BOE name the school after Lucy Flower, the former BOE member and CWC president who brought sewing into the elementary schools in the 1890s. The Lucy Flower Technical High School for Girls—popularly known as Flower Tech—opened in the fall of 1911 as Chicago's first public school for girls.[45]

Flower Tech was the result of successful activism by women reformers who argued that public school officials must invest in the future labor lives of working-class girls. Flower Tech was originally housed in a vacant schoolhouse in the South Loop. School officials renovated the building with factory-style classrooms filled with foot-powered sewing and buttonhole machines, where girls learned various techniques for working with garments and gloves. Along with a traditional high school curriculum, students enrolled in either two- and four-year needle trade programs for aspiring dressmakers, milliners, and designers. Flower Tech's design department featured a display room where girls practiced dressing mannequins as preparation for department store jobs. Flower Tech also had an on-site laundry department in the school's basement, a dining room, and a cooking laboratory for required household arts instruction. Flower Tech remained the city's only all-girls public school for the next half century.[46]

Flower Tech's curriculum reflected middle-class women's preoccupation with preparing working-class girls for respectable womanhood. Education for domesticity outweighed trade training in the Flower Tech curriculum. "A technical school for girls," Young explained of the school, "must provide first for a general training in the art of homemaking and second a marketable skill in occupations suitable for women." Young designed the Flower Tech curriculum with her colleague Dora Wells, who served as founding principal. Wells was a graduate of Wellesley College who spent most of her postcollege career training future teachers at the Chicago Normal School. Wells echoed Young that a "school built around the girl" must offer education for both "women's work" and "women's needs." Wells argued that training for domesticity was a need because the average American woman spent more time working in the home than in the paid labor force. Some girls wanted training for work, but all girls needed education for the home.[47]

Members of the Chicago WTUL were quickly disillusioned by Flower Tech's emphasis on domestic instruction. Chicago labor women resented their lack of involvement in teaching trade courses in the school, which was common practice in the girls' trade schools in Boston and New York. Male labor leaders were also partners in boys' vocational training in Chicago. By 1912, school officials allowed select craft unions to run apprenticeship programs for boys enrolled in the city's technical high schools. The International Brotherhood of Electrical Workers, among others, had seats on an advisory committee with the school board that oversaw some 600 high school apprentices a year. Trade women in the Chicago WTUL hoped that Young would similarly engage "women of experience" in the training of future garment workers at Flower Tech. They wanted apprenticeship programs for girls run by tradeswomen. Instead, middle-class women with teaching degrees oversaw the vocational programs at Flower Tech.[48]

Young and Wells responded to this criticism by stressing the practicality of homemaking education for working-class girls. Young argued that apprenticeship programs overemphasized "the money side" of vocational education rather than "the joy of working." She suggested that girls' character development was the goal of trade education rather than improving wage earning. Flower Tech students practiced trades to learn "the most valuable asset in the world: initiative." Wells echoed these points in defense of the school. She admitted that Flower Tech students lost some "wage-earning power" because the curriculum emphasized homemaking skills. But wage earning was only a temporary pastime of premarital girlhood. Wells argued that only some girls earned wages. All women cared for the home. The loss of wage-earning power for Flower Tech students, she concluded, "must be accepted as inevitable under the present organization of society."[49]

Disappointment with Flower Tech led members of the Chicago WTUL to open their own trade schools for girls. With financial support from the CWC, Jane Addams established the Hull-House Trade School for Girls in 1912. The school offered dressmaking education and apprenticeship opportunities for girls over the age of fourteen who graduated from the city's elementary schools. Two years later, Agnes Nestor and Margaret Dreier Robins opened a school for garment workers in the Chicago WTUL's headquarters building. The Training School for Active Women Workers was the first full-time labor school in the United States. The school catered exclusively to young women and girls over the age of fourteen. Students studied existing labor legislation, the history of the women's movement, and the history of capitalism in courses led by local WTUL members. Students had the opportunity to apprentice with skilled dressmakers and glove stitchers and engaged in "field work" by visiting union offices and participating in strikes.[50]

These short-lived schools highlight the Chicago WTUL's desire to train working-class girls for active participation in the labor movement. Both schools offer an alternative vision of vocational education for the working girl rooted in working-class values and not just working-class skills. Like Flower Tech, both schools privileged trade education in garment work to preserve and uplift the female-dominated needle arts. The next generation of working-class women, however, often had different priorities when pursuing vocational schooling.

A Poor Man's Vassar

Flower Tech struggled to attract its target demographic of white working-class girls bound for the needle trades. When Flower Tech opened in 1911, social workers with the Chicago Commons settlement house visited tenement neighborhoods near the stockyards to tell immigrant mothers about the school. They were frustrated by the lack of interest among first-generation woman who said the school was not worth the carfare or the lost wages of their daughters. Settlement house workers only convinced six mothers in the meatpacking district to enroll their daughters at Flower Tech. All but two dropped out to join the workforce within two years. Flower Tech was the least-populated high school in Chicago with only 158 full-time students by 1913. When the school opened, Young estimated an enrollment of at least 500 girls. The reality remained that most working parents expected their children to leave school and support the family through paid or unpaid labor. Investing time and money in secondary education was not often feasible.[51]

Many immigrant parents who chose to send their daughters to Flower Tech were not interested in the school's vocational programs. Immigrant parents from South Side enclaves like Bridgeport and Englewood enrolled their daughters at Flower Tech simply because the school was girls only. Flower Tech had no male students, teachers, or even staff members. Boys were not allowed within two blocks of the schoolhouse. The total gender segregation of Flower Tech appealed to parents who hoped to protect their daughters' modesty for the marriage market. In oral histories, alumnae

Practical Cooking—Preparation of Lunch for the Rest of the School

Costume Designing and Draping

Students in cooking and garment design courses at Lucy Flower Technical High School, 1921 (Library of Congress)

recalled how Flower Tech felt like "a boarding school that you didn't live in." Some immigrant parents gave their daughters the choice to either attend Flower Tech or a Catholic school for girls. Encouraging respectability—not vocational training—was the draw for protective immigrant parents. "You could always tell a Flower Girl," recalled the daughter of Italian immigrants. "We always acted like ladies."[52]

Black families also valued the respectability of Flower Tech's all-girls environment more than its vocational curriculum. Flower Tech first opened in the city's former South Division High School building at Twenty-Sixth and Wabash near Chicago's Black business district. Middle-class families who worked in the Black Metropolis enrolled their daughters immediately. By 1918, 20 percent of Flower Tech students were Black. Black girls made up roughly a third of students in the 1920s. Many of these "Flower Girls" were not working-class daughters as the WTUL had in mind for Chicago's female trade school. On the contrary, they were the daughters of Black bankers, lawyers, and other prominent South Side community leaders. They hoped to use a four-year education to pursue teaching careers, college, and nursing school. These students included Mabel Wheeler, the daughter of the first Black lawyer in Illinois, and Alfreda Barnett, the daughter of civil rights activist Ida B. Wells-Barnett.[53]

The school's all-girls environment and emphasis on domestic respectability made Flower Tech desirable for these "daughters of the race." In oral histories, Black alumnae also described Flower Tech as a classy school for "ladies." Black clubwomen helped foster this reputation in its early years. In 1915, Black clubwoman Marie Clay Hudlin received special permission from Ella Flagg Young to attend Flower Tech alongside her fifteen-year-old daughter, Irene Bernice. The *Chicago Defender* praised the "wholesome example" set by the "charming and brilliant society matron" who devoted her spare time to taking courses at Flower Tech. The *Defender* also "took pride" in the respectability of Flower Tech students like Irene Bernice, whose coming-out party was publicized in the paper the following year. The *Chicago Defender* increased Flower Tech's reputation as a prestigious school for high-achieving girls throughout the 1920s and 1930s by publishing profiles of Black students that detailed their college and career ambitions alongside a glamorous headshot.[54]

Some Flower Tech students wanted to attend the city's first and only vocational school for girls to work as tradeswomen, often against the wishes of parents. These alumnae recalled how the school attracted "dreamers" who wanted to run their own stores or become bridal designers. Flower Tech was a school for girls of a "different type of personality" who hoped to do something creative with their hands in the female economy. Mary

Brooks Staver, the daughter of Jewish immigrants, convinced her parents to let her enroll in a two-year millinery program at Flower Tech. Her parents preferred that Staver leave school by age fourteen with a work certificate to help support the family income. Staver insisted the training would help her land a better position when she turned sixteen. After two years at Flower Tech, Staver found a position as a hat saleswoman at the Marshall Field department store in downtown Chicago. She earned enough money at Marshall Field to support herself as a single working woman for eleven years. As an adult, Staver felt proud of her job and grateful for access to trade training. People joked that "all the old maids come from Lucy Flower," she recalled. "I was so glad to get a chance to go to school."[55]

The trade programs at Flower Tech were most useful for white American-born girls like Staver. These courses proved unrealistic for Black students, who rarely found work in downtown department stores and dress shops. Black girls who embraced the specialized trade programs at Flower Tech struggled to find jobs when they graduated. While some found work in Black-owned businesses with their high school diplomas, many Black alumnae who studied needle trades for two years later worked in factories. One student, Willetta Yates Greer, pursued a millinery degree at Flower Tech. Greer worked at a lampshade factory after graduation along with her sister, a fellow Flower Tech alumna.[56]

The vocational interests of Black students were never the priority of Flower Tech's founders and early administrators. In fact, the school's growing popularity among South Side Black girls likely encouraged the BOE to relocate Flower Tech across town after World War I. In 1915, school officials argued that Flower Tech should be moved to protect girls from "vice" and "evils in its neighborhood." Flower Tech's proximity to the downtown red-light district stoked these concerns about protecting girls' sexual purity. But talk of a Flower Tech move coincided with controversy over racial integration in other South Side high schools, most notably Wendell Phillips High School. Black parents argued that local officials tried to segregate their children in the "Jim Crow School" throughout the 1910s. The Negro Fellowship League launched an investigation into these complaints and put pressure on the BOE to fire the school's dean of girls, whom they accused of segregating Black students in social activities. School officials announced that Flower Tech was "unable to cope with surroundings" a month after the league's investigation into Wendell Phillips High School. They temporarily moved Flower Tech to an unused schoolhouse forty blocks away at Sixty-First Street and Wabash Avenue. School officials constructed a dedicated four-story schoolhouse for Flower Tech on the West Side of the city in 1926, directly across the street from the scenic Garfield Park Conservatory.[57]

Lucy Flower Technical High School for Girls, 3545 West Fulton Boulevard, 1928 (Chicago History Museum, ICHi-069982)

Black students followed Flower Tech to Garfield Park and took advantage of its more modern facilities. Migrant daughters from the Jim Crow South made up a large contingent of Black enrollment at the new schoolhouse in the 1920s. Migrant families viewed this racially integrated, all-girls public school as the height of a prestigious northern education. Alumnae from this era recalled their hourlong commutes to the Garfield Park neighborhood and the strain on their families to cover the carfare. But the experience was well worth it for girls with teaching and college ambitions. Mildred Tolliver Hoskins migrated to Chicago from Alabama with her parents and enrolled at Flower Tech in the 1920s. Hoskins later described the school as "a poor man's Vassar" for migrant girls from working-class families like her own. The modern, multilevel institution of brick and limestone stood in stark contrast to the dilapidated one-room schoolhouses available to girls like Hoskins in the South. She recalled her pride in the new Flower Tech building decades after graduating. "Like moving from a kitchenette to a ten-room mansion. Everything was new and wonderful."[58]

This early history of Flower Tech highlights the disparate goals of vocational school reformers and the communities they served. Members of the CWC and Chicago WTUL lobbied for an all-girls trade school to promote their visions of working-class girlhood. The next generation of working girls were largely uninterested. Immigrant parents showed little interest while Black girls reimagined Flower Tech as a school for "ladies." Moving Flower Tech away from the South Side did not change how students used the school. On the contrary, relocating Flower Tech to a more modern facility only increased its reputation as a respectable institution for high-achieving girls of color. White women's groups successfully established a public trade school for girls by 1911. But girls decided why the school mattered. For many of them, the trade programs mattered very little.

Conclusion

This history of girls' vocational education highlights the centrality of school reform to the broader social reform agendas of Progressive Era women's groups. Members of the Chicago WTUL looked to the emergence of vocational education as an opportunity to insert the values of the women's labor movement into the public school curriculum. Reformers with roots in the settlement house and women's club movements argued that vocational education would encourage cleaner homes and healthier urban children. They shared high hopes that vocational education could improve the lives of working-class girls who left the school system to labor in factories, shops, and within their own homes. Their support of vocationalism helped gender the high school curriculum and confirm its new function of educating boys and girls for separate work roles.

Women school reformers were limited by a narrow focus on needle trades during the vocational education movement. The joint activism of CWC and Chicago WTUL members reveals a common interest in promoting the needle trades for their cultural value more so than their economic benefit for girls. Needlework offered transferable skills for the home and protected sexual purity by keeping girls out of mixed-gender offices. For labor women like Agnes Nestor, education for needle trades uplifted the work and social respectability of blue-collar women. These school reformers rarely, if ever, discussed the challenges of finding work in the shrinking needle trade market or the material benefits of office work for girls. Using school reform as social reform led women's groups to overlook the vocational interests of actual working-class girls: upward class mobility.

Students and families used Chicago's public school system to meet their own goals, as they had before the vocational education movement. The daughters of immigrants embraced commercial classes to prepare for white-collar work. Black students attended Chicago's only trade school for girls to improve their academic record for college. Most working-class girls left the school system by (or before) the legal working age and ignored these reforms altogether. Over the next decade, however, the vocational education movement became harder to ignore as women's groups created new bureaucracies to guide working-class children back into the classroom.

[CHAPTER FIVE]

Sex, Spending, and "Going Astray"

Vocational Guidance Counseling for Girls
of Legal Working Age, 1910–1920s

The Chicago Vice Commission conducted the nation's first municipal investigation of sex work in 1910. The commission of social reformers, doctors, and members of the clergy aimed to uncover "the social evil" of the urban sex trade, which was legal in Chicago's designated red-light district. They interviewed sex workers, brothel owners, and customers to understand the "torturing temptation" to pursue sex work among working-class women and girls. Their widely read study, *The Social Evil in Chicago* (1911), concluded that the average sex worker in Chicago was white, American born, and left school for work between ages fourteen and sixteen. Without a secondary education, these working-class girls chose to triple their wages in the sex trade rather than succumb to "city poverty" as domestic servants or factory hands. The commissioners recommended that school officials invest in high school vocational programs to dissuade "tempted girls" from entering the sex trade on the promise of higher wages. Reforming the public education of girls could serve the interests of urban vice prevention.[1]

Urban reformers argued that criminalizing sex work would protect working girls from moral corruption and sexual abuse. Former president of the Chicago Woman's Club (CWC), Ellen Martin Henrotin, demanded the mayor appoint her to the all-male vice commission in 1910. "Without the aid of women, the evil will never be abolished," she asserted. Like many of her reform efforts, Henrotin believed that working-class girls were not safe to enter the labor force without the moral and vocational guidance of women like herself. She argued that men seduced or tricked white American-born girls into the sex trade and confined them as "white slaves" to brothels. To protect white girls from the real and imagined dangers of sex work, vice reformers like Henrotin not only helped shut down brothels and incarcerate alleged sex traffickers; they also policed urban girlhood through public education. In the 1910s, women's groups used the threat of sex work and "white slavery" to introduce a new bureaucracy into the school system that oversaw when students exited the school system for work.[2]

Panic over working-class girls, sex, and delinquency brought vocational guidance counseling into Chicago public schools and juvenile courts in the 1910s. A group of social reformers and clubwomen in Chicago organized the Vocational Supervision League (VSL) to offer employment guidance to girls in the "dangerous age" of fourteen to sixteen years old. The VSL promoted vocational guidance as vice prevention, arguing that white American girls in this age range were particularly vulnerable when leaving school without maternal supervision. They helped organize the women-led Vocational Guidance Bureau, a public school agency that encouraged working-class children to pursue a high school education. They funded scholarships that helped mostly white working-class children stay in school and prepare for "respectable" careers. Black social reformers also engaged in vocational guidance campaigns to steer working-class girls away from "vice" and encourage their continued education. In the 1910s, the VSL successfully leveraged racialized anxiety about the white working girl's sexual purity to make guidance counseling a formal function of Chicago's public school system.

Women's vocational guidance reform was not unique to Chicago. School officials throughout the urban North used vocational guidance to standardize students' transition from school to work and, as historians have noted, to curb juvenile delinquency and promote productive citizenship among the children of immigrants.[3] Yet scholars have neglected the gendered and racialized nature of this movement. Girls of legal working age raised distinct fears about sexual delinquency, prostitution, and the moral future of American cities. Vocational guidance counseling in the 1910s reflected "white slavery hysteria" in which reformers demanded state intervention to protect the sexual purity of white girls while ignoring the sexual exploitation of Black girls. Women guidance professionals and probation officers feared that the new financial autonomy of second-generation working girls could expose them to alleged "sex traffickers" and increase sexual delinquency. Women in the guidance movement worked together to guide these "problem girls" back to school, policing their labor and leisure lives in the process.

The popularity of office work among second-generation immigrants heightened anxieties about the white working girl's sexuality and financial freedom. Women in the guidance movement argued that a new obsession with urban nightlife and consumerism encouraged girls to pursue "indecent" employment as stenographers for higher wages. As a mixed-sex workplace, the downtown office stoked fears that male managers could sexually assault or even traffic stenographers as "white slaves." Demographic changes in the urban workforce during World War I alleviated these fears by feminizing office culture and racializing office work as white. In the postwar decade, second-generation girls benefited from a new cultural acceptance of office work and received scholarship support from the VSL to stay in school and study stenography. These white-collar skills helped the daughters of immigrants join the clerical sector and assert their American identities through the social cachet of downtown office culture. While second-generation girls ultimately benefited from the vocational guidance movement, their support from the VSL reflected a persistent effort to contain white working girl sexuality by guiding these students toward "respectable" labor.[4]

Peril to the Girl of Fourteen

Urban reformers blamed weak child labor laws for rising rates of juvenile delinquency in the 1910s. In a 1912 study, the City Club of Chicago reported that over 23,000 children left school each year to "flit about" from job to job. The City Club pinned this problem on the work certificate system. School and state officials allowed children to receive work certification by age fourteen without verifying if they had secured safe or stable employment. The City Club concluded that the work certificate system thus encouraged "irregularity of habit" among adolescents, which constituted "the undoing of manhood and womanhood." The Chicago problem mirrored national trends. According to the US Bureau of Labor Statistics, two-thirds of all children arrested by police in American cities were in their "transitional period" between school and work. Crimes of "sexual delinquency"—alleged sex work or sexual activity—were the most common offenses for girls arrested during their transition out of the school system.[5]

School officials created vocational guidance programs to curb juvenile delinquency and promote productive citizenship among urban children leaving school for work. Two professors and social reformers, Meyer Bloomfield and Frank Parsons, introduced the first vocational guidance program in Boston public schools in 1909. Bloomfield and Parsons were leaders in the national vocational guidance movement. In his influential *Choosing a Vocation* (1909), Parsons argued that working-class children needed more than vocational training in public schools. Educators also needed to guide students out of the school system by directing them toward decent employment. "We guide our boys and girls to some extent through school then drop them into this complex world to sink or swim," he wrote. Bloomfield and Parson proposed that school systems invest in a new group of counseling professionals who protected children from adopting vagrant lifestyles, "wasting their golden years," and "drifting through life like a rudderless boat." School districts in the industrial North from Milwaukee to New York organized vocational counseling bureaus in the years that followed.⁶

Urban women's groups used terms like "drifting" and "going astray" as euphemisms for the moral danger of unsupervised girlhood. "Drifting" conjured images of isolation and vulnerability in the turbulence of the city. The word connected the problem of young girls leaving school for work to the larger social conversation surrounding adult working-class "women adrift" who operated outside the domestic security of their families while earning wages. "Going astray" suggested the criminal implications of drifting. Often used to imply sex work, girls described as "going astray" had already deviated from socially acceptable behavior. These terms had roots in nineteenth-century child-saving movements and were reflected in legal language describing dependent and delinquent children. The continued use of this language in the 1910s highlights the persistence of nineteenth-century fears about working-class girlhood, sex, and public labor in industrial cities.

Urban women's groups funded vocational guidance and job placement services to prevent girls of legal working age from "drifting" into the sex trade. Members of three Chicago women's groups formed the VSL in 1910 to offer job guidance to fourteen- to sixteen-year-old girls. League founders included elite representatives of the two most influential women's clubs in the city: the CWC and the Woman's City Club (WCC). Clubwomen in the VSL funded investigations of industries to better understand what job opportunities awaited the fourteen- to sixteen-year-old girl with a work certificate. Most of the guidance work was overseen by members of the VSL's third organizing group, the Association of Collegiate Alumnae (ACA), whose college-educated members advocated for the rights of women in higher education. These VSL leaders included social reformers Jane Addams, Edith Abbott, and Sophonisba Breckinridge. Abbott and Breckinridge lived with Jane Addams at Hull House when they organized the VSL and taught courses in social work at the Chicago School of Civics and Philanthropy at the University of Chicago.⁷

The VSL viewed their work as an extension of anti-vice reform in Chicago. Founding members like Addams were active in municipal efforts to criminalize sex work and shut down red-light district brothels. These reformers argued that criminalizing sex work and promoting vocational guidance would protect the sexual purity and future marriage potential of white working-class girls. Sex work, they presumed, shut girls out of both the respectable labor market and the marriage market due to loss of reputation. They also assumed that the vice market guaranteed girls an early death by suicide, addiction, or venereal disease infection. This fate was promoted in

Jane Addams (1860–1935), 1914
(Library of Congress, Prints & Photographs Division)

pop culture of the period, as fictional accounts of sex workers always concluded with the woman's death. Introducing the VSL in 1910, the *Chicago Tribune* suggested that the group would both curb prostitution and protect school-age girls from utter demise. "Peril to Girl of 14 Who Leaves School to Work" read the headline.[8]

Black urban reformers shared similar concern for unsupervised girls searching for work in northern cities. The National League for the Protection of Colored Women (NLPCW) organized in 1906 to help migrant Black women and girls from the South find respectable jobs in the North. The NLPCW set up stations in Philadelphia, Baltimore, and New York that provided vocational guidance services, including sharing lists of "reliable" employers with new arrivals. In Chicago, Black sororities like Alpha Kappa Alpha organized an annual "vocational guidance week" for girls to direct their "youth power" toward pursuing a secondary education and college. Black urban reformers also worried that migrant girls could "drift" into the sex trade without this maternal intervention. Victoria Earle Matthews, who founded the White Rose Home settlement house in New York, argued that Black working-class girls needed "corrective influences" because their choices could reflect poorly on entire northern Black communities. She feared that letting girls drift into the sex trade might convince white society that all Black urbanites "are naturally low."[9]

Through vocational guidance work, urban women's groups sought to police the sexuality and labor of working-class American girls. These groups devoted fewer resources to foreign-born women and girls, who were underrepresented in the sex trade due in part to social customs. Unmarried immigrant women and girls often lived with their families and earned wages out of a sense of familial responsibility to support the household income. Working-class American girls were most likely to live alone or with fellow working girls in the city. By 1900, 70 percent of sex workers in Chicago's Levee red-light district were young native-born white women. Historian Cynthia M. Blair found that African American women were also overrepresented in Chicago's brothels. Black women and girls represented 17 percent of sex workers in 1900 while making up 2 percent of the city's population. According to the Chicago Vice Commission, roughly 5,000 American-born women and girls made a living as professional sex workers in the city in 1910.[10]

American-born sex workers challenged middle-class gender norms through their financial and sexual autonomy. Working-class girls chose the sex trade because it offered higher wages and more flexibility than most jobs in factories and domestic service. In the early twentieth century, the average domestic servant in Chicago lived on wages of $5 a week. Chicago's department stores paid female workers between $6 and $8 a week, although the youngest workers (girls under sixteen) were paid as low as $3 a week. Other jobs in the female economy—like garment work or packhouses—were often seasonal and required that women look for supplemental wages in periods of underemployment. In contrast, the average sex worker in

Chicago's brothel district earned at least $25 a week. Some girls testified to the Chicago Vice Commission that they earned at least $50 a week. The higher-end brothel keepers reported that their workers made between $100 and $400 a week. Furthermore, sex workers made their own money rather than embrace chastity to prepare for financial dependence on future husbands. The young sex worker lacked parental supervision and a family-centered home life that middle-class women viewed as hallmarks of respectability.[11]

White women's groups relied on racial stereotypes about "white slavery" to suggest that only white American girls needed protection from the sex trade. Vice reformers claimed that an illegal ring of sex traffickers forced young white women to perform sex work across the industrial North. The term "white slavery" reveals racialized assumptions about the sex trade (white) as well as the presumed lack of agency among sex workers (slavery). The Chicago Vice Commission, for example, referred to workers in brothels as "inmates" to suggest their lack of autonomy in the sex trade. Newspapers and pulp fiction movies and books of the period popularized unsubstantiated claims of white slavery. They featured sensationalized stories of young white women who came to the city in search of work only to be seduced into the sex trade by corrupt men. White slavery hysteria had serious legal consequences on the local and federal levels despite the exaggerated claims of vice reformers. Most notoriously, Congress passed the White Slave-Traffic Act (Mann Act) in 1910 that criminalized the transport of women across state lines for "any immoral purpose" in defense of white women's sexual purity. The federal crackdown on "white slavery" cemented a racialized view of the sex trade and implied that Black women and girls did not need protection from sexual abuse.[12]

Members of the VSL believed that a lack of vocational guidance left white American girls vulnerable to the manipulation of alleged "white slave traffickers." Jane Addams published *A New Conscience and an Ancient Evil* two years after she helped organize the VSL in 1910. She told the story of a seventeen-year-old girl who moved to Chicago from the countryside seeking office work. The "pretty and attractive" girl found a typing position advertised in the daily paper and pursued her dream of employment in a downtown office. According to Addams, this led to her downfall. One day the girl accepted the invitation of a male colleague "to see more of the wonderful city" after work. Instead, he took the girl to a "disreputable hotel" in the red-light district. Addams implied that the girl was then tricked, seduced, or exploited against her will to pursue sex work, "the worst vice of the city." The story demonstrated why girls needed formal supervision in their transition into the urban workforce. Girls could escape this fate if women took an interest in their employment and ensured "the respectability of their employers."[13]

The VSL promoted a central fallacy of "white slavery hysteria" that working-class girls always entered the sex trade unwillingly. Members argued that most teenage sex workers in Chicago were duped into the sex trade while "despairing and hopelessly hunting for work." Women in the VSL hoped to offer guidance to these girls and serve as an employment bureau to connect them with respectable jobs in the female-dominated needle trades. Echoing the Chicago Vice Commission, representatives of the VSL told the press that "a large proportion" of sex workers were "untrained children" who left school by age fourteen without a secondary education. Many of these girls needed vocational guidance to understand the benefits of staying in school and studying a respectable trade like dressmaking. "The work of caring for these girls by securing them proper vocational employment is preventative," one member told the *Chicago Tribune*. "It is to prevent girls from going astray."[14]

Anne S. Davis served as "chief investigator" of the VSL tasked with researching where working-class girls labored after leaving school with their work certificates. The daughter of Welsh immigrants, Davis was twenty-seven years old and had recently graduated from the Chicago School of Civics and Philanthropy, where she was likely mentored by VSL cofounders, Abbott and Breckinridge. Davis spent her first four months interviewing wage-earning girls and collecting data on their working conditions. She visited over a dozen industries for the VSL including shoemaking, garment factories, artificial flower construction, engraving, stenography, telephone operating, hairdressing, and laundry. Davis's investigations reflected the concern of VSL members that girls needed guidance to avoid both physical and moral dangers in the public workplace. Davis reported that fourteen- to sixteen-year-old girls suffered from "continual nervous strain" in factories due to poor lighting and ventilation. She argued that many young wage earners also faced sexual threats in "undesirable" mixed-gender work environments full of "temptations."[15]

Davis provided vocational guidance counseling during her investigation and helped many girls secure higher wages. During her first year with the VSL, Davis helped forty-eight girls find better positions in the garment trades. She convinced at least seven to return to school until their sixteenth birthdays, arguing that a few extra years of English, math, or sewing classes would help them find better work. Davis counseled girls and a few boys referred to the VSL by settlement house workers and Protestant charity groups. She advised one fifteen-year-old, Emma, who worked in a department store making $2.50 a week. Davis found Emma a job in an embroidery shop for double the wages. Another girl referred to the league had some sewing skills from elementary school, which helped her fill a seasonal position in a tailor shop. Davis found her a job in a dress shop on Michigan Avenue making $4 a week, nearly twice her previous income. Davis routinely checked in on girls after placing them in new industries as part of the VSL's effort to ensure that girls remained safe from sexual corruption.[16]

Founders of the VSL argued that the public schools should fund Davis's vocational guidance counseling to prevent American girls from being "led astray by the gayety and glamour of the streets." In 1911, the VSL sent Davis's first investigative report to the Chicago Board of Education (BOE) to demonstrate the material benefit of their counseling on working-class girls. They also sent an essay stressing the importance of funding Davis's work. In "A Plea for Employment Supervision in the City Schools," Abbott and Breckinridge wrote that fourteen- to sixteen-year-old girls were too vulnerable to exit the school system without formal counseling. These girls were "very helpless and ill equipped to enter alone and unguarded upon her wage-earning life." Abbott and Breckinridge criticized school officials for being "inactive" in considering what happened to children after leaving the school system. "It is the proper function of the school," they argued, to make sure that children find the right "wage-earning opportunities and industrial possibilities."[17]

Abbott and Breckinridge suggested students enrolled at the Lucy Flower Technical School for Girls (Flower Tech) would benefit most from the VSL's counseling. In 1911, they asked Superintendent Ella Flagg Young to let Davis counsel Flower Tech students. Young gave Davis a permanent office in the basement of Flower Tech from which she continued researching employment opportunities available to girls in Chicago. School officials required all Flower Tech students to meet with Davis for an advising appointment before leaving school. Davis interviewed each student and conducted a house visit to determine her financial needs. If a student and her family convinced Davis that immediate employment was necessary, her goal was to find the student a better job "than the girl could have found for herself."[18]

Through her work at Flower Tech, Davis became the first guidance counselor in Chicago public schools and initially catered exclusively to female students. Vocational guidance counseling expanded in the public schools over the next three years. League members paid the salaries of three full-time "vocational supervisors," who assisted Davis with her investigative and counseling work. Their advising work extended to boys under the age of sixteen with financial support from affiliated women's groups. According to their meeting minutes, Chicago Woman's Aid devoted 50 percent of their annual budget to vocational guidance in the public schools between 1912 and 1914. The Chicago BOE voted to assume financial responsibility for the counseling and investigative work of the VSL by 1915. They gave vocational guidance counselors a permanent department of the public school system known as the Vocational Guidance Bureau. The BOE appointed Anne Davis as bureau director, a position she held for the next twenty years.[19]

Moral concern for the sexual purity of white working girls brought vocational guidance counseling into Chicago's public schools in the 1910s and expanded the role of public schools in the lives of all working-class children. The VSL's vocational guidance work had real material benefits for working-class girls. Davis helped girls earn higher wages and secure more stable positions in the garment trades. Vocational guidance initiatives also reveal the class assumptions of middle-class reformers who hoped to protect working-class girls from mixed-sex workplaces and, ultimately, police their sexual labor. The success of their movement also relied on racialized falsehoods about "white slavery," which confirmed popular views that white American girls were most worthy of public investment.

Vocational Guidance as Child Protection

Under Davis's leadership, the Vocational Guidance Bureau hired counselors to advise fourteen- to sixteen-year-old students in over a dozen neighborhood districts with the lowest rates of high school attendance. The power of the Vocational Guidance Bureau expanded in 1916 when the BOE placed the work certificate system under Davis's purview. School officials required all students to meet with Davis or a vocational guidance counselor to receive their work certificates and leave school legally after 1916. Through the lobbying efforts of the VSL, the Vocational Guidance Bureau brought women's counseling services into Chicago's school system. Perhaps most importantly, Davis's bureau had the regulatory authority to issue or deny working papers to all working-age children.

Vocational guidance counselors hoped to convince immigrant families to keep their children enrolled in school for as long as possible. The Vocational Guidance Bureau distributed pamphlets with titles like "Why Boys and Girls Should Go to High School" that listed information on vocational programs available in Chicago high schools. Davis wrote personal letters to parents explaining the value of a vocational education for their children. "There is little chance for boys or girls to secure good work until they are sixteen years of age," she explained in one letter. "As a result, children who leave school at fourteen are compelled to take up factory or errand work." Davis suggested that longer school attendance would protect children from physical and moral danger. In one letter, she explained that children who left school before age sixteen had bouts of "idleness" that left them "on the streets where they often get into trouble." Davis's letters imply that a lack of awareness about the importance of secondary education increased the child labor problem. Fewer children would end up on the streets if their parents understood the importance of a secondary education for their children's future.[20]

Vocational guidance professionals viewed their work as a solution to exploitative child labor practices in their cities. The director of the New York City Vocational Bureau, Alice Barrows, argued that vocational education should address "the general welfare of workers" rather than "the immediate interests of employers." She argued that vocational programs placed children in narrow tracks that often led to dead-end jobs. Guidance professionals could better serve the needs of working-class children through individualized counseling. One of Barrows's colleagues, Henrietta Rodman, pursued vocational guidance reform because of her own experience as a low-paid child worker in New York. "I went to work when I was 15 years old at $2.50 a week," Rodman recalled in 1913. "My interest in Vocational Guidance dates from that moment." Rodman was able to attend night classes toward her teaching certification while working as a domestic servant in her teens. As an adult, Rodman wrote vocational guidance literature to protect "her girls" from the same fate while teaching in an all-girls school.[21]

The US Children's Bureau promoted vocational guidance counseling as an anti–child labor initiative at the national level. Julia Lathrop began her social work career while living at the Hull House settlement in Chicago in the 1890s. She was appointed by President William Taft to direct the US Children's Bureau in 1912, a new agency dedicated to addressing national youth welfare issues including child labor, infant mortality, and juvenile delinquency. As the first woman to oversee a federal bureau, Lathrop was also active in professionalizing vocational guidance work. The Children's Bureau published reports on vocational guidance programs in urban public schools, and Lathrop spoke at meetings for the National Vocational Guidance Association. At a 1914 conference, Lathrop argued that vocational guidance counselors should not help children find jobs. "Vocational guidance for child labor is a grotesque travesty that we set aside," she argued. Instead, vocational guidance counselors should advise children to engage in their schoolwork.[22]

Vocational guidance programs expanded throughout the 1910s to help prevent child labor and juvenile delinquency. In 1917, members of Chicago's VSL asked Lathrop to spearhead a national study of vocational guidance programs in American cities. On behalf of the Children's Bureau, Lathrop surveyed 233 urban school districts that offered vocational guidance services. When asked the primary goal of vocational guidance, only 45 school districts—the smallest number of respondents—reported a priority of connecting students with "suitable opportunities in industry." Instead, the majority reported a central strategy of anti–child labor activism: "to keep children in school." The largest group of school districts (183) used guidance counseling to convince students to attend high school by discussing "the value of education in wider opportunities."[23]

References to "students" and "children" in national surveys obscure the gendered and racialized nature of vocational guidance work. Attention to the role of vocational guidance reformers on the local level shows how urban anxieties about white working-class girlhood and vice shaped this bureaucracy building. Chicago reformers in the VSL were also concerned about the sexual exploitation of Black girls who lived near the South Side brothel district. Addams and Breckinridge—both members of the NAACP—argued that housing discrimination forced many Black families to settle near red-light districts and exposed girls to immorality. They did not use these stories to demand state or school protection of Black girls. Instead, they conjured cultural images of "white slaves" to promote vocational guidance for the daughters of European immigrants. In a 1911 article in *The Crisis*, Addams explained that Black girls in Chicago were often "without protection" in the city because their mothers worked and left them unattended. She suggested that Black mothers (not public schools) were responsible for guiding girls away from vice districts to protect their sexual purity. The daughters of Italian immigrants, in contrast, rarely entered the sex trade by choice because their mothers kept a watchful eye on them out of "social tradition." Her comparison suggested that the American-born daughter of an Italian mother would only pursue sex work if coerced, an assumption at the heart of white slavery hysteria.[24]

The Vocational Guidance Bureau devoted few resources to supporting Black students. Instead, Black settlement houses like the Wendell Phillips Settlement and civic organizations like the Chicago Urban League offered job guidance and served as employment bureaus in Black neighborhoods. Black parents and reformers understood that their children were not the intended recipients of vocational guidance reform, and many advised their children to avoid white counseling services in the public schools. T. Arnold Hill, president of the Urban League, summed up Black parents' perspectives on vocational guidance in Chicago public schools in the 1930s: "Very little has been done by vocational guidance to help the Negro children because a more favored group refused to change its early concepts of them." Indeed, the goal of vocational guidance counseling in Chicago public schools was not often job placement or even career advice. The goal was student retention.²⁵

Davis made at least one attempt to better address the vocational needs of Black girls at Flower Tech as director of the Vocational Guidance Bureau. In addition to counseling services, the bureau used school resources to continue Davis's investigative work into Chicago industries that employed girl workers. In a 1926 investigation, a vocational adviser with the bureau, Ruth Bartlett, reported that "beauty culture" was one of the only industries that employed both Black and white women in Chicago. She found that the beauty industry was a rare field in which Black women could run their own hairdressing businesses and cosmetology schools. Beauty parlors also offered moral protection for working-class Black and white girls because they were run by other women who could serve as maternal guides. Davis encouraged school officials to introduce a "beauty culture" program at Flower Tech when the school relocated to a new building in Garfield Park. In oral histories, however, Black alumnae recalled that they were unwelcome in new courses for aspiring manicurists, cosmetologists, and hairdressers. Despite the bureau's good intentions, Flower Tech students understood that beauty culture was unofficially for "the white clique."²⁶

Women in Chicago's vocational guidance movement suggested that Black girls should stay in school and study needle trades despite racist hiring practices in the industry. Social reformer Louise deKoven Bowen served as president of the CWC and the WCC, the two women's clubs that helped found the VSL in 1910. In a 1911 article, Bowen wrote that the absence of Black women in the needle trades was the result of girls' lack of investment in their own vocational training. She argued that white dressmakers had "little feeling against the employment of Negro seamstresses." Rather, Black women and girls "little tried" to learn skills to succeed in the field. "Without doubt one fundamental reason for the difficulties the colored woman meets in seeking employment is her lack of industrial training." Bowen's assertion that vocational education could uplift Black working-class women reflects a flawed assumption at the heart of women's public school reform: that the right education could solve structural problems.²⁷

Like the VSL, the Vocational Guidance Bureau focused their work on studying the employment of white American-born children and protecting them from child labor through longer school attendance. Vocational guidance professionals, however, had limited success keeping working-class children out of the labor force. During the 1914–15 school year, only 17 percent of students (or their parents) decided to attend high school after meeting with a Vocational Guidance Bureau counselor. Ninety-three percent of Chicago children left school before high school to earn wages or help care for family members at home in 1917. Mandatory counseling on the value of a secondary education proved insufficient.[28]

Clubwomen in the VSL maintained a relationship with Davis by arranging scholarships for "worthy poor" students whose families could not afford to keep their children enrolled in public school. The VSL began paying families for their children's lost wages in 1916 when the BOE established the Vocational Guidance Bureau. On average, the VSL awarded fifteen to twenty dollars a month to students in the "dangerous ages" of fourteen to sixteen years old. The number of scholarship recipients varied from year to year but fell somewhere between 140 and 200 students during the 1910s. Scholarship funds were supported by more than 200 dues-paying members of the VSL who representing more than 50 women's groups in Illinois. Ella Adams Moore, a child welfare reformer and English professor at the University of Chicago, served as VSL president when the league shifted their work from guidance to scholarships in 1916. Moore believed in the importance of extending the school lives of working-class children to prevent them from escaping "into the real world" as soon as "the compulsory education act will allow." Funding scholarships also supported the initial goal of the VSL to protect working-class girls from drifting into the sex trade. According to Moore, boys who left school too early became the "raw material from which the ranks of criminals are recruited." But girls who left school too early joined "that other army of which we do not think without a shudder."[29]

The VSL used scholarships to extend the school lives of working-class girls and help them prepare for respectable work. In 1916, female students accounted for only one-third of work certificate applicants in the public schools. Yet girls made up more than 50 percent of students who received scholarship support from the VSL. Members had long suggested that low wages—or the lack of wages—led girls to pursue sex work. Paying girls to stay in school solved the problem of girls leaving school too young and finding work in disreputable fields. Before World War I, the VSL offered scholarships for girls to attend high school and study the needle trades. This included girls like fourteen-year-old Loretta, who received a four-year scholarship to study dressmaking at Flower Tech. After she graduated, the Vocational Guidance Bureau found her a dressmaking apprenticeship in a department store. Through scholarship services, the VSL supported a reform goal of women labor activists who wanted to uplift working-class girls through "the higher branches" of needle work.[30]

The VSL required some of their scholarship recipients to study homemaking in the summer months at their summer camp, Sunset Lodge. The two-week camp opened in 1915 and was located forty miles northwest of Chicago on placid Diamond Lake. Sunset Lodge originally catered mostly to the daughters of Russian Jewish immigrants and was supported by the charity work of the League of Jewish Women. The VSL took over the camp from the League of Jewish Women and expanded services. By World War I, the camp had beds for 130 girls, most of whom were scholarship recipients judging by VSL records. The goal of Sunset Lodge was to provide urban girls with an escape from the city in the summer and introduce them to the joys of housekeeping. Along with recreational activities in the countryside, girls learned to care for their "beautiful house, model in every way." After their two-week stay, camp organizers expected girls to return to their neighborhoods "an inspiration to others" with new knowledge of the home and appreciation for the countryside.[31]

Sunset Lodge was the VSL's solution to the problem of summer breaks for working-class girls. Beginning in the 1890s, urban school districts created "vacation school" programs to keep children off the streets and out of workplaces. The precursor to summer schools, vacation schools were part of the larger reform effort to increase the role of public education in the lives of urban youths. School officials argued that vacation schools would decrease summertime spikes in juvenile delinquency caused by working-class children enjoying the unsupervised freedom of warm nights on city streets. Like Sunset Lodge, many vacation school programs brought children into the countryside to both escape the heat of the city and to receive the health benefits of fresh air, swimming, and nature walks. But Sunset Lodge was also designed for domestic instruction. In its early years, the daily chores of campgoers resembled the labor of girls in carceral schools who sewed, dusted, and beautified the institution.[32]

The VSL was not the only urban women's group that supported the public education of working-class children through financial aid. The Jewish Women's League organized scholarships for Russian Jewish children in the public schools at the turn of the twentieth century. The VSL's scholarship program absorbed those donations (along with Sunset Lodge) in 1916 to support the American-born children of Russian Jewish families. Black clubwomen also funded scholarships for schoolchildren on an individual basis. They paid for carfare and school supplies for at least one fifteen-year-old homeless girl in 1894 so she could become "a useful member of society." Records suggest the VSL did not work with Black clubwomen to arrange scholarships for Black children. Instead, the VSL created a formal relationship with school officials to keep mostly second-generation children off the city streets and out of the urban workforce. Their relationship with the school system would persist in Chicago for the better part of a century. The VSL was renamed the Scholarship and Guidance Association in 1942, which it remains today.[33]

The Lure of the City

School officials partnered with women working in the juvenile court system to guide Chicago girls toward school and respectable labor. The CWC helped establish the Cook County Juvenile Court in 1899, the world's first court specifically for minors. They also hired the first probation officers to counsel children and advocate on their behalf in Chicago's juvenile court system. The salaries of juvenile probation officers were initially paid by the CWC except for Elizabeth McDonald, the first Black probation officer in Chicago who advocated for Black children as an unpaid volunteer.[34] The city professionalized and expanded probation work in the juvenile court during the 1910s alongside vocational guidance in the public schools. School officials encouraged the expansion of probation work, arguing that women probation officers could guide girls away from delinquent behavior. "If these girls are to be saved," wrote one BOE member in 1914, "women alone can save them." By 1920, over one hundred women worked as juvenile probation officers in Chicago. They made up the largest juvenile probation force in the country.[35]

Juvenile probation work was a feminized "helping profession" much like vocational guidance counseling. The courts expected officers to serve as maternal guides to wayward children and evaluated women on their modest clothing choices, feminine poise, "moral character," and "temperate habits" into the 1930s. Black and white women who served as juvenile probation officers viewed their work as preventive of delinquency and vice. They counseled children on the value of returning to school and convinced working-class parents that vocational education was a worthwhile investment for their children. Anne Davis advised delinquent girls in the juvenile court system before joining the VSL as an investigator. Reformer Ethel Kawin worked with Davis as one of the first guidance counselors in the public schools while her sister, Irene Kawin, worked as a juvenile probation officer. The close relationship between vocational and probational guidance counseling reveals how urban women reformers used both the juvenile carceral state and public education to regulate the public behavior of urban children.[36]

Women court officials agreed that a lack of vocational guidance led fourteen- to sixteen-year-old girls to "drift" into the sex trade. Cook County opened a separate court specifically to hear the cases of girls accused of "delinquency" in 1912. The first woman to oversee her own courtroom in America, Mary Bartelme, ran the Cook County Court for Delinquent Girls into the 1920s. Bartelme was a former Chicago public school teacher and the first woman to receive a law degree from Northwestern University in 1894.

She spent the first decade of her career working with probation officers in the juvenile court system. In 1913, the *New York Times* interviewed Bartelme about her historic appointment to the bench. When asked about the leading cause of girlhood delinquency, Bartelme credited the twin problems of "lack of employment" and sexual coercion by men. She explained that girls without full-time jobs spent their days wandering the downtown business districts in search of work, where they were "stalked and hunted like game in the fields."[37]

Bartelme supported the work of vice reformers and school guidance counselors by ordering working-age girls back to school. Bartelme shared the view of child labor activists that all girls under sixteen were too young to earn wages. Her remaining court transcripts feature numerous cases in which a girl's age alone led Bartelme to order her return to school regardless of having legal working papers. For example, fifteen-year-old Ruth appeared before Bartelme's bench after being arrested for stealing wallets at a department store on State Street. Bartelme ruled that Ruth was too immature to earn wages and told her probation officer to ensure she return to school until at least age sixteen, at which time the Vocational Guidance Bureau could help her find a job. Bartelme viewed her rulings as a form of sexual protection for working-age girls like Ruth. Bartelme told the *New York Times* that no girl under sixteen was mature enough to "fight against temptation" and should therefore stay in school.[38]

Juvenile probation officers advised "delinquent" girls to return to school and further their vocational education. In 1922, Bartelme heard the case of a fourteen-year-old Black girl named Betty who was confined to the court's Detention Home for skipping school and falling "into very bad company." A representative in court (likely her probation officer), Miss Wiggins, explained to Bartelme that a previous judge recommended Betty work as a domestic servant because she was of legal working age. "Judge Arnold recommended that she do housework, but she didn't want to do housework." Wiggins argued that Betty's mother was able to care for her and keep Betty "right." Betty agreed that she would stay with her mother and follow her rules if the court gave her permission to pursue a vocational program at Wendell Phillips High School. In this example, probationary guidance supported the future education of a working-class girl caught in a racist court system. Not all girls were fortunate enough to have an advocate like Wiggins. On average between 1910 and 1920, court officials sentenced 42 percent of "delinquent" girls to carceral schools like the Illinois State Training School in Geneva each year. Black girls were overrepresented among them, accounting for 20 percent of all "delinquent" girls brought to the Cook County Juvenile Court in 1920.[39]

Juvenile court systems in other American cities also enlisted women to guide working girls back to school as delinquency prevention. Some social reformers created independent vocational guidance bureaus specifically for "problem girls" who were arrested, skipped school, and stayed out too late. Both juvenile probation officers and school officials in New York City referred girls to the Vocational Adjustment Bureau for Girls, which helped "pre-delinquents" return to school and pursue vocational training. The bureau's placement director argued that girls displaying "problems of behavior" needed women's guidance before they "drift into delinquency." She explained: "By identifying these cases early, we are enabled to help the girl become a useful member of society instead of a destructive one." The use of the word "destructive" is telling. In the eyes of reformers, "drifting" into sexual delinquency reflected the ultimate breakdown of morality and the social unit of the American family.[40]

Cultural anxieties about girls' growing economic freedom dictated how both court and school officials counseled "problem girls" of legal working age. In the 1910s, working-class girls increasingly spent their wages on new commercialized leisure activities in industrial cities. They frequented nickel theaters and dance halls with their girlfriends on weekday evenings, in part due to their shorter workdays secured by labor activists. In the warmer months, Chicago girls explored new parts of the city on the streetcars and took weekend boat excursions on Lake Michigan. Groups of girls in New York City traveled to leisure attractions like Coney Island. This pursuit of "cheap amusements" worried reformers for multiple reasons. Urban leisure brought single women and girls into public venues that were also frequented by men. Leisure venues like dance halls that encouraged interactions with men most concerned women involved in municipal vice reform during the 1910s. Urban reformers viewed the dance hall as a dangerous breeding ground for sex traffickers, as conveyed in the sensational title of popular reform treatises like *From Dance Hall to White Slavery: The World's Greatest Tragedy* (1912).[41]

The choice to spend wages on personal leisure also challenged middle-class expectations of a protected, respectable girlhood. By the 1910s, many reformers accepted that some working-class daughters needed to earn wages out of familial responsibility. According to the Chicago Vice Commission, most girls left school for work only when "spurred on by the necessity of gaining her daily bread." They worried, however, about a new class of working-class girls who exited the school system looking for "adventure" and "independence of feeling." Studies conducted by the Vocational Guidance Bureau confirmed this trend. During her first years with the bureau, Davis asked nearly 7,000 fourteen- to sixteen-year-old students why they planned to leave school for work. She categorized the largest group (35 percent) as leaving school for "economic necessity," such as supporting a widowed parent. The second largest group of students (22.3 percent) fell into the concerning category of "earnings desired, but not necessary." It was one thing for working-class girls to earn wages out of daughterly duty to their families. It was another for girls to pursue work in service of their own financial freedom and consumer desire.[42]

The spending and leisure habits of working-class girls challenged expectations for appropriate girlhood behavior in Black migrant families as well. The *Chicago Defender* chastised Black girls in 1917 who left school too early to earn wages because they were "anxious for a good time and a few clothes." In her study of Black women's reform in New York, Cheryl Hicks found that Black urban parents relied on the juvenile court system to police the "wild" behavior of single daughters in the city. These parents had faith that putting their "problem girls" on probation would encourage respectability by keeping girls off the streets and guiding them back to school. This faith in the court often backfired, as Black girls faced higher rates of institutionalization on "delinquency" charges due to racial stereotypes about Black feminine sexual deviance. But Black parental use of the court system reveals the central importance of respectable public behavior for girls to the politics of racial uplift.[43]

Parents and urban reformers assumed that the financial and leisure freedom of working-class girls could lead to sexual delinquency. They feared that girls who traveled unsupervised to movies, dance halls, and shopping centers after work would become victims of sexual abuse or trafficking. They also suggested that the consumer desires of working-class girls were signs of pre-delinquency. As Jane Addams argued, impressionable young girls were corrupted by their "quest for adventure" and "the lure of the city." She wrote in 1911 that a new world of nightlife and shopping "seduced" the working girl into privileging consumer pleasure over their gendered obligations to their family or future husbands. Reformers linked this "seduction" of consumerism to sex work. The Chicago Vice Commission reported that many girls left school for work because they wanted to afford "entertainment" and "attractive clothes." According to the commissioners, many Chicago girls were often disappointed to find that the pay of most day jobs could not support a lifestyle of "ease and luxury." These girl workers were the most likely to succumb to the seduction of the sex trade for extra cash. One commissioner who worked in the court system, Anne Dwyer, wrote elsewhere that "a love of fine dress" was just as dangerous for working girls as "the lure of vicious men." In other words, both where and how girls spent their wages could threaten morality.[44]

Bartelme routinely asked girls about their spending habits to assess their level of delinquency. Bartelme echoed Addams in a 1913 interview, saying that "the lure of the city" and its commercial attractions encouraged girls to become sexually active. She argued that "a new and brilliant world" of consumer luxuries seduced teenage working girls by distracting them with money and entertainment rather than wholesome living. "These poor, foolish girls think only of the pleasure of the moment," she lamented. Bartelme's court records reveal a common line of questioning focused on girls' consumerism. She often asked girls how many hats they owned, how many pairs of shoes, if they owned stockings, and whether those stockings were silk. Of all "immoral fashions," Bartelme had a particular vehemence against girls who bought silk stockings. She told the *Washington Post* in 1915: "I wish all the silk stockings in the world were in the bottom of the Atlantic Ocean!" Bartelme argued that girls who spent their wages on "foolish things" like silk stockings were not mature enough to earn wages and should return to school.[45]

Middle-class reformers associated girls' purchase of consumer luxuries—particularly silk stockings—with sex work and the practice of "treating." White American girls who worked in garment factories and stores wanted higher wages to participate in the ready-made consumer market that their labor supported. Reformers viewed department stores as dangerous work environments for this reason. As one reformer explained: "Some of the girls who are most tempted, and enter lives of prostitution, work in the big department stores, surrounded by luxuries, which all of them crave." Department store girls participated in the "treating" economy where sexual favors were exchanged for consumer goods rather than wages. The Chicago Vice Commission asked one department store worker who made eight dollars a week how she afforded her fashionable outfit, which, including shoes and hat, was worth over $200. According to commissioners, a treating man who lived "a sporting life" bought the girl clothing in exchange for her "good looks and physical charms." Black reformers viewed a girlhood interest in finery as lowbrow and not respectable. Erica L. Simpson, who wrote an advice column for Black women in the *Chicago Defender*, encouraged working girls to avoid "startling colors" and garish fashion "no matter how much tempted."[46]

Bartelme interpreted a girl's spending and leisure habits as evidence of sexual delinquency. Linda, the seventeen-year-old American daughter of Italian immigrants, appeared before Bartelme for "incorrigible behavior" in 1923. According to her probation officer, Linda was unemployed after quitting her job in a mail-order house and spent most weekday evenings at dance halls. Bartelme questioned Linda extensively about her dress, shoes, and silk stockings. She asked how much clothing Linda owned, how often she shopped, and how much each item in her closet cost. Bartelme concluded that Linda was delinquent for shopping frivolously while in between jobs, which made her a burden on her single mother. "No girl is a good girl that becomes a beggar," Bartelme explained, and ordered Linda to a carceral school for delinquent girls.

Linda rejected this ruling. While Bartelme viewed her shopping and dancing habits as signs of delinquency, Linda maintained she was not delinquent because she never had sex. Their exchange highlight competing definitions of girlhood delinquency:

> LINDA: I am not delinquent.
> BARTELME: But, my dear little girl, you are delinquent.
> LINDA: I am not.
> BARTELME: Define delinquency.
> LINDA: I have not lost my virtue.
> BARTELME: The law says that girls who defy their parents and that run the streets are delinquent.
> LINDA: I am not delinquent. I have not lost my virtue.
> BARTELME: [The State Training School in] Geneva takes girls for any delinquency.
> LINDA: They are bad.
> BARTELME: But you are bad.
> LINDA: I am not bad.
> BARTELME: My dear girl, you may be virtuous, but are not a good girl.
> LINDA: I am.
> BARTELME: You are a street bum. Now that is bad. Where a dance hall keeps open until 4 in the morning—
> LINDA: —It was not a dance hall.
> BARTELME: Then what was it?
> LINDA: It was a party.

Bartelme and Linda sparred for several minutes about whether her nightlife activities truly made her "bad." Bartelme assumed that girls who spent their wages at late-night dance halls (or parties) must be sexually active and therefore sexually delinquent. Bartelme ultimately conceded after Linda insisted on her virginity. She rescinded her decision to institutionalize Linda in a state-funded carceral school. Instead, she switched her line of questioning to assess what vocational training Linda had pursued in her neighborhood high school, and whether she was ready to find a job.[47]

Women court officials supported the vocational guidance movement by advocating that "problem girls" return to school and prepare for respectable work. Bartelme's court records demonstrate discomfort not only with where girls worked but how they spent their wages. Consumerism implied sexual immorality by challenging gender norms for respectable daughters. Bartelme's anxiety about commercial freedom contributed to employment regulation and a return to school for many working-class girls. Linda's outcome was maybe an exceptional one. As the above example demonstrates, Bartelme pointed to girls' consumer choices to justify institutionalization in carceral schools during the 1910s. Girls who were not white, American born, and English speaking like Linda undoubtedly had greater difficulty convincing court officials of their "virtue."

Frivolous Stenographers

School and court officials often dissuaded working-class girls from pursuing clerical jobs in downtown offices. Bartelme attempted to convince Linda that she should enter the needle trades after the above exchange about her status as a "delinquent." Bartelme judged that Linda was mature enough to earn wages because she was seventeen years old and had completed two years of high school. Bartelme asked Linda what type of position she wanted and ignored Linda's response of "office work." Instead, Bartelme asked what needle trade training Linda received in her neighborhood high school. Linda responded that she learned to embroider, bead, and make lampshades in household arts. "Lamp shade work pays very well, I understand," Bartelme commented. Linda countered that the work did *not* pay well, and that stable jobs in lampshade factories were difficult to find. Bartelme pressed Linda on whether she had truly looked hard enough for lampshade jobs in the local paper. Linda's probation officer agreed to help Linda find an office job with a telephone company, and Bartelme dropped the discussion.[48]

Bartelme likely shared the concern of women in guidance roles that mixed-sex work environments were not respectable for working-class girls. In the 1910s, Davis was also hesitant to refer female students to white-collar jobs for this reason. She distrusted the work hierarchy of young female stenographers toiling under the command of male managers who could be sexually abusive. In one report as director of the Vocational Guidance Bureau, Davis told counselors to keep girls away from telephone operating offices. She wrote that telephone operators were exposed to "temptations" working under male managers and sometimes required to work evenings. Evening work, she wrote, was "always bad for the young girl." Furthermore,

Davis asserted that the downtown locations of most offices were unsafe because they required girls walk through "undesirable" sections of the city to get to work.[49]

Davis recommended that girls pursue vocational training for needle trades instead. Like other women in vocational school reform, Davis believed the female-led garment industry offered the most respectable wage-earning environment for the single girl worker. Millinery was "exclusively a woman's trade," she wrote in a promotional pamphlet for the bureau, and therefore offered sistership for female workers. Most girls who came to the Vocational Guidance Bureau, however, requested help finding office jobs. Stenography positions offered more wage security than positions in shops and department stores because office work was rarely seasonal. Female office workers with basic commercial training earned an average of six to eight dollars a week in Chicago. Their interest in office work was a source of frustration for Davis, who worried the "stenography craze" distracted girls from more respectable jobs in the needle trades. "The girls have been so intent upon securing stenography," Davis complained in one of her annual reports.[50]

Black reformers dissuaded girls from pursuing office jobs in the 1910s for a different reason: racial discrimination in the field. In 1918, the *Chicago Defender* told Black high school students to ignore the new two-year stenography program in neighborhood high schools that was so popular among their white peers. "Many white girls are taking this course, but a white girl has a hundred chances to your one," they reported. Black girls who ignored this advice were cautionary tales of the overt racism in the corporate world. In 1912, a Black female student at Wendell Phillips High School applied to three different business colleges in Chicago. According to the *Defender*, all three colleges refused to admit her due to "colorphobia." While most college representatives denied her enrollment through "evasion and subterfuge," one openly admitted that the school had never accepted a Black student and did not plan to start now. Black girls were advised to focus on their academic studies to avoid prejudice and a wasted education.[51]

Urban reformers argued that young office workers could be sex trafficked by male managers during the "white slavery" hysteria of the 1910s. While they often made better wages than factory or department store workers, stenographer-typists were still the lowest-paid workers in a male-dominated field. Reformers worried that stenographers were vulnerable to not only sexual harassment but coercion into performing sexual favors for higher pay. In 1912, Jane Addams wrote that "perhaps no woman is more exposed to the temptation" of sex work "than the one who works in an office where she may be the sole woman employed." Addams continued that the needle trades offered a much safer environment for working girls through "the companionship of other working women." When a young woman enters a downtown office alone, she cautioned, "her isolation in itself constitutes a danger."[52]

Guidance professionals implied that girls' interest in stenography reflected an immature and immoral obsession with leisure and consumerism. In 1916, a fourteen-year-old student wrote to a weekly job advice column for "business girls" about her desire to leave school and work in a downtown office. "I feel that I am old enough and sufficiently educated to earn my own living," she explained in her letter. "So many girls I know, who are not much older than I, are working, and they are able to buy such pretty clothes for themselves, and seem to have such a good time.... I want to be able to earn my own living and be independent." The *Chicago Tribune* advice columnist Mary King viewed this eagerness to join the clerical workforce as the height of girlhood immaturity. After printing the fourteen-year-old's letter in full, King wrote in her Sunday-morning column: "So many of the letters which have reached my desk lately have been from young girls who are anxious to give up their school work, and make themselves 'independent' by going to work." King chastised the young letter writer for not appreciating "the advantages of a good, substantial education" and urged her to pursue a high school education. The real problem for King was the girl's desire for financial freedom and urban consumerism.[53]

Other members of the press associated a frivolous interest in consumerism with the girlish "stenography craze." The *Chicago Tribune* mocked teenage stenographers for their obsession with fashion, describing their clothing as "too gaudy of color" and "too extreme of style." Serious moral consequences arose from their fashion choices, according to reporters. Press coverage framed these young workers as temptresses who could distract married men from their work and encourage infidelity. In a 1905 article, the *Chicago Tribune* described the popularity of stenography positions among both poor immigrant girls—"the Ellis Island kind"—and American-born girls with "golden pompadours and dashing smartness." The reporter assumed these young women pursued a mixed-sex workplace to find middle-class husbands. This was often not the case. He asked one young stenographer if she had plans to marry. "I get over a thousand dollars a year," she responded. "Do you suppose I am going to give that up?" Another girl quipped that a job offered more financial security than a husband. "I have never seen a man yet who would give me $80 a month with no questions."[54]

A young stenographer, Barbara Walters, working among men at the W. D. Allen Manufacturing Company, 1908 (DN-0006621, Chicago Daily News collection, Chicago History Museum)

These accounts reveal contradictory assumptions about the young white stenographer. On the one hand, middle-class professionals like Bartelme and Davis argued that the mixed-sex office was morally and potentially physically dangerous for vulnerable girls toiling under older men. On the other hand, the press often blamed "frivolous and immoral stenographers" for threatening the sanctity of marriage and encouraging infidelity in the corporate workplace. In the 1910s, the young white stenographer was painted as both seducible and seductress, both symptom and cause of sexual immorality. Above all, the young stenographer was controversial because she represented a new type of working girl who embraced "the lure of the city" with her independent wages.[55]

Guidance professionals reimagined stenography as a respectable field for white working girls after World War I. The wartime economy helped femininize office jobs and further racialized office environments as white spaces. More than one million white women and girls worked as stenographers and bookkeepers during the war to fill positions made vacant by men drafted into service. In 1918, the Chicago BOE received more than one thousand calls from employers requesting female students who could fill in for their absent male clerical staff. Urban school officials responded quickly to the demand for female office workers by expanding evening classes for current and returning students to learn typing and accounting skills. In Chicago, school officials introduced an accelerated five-month stenography program for female students in six high schools, including Flower Tech, to fill the wartime shortage. The program was attended by thousands of female students and returning alumnae eager to leave manufacturing work behind and join the clerical sector.[56]

Observers framed women's pursuit of office work in patriotic terms during the war. No longer a sexual threat to male office culture, the young stenographer was commended for performing an economic necessity to keep American business moving smoothly during the conflict overseas. The draft was not the only factor pulling young women and girls into downtown offices. World War I also led to a general expansion of the corporate sector in urban economies and a demand for more entry-level office workers. Companies engaged in communication, insurance, and financial services all required more clerical workers by the end of the war. In addition to typist-stenographers, women started to fill higher-paid office positions in accounting during World War I. For these reasons, offices were no longer coded as male or even mixed-sex environments by the end of World War I. Women who filled wartime manufacturing jobs generally lost their positions when men returned home from combat. This was not the case for office jobs, as the growing corporate sector continued to rely on women workers when the war ended. By 1930, white women made up more than 60 percent of bookkeepers in American cities.[57]

Guidance professionals after World War I argued that offices were good environments for working girls to prepare for future duties as wives and homemakers. In her 1919 vocational guidance textbook for girls, Boston clubwoman Marguerite Dickson argued that office jobs offered transferable skills for the home. Office work taught "neatness, accuracy, precision," which were essential to "the housekeeper's routine." She continued: "The calm atmosphere of the well-kept office, even when typewriters and calculating machines are rattling, is a better preparation for an orderly home than the rush of the department store or the factory." The femininization of white-collar work desexualized office culture. Now dominated by single women workers, guidance professionals recast office work as useful domestic training for the ever-organized and helpful American homemaker.[58]

The wartime economy also destigmatized office work by widening the racial gap between Black and white women's labor in northern cities. Black women and girls who migrated to Chicago after World War I worked in domestic service or, increasingly, filled manufacturing jobs left behind by white women entering the clerical sector. Despite the demand for female typists, very few offices hired Black women and girls due to racial prejudice. Only 2 percent of white-collar workers in the United States were African American by the end of the 1920s, and these women worked almost exclusively in Black-owned businesses. The new gender dynamics of office work assuaged earlier fears about sexual exploitation in the corporate world. By the 1920s, offices provided "the companionship of other working women" that Jane Addams argued would protect girl workers from sexual abuse. But this reimagining of office work also reflected racist views of "respectable" work. The more office jobs became dominated by white women specifically, the more women guidance professionals promoted the field as proper for girls.[59]

White American-born girls used scholarship support from the VSL to study stenography during World War I. By 1919, nearly 70 percent of scholarship recipients were girls enrolled in two-year stenography or four-year business programs in neighborhood high schools. By 1923, these students accounted for 75 percent of VSL scholarship recipients. Some of these students, like fourteen-year-old Annie, found scholarship support after visiting the Vocational Guidance Bureau for a work certificate. Annie failed her mandatory health screening when the examiner reported she had "a weak heart" not suitable for wage earning. Annie's mother could not afford to have her daughter attend high school, so a school counselor arranged for her to receive a scholarship from the VSL and pursue a two-year stenography program. White girls from working-class families benefited most from scholarship support after office work became "respectable." When Annie turned sixteen, she returned to the Vocational Guidance Bureau for placement in an office job.[60]

Immigrant daughters viewed offices as distinctly American workplaces that offered cultural cachet along with more financial freedom in the postwar decade. In 1922, Ella, the fourteen-year-old daughter of Polish immigrants, was arrested after running away from her parents. Appearing before the Juvenile Court for Girls, Ella told Bartelme that she ran away because her parents insisted she attend her Polish parochial school. She wanted to attend her local public school instead where she could learn to type and strengthen her English skills. "I want to have an American education," she told Bartelme. "I want to go to Public School and be an American girl." Learning white-collar skills in her local public school was critical to Ella's American identity as a second-generation immigrant. White-collar work was also "respectable" and "American" because offices were populated by other American-born white workers.[61]

Access to white-collar skills and employment opportunities helped immigrant daughters like Ella become fully "white" after World War I. Second-generation immigrants held a quasi-white social status in the early twentieth century as American-born citizens with ethnic cultural backgrounds. In the hyper-patriotic postwar period, many "ethnic whites" downplayed their cultural distinctions and asserted white American identities. The downtown skyscraper—an icon of the American city and American capitalism—was also the quintessential American workplace. Office work and office culture helped "whiten" second-generation girls and allowed them to assert their rights to "white social citizenship" in the postwar decade. Their access to white American identity was made possible by racial discrimination in the clerical sector. The respectability of white women's office work was forged partially in contrast with Black women's domestic labor.[62]

The swift cultural acceptance of girls in office jobs during World War I was profound. Women reformers resisted girls' pursuit of office work in the early 1910s, using the threat of mixed-sex offices to justify municipal crusades against an alleged "white slave traffic." Ten years later, the VSL's primary work was funding scholarships for future stenographers in neighborhood high schools. Women's support of white-collar education was new, but the rationale was not. Reformers embraced clerical work for girls after the war only because the field was femininized and desexualized. Shifting racial demographics in the urban workforce also supported this cultural acceptance by imbuing downtown offices with the respectability of whiteness.

Poster encouraging women to fill the stenography shortage in Washington, DC, c. 1918 (Prudential Litho. Co., Library of Congress, Prints & Photographs Division)

Conclusion

Members of the VSL brought vocational guidance and scholarship services into the public high schools to address their anxieties about white working-class girls, vice, and sexual delinquency. They looked to the public schools to solve social issues facing the white working girl, notably the alleged "white slave traffic" in Chicago that was largely a fiction. Their guidance and scholarship work supported racialized assumptions about girlhood respectability in the public workforce. Black reformers also policed the public behavior of working-class girls in this period through vocational guidance and juvenile probation work. But the VSL made protecting white working-class girls a formal function of Chicago's public schools. These women helped establish a new public school bureaucracy that regulated how *all* working-class children made their legal transition from school to work.

Women guidance professionals and court officials perpetuated the idea that working-class girls in the city were potential "pre-delinquents" vulnerable to sexual corruption. This concern was not new in the 1910s. Anxiety about public girlhood shaped juvenile delinquency law in the nineteenth century and led to the creation of carceral schools for girls (analyzed in chapter 1). Yet the moral hysteria about unsupervised girlhood took on new dimensions during municipal vice reform campaigns. Women reformers emphasized the moral threat of sex work and "white slavery" to demand greater regulation of girls' transition from school to work by school and city officials alike. The growing financial freedom and consumer autonomy of urban working girls also inspired greater concern for girlhood morality in the 1910s. Spending habits were viewed as both a cause and symptom of girlhood sexual delinquency that demanded state intervention.

The vocational guidance movement reflected a growing acceptance that most urban children needed to earn wages to support themselves and their families. The VSL's scholarship program helped hundreds of working-class children remain in school each year and gain access to a secondary education. Yet members also hoped to police the sexual agency and work environments of white American girls through their support. They funded scholarships to incentivize white girls to stay in school, avoid selfish spending, and pick jobs that offered transferable skills for the home. Second-generation girls benefited from these scholarships during World War I by using VSL support to prepare for desirable jobs in the clerical sector. This education helped immigrant daughters assert their American identities and distinguish their "respectable" labor from the limited wage-earning options open to Black migrants. In the postwar decade, urban school officials relied on new government funds to further Americanize second-generation girls through vocational education in urban high schools. Federal investment in girls' vocational training also promoted distinct citizenship expectations for American girls delineated by race after World War I.

[CHAPTER SIX]

A Nation of Good Homes

Labor, Citizenship, and Home Economics for Girls, 1917–1930

Adelaide Steele Baylor was among a handful of home economists employed by the federal government in the 1920s. As chief home economist for the US Bureau of Education, Baylor traveled to all forty-eight states and the territory of Hawai'i to share "the general cultural value" of girlhood education in childcare, cooking, and housekeeping. Baylor argued that the government should invest in these home economics courses to encourage good citizenship in public schools and promote American gender expectations in US territories. In the postwar decade, white college-educated women like Baylor harnessed the power of federal and state agencies to expand the role of domestic training in the school lives of all American girls. They brought urban school reforms like scientific cooking and "little mothers" classes out of the city schools to achieve a standard national curriculum for American girlhood. "If we are interested in having national life of the right type, it is necessary to have home life of the right type," Baylor explained in 1928. "National standards are simply home standards on a larger scale."[1]

Schooling the working girl became a national priority in the postwar decade. Urban clubwomen and labor activists shaped the landmark Smith-Hughes National Vocational Education Act (Smith-Hughes) of 1917 that funded agricultural, industrial, and "vocational home economics" programs in American high schools for the next half century. The Smith-Hughes Act signaled the success of the vocational education movement and solidified the expectation that public high schools should prepare American students for gendered work roles. While labor women like Agnes Nestor fought to keep domestic education out of the original bill, urban clubwomen demanded federal funding for home economics to ensure the health and citizenship development of second-generation immigrant girls. City school districts used Smith-Hughes funding to require wage-earning girls return to school and study American homemaking in public "continuation schools." Through the Smith-Hughes Act, urban women's groups achieved their goals of bringing working-class girls back into the school system and educating them for respectable womanhood.[2]

The Smith-Hughes Act empowered white college-educated members of the American Home Economics Association (AHEA) to advance their own careers through oversight of the working girl's curriculum. Founded in 1909 by domestic scientist Ellen Swallow Richards, the AHEA continued to professionalize domestic education for women at the college level and emphasize the public health principles of the domestic science movement. AHEA members promoted racialized assumptions about gender, labor, and citizenship by linking their field to Americanization efforts in urban school districts during the 1920s. The AHEA defined home economics as a "social study" that taught second-generation girls that women's good citizenship was defined by unpaid service to their husbands, children, and healthy homes. Members encouraged local school officials to educate Black girls for these American homemaking expectations while also stressing the value of home economics education for future employment as domestic servants. As a "social study" of American work roles, vocational home economics promoted unequal citizenship expectations for Black and white girls in American public schools.[3]

In the post-suffrage decade, national women's groups like the League of Women Voters lobbied to expand home economics outside the city schools as a matter of women's equality. They wanted federal and state governments to make the same investment in home economics for girls as they did nationally in agricultural and industrial education for boys. Securing greater resources for home economics, however, further solidified gender segregation in American public schools. Rather than achieve "equalization" for women, home economics courses promoted race-based citizenship expectations for American girls. To use Elizabeth Cohen's term, the AHEA enforced the "semi-citizenship status" of Black women through teaching a double labor burden of homemaking and breadwinning in government-funded education. New home economics requirements in the Jim Crow South and the colonized territory of Hawai'i allowed AHEA members to confer varying degrees of Americanness on new groups of working-class girls after World War I. With help from the federal government, women education reformers exported a narrow vision of gender, labor, and American citizenship far beyond the urban high school.[4]

We, Too, Loved the Home

The National Society for the Promotion of Industrial Education (NSPIE) urged President Woodrow Wilson to support the vocational education movement through federal aid in 1914. As Europe erupted in World War I, Wilson was moved by NSPIE's assertion that vocational education would help America win its industrial competition with Germany. In a speech to members of Congress, Wilson argued that Americans needed to defend themselves against Germany on two fronts: the "military side" and the "vocational side." Like Germany, their "great country" needed "a system of industrial and vocational education under federal guidance and federal aid." President Wilson placed his support behind the economic power of school reform in 1914. In doing so, he suggested that vocational education would make America's children better workers and better citizens by helping America's struggle for global economic supremacy.[5]

Wilson established a special commission of legislators and education reformers to draft a bill that would allocate federal funds to vocational programs. Most of his appointees represented northern states and industrial interests. Senator Carroll S. Page (R-VT) and Representative Simeon D. Fess (R-OH) hoped to expand trade education to urban children in their states. Charles Winslow, who served on the Massachusetts Commission on Industrial Education and the US Bureau of Labor Statistics, supported their goals with a wealth of employment data on manufacturing needs in the industrial North. Wilson also appointed two sociologists and trade school experts, Charles Prosser and John A. Lapp, who were affiliated with NSPIE. Southern legislators complained that the needs of rural students would be neglected by these commissioners. Wilson responded by appointing two southern legislators, Senator Hoke Smith (D-GA), who served as chair, and Representative Dudley Hughes (D-GA). Smith and Hughes submitted the commission's final recommendations to Congress and drafted the subsequent Smith-Hughes bill for federal aid to vocational education in public high schools.[6]

Wilson appointed two women to the Commission on Federal Aid to Vocational Education: Agnes Nestor of the Women's Trade Union League (WTUL) and Florence Marshall of the Manhattan Trade School for Girls. Both Nestor and Marshall supported the women's labor movement in their cities and trade education for working-class girls. But Nestor was the only working-class member of the commission. The American Federation of Labor (AFL) and local union leaders endorsed her appointment for this reason. Letters of support poured into her office at the Chicago WTUL headquarters from union men and women who hoped she would be a voice of working people on a commission of "peanut politicians." Even Ella Flagg Young wished Nestor luck achieving what she had failed to implement in Chicago. She wrote Nestor: "Hoping you have powers granted in the Committee that will enable you to make your ideas effective."[7]

During their proceedings, the commissioners agreed that Congress should equally distribute federal aid for agricultural education in rural school districts and industrial education in urban school districts. Congress could also reimburse states for developing vocational teacher training programs at land-grant state colleges and partially pay the salaries of vocational teachers in public high schools. A state requesting federal aid for vocational education could use funds for all-day, part-time, or evening schools at the high school level. But they could use no more than 50 percent of their budget for agricultural education and 50 percent for industrial programs. As Smith and Hughes explained in their final report, students who left school to work "in the shop and in the factory" deserved the same federal support as rural boys who "work on the soil." The commissioners suggested that expanding vocational education would enrich two sides of the American economy. The bill would support a new generation of expert farmers through professionalizing agricultural trades and would prepare skilled tradesmen through urban school investments in industry.[8]

Smith and Hughes framed this division of labor as essential to prepare rural and urban children for "efficient citizenship." The commissioners argued that Congress could help standardize citizenship training by funding vocational programs. Government-funded vocational classes would teach American boys to value productivity and financial responsibility, the hallmarks of "useful and happy citizenship" under American capitalism. These programs would train a generation of farmers and laborers to invest in America's "commercial prestige" that was threatened by competition from Germany, France, Britian, and "far-off Japan." In their report to Congress, the commissioners framed vocational education as both a "social and economic need" of the government to ensure "the happiness and welfare of its citizenship."[9]

Commissioners struggled with where to place girls in their proposal for agricultural and industrial education. Transcripts of their proceedings show that debates surrounding girls in rural school districts were less contentious. All nine commissioners agreed that rural school officials could use federal aid to fund both "farm and home" education. They reasoned that the economic distinction between breadwinner and homemaker was less defined in agricultural economies because labor "on the farm and in the home are so closely interrelated." Classes on food storage, canning, cooking, laundry, sanitation, and household budgeting would prepare girls for "useful employment in the farm home" and could therefore receive aid under a state's budget for agricultural education. The education of future farm wives was equally important to "the welfare and happiness of the Nation."[10]

Nestor argued that unpaid household labor was not vocational in cities because the industrial economy relied on the wage. During the proceedings, Nestor urged her colleagues to focus on the wage-earning pursuits of urban girls only. Nestor later recalled the difficulty of convincing fellow commissioners to interpret "vocational education" for girls in city schools strictly in terms of waged work outside the home. "We, too, loved the home," Nestor wrote in her 1954 autobiography, "but the girls needed training to earn a living." Nestor worried that any reference to "domestic science" or "home economics" in the Smith-Hughes bill might confuse urban school officials or make it "too easy to push all the girls into that field." For this reason, Nestor worked to ensure that the language of their recommendations to Congress clearly distinguished between vocational education for girls in rural and urban school districts.[11]

Nestor called fellow WTUL member Leonora O'Reilly to speak before the commission on the importance of trade education for girls in urban school districts. O'Reilly was a union seamstress who taught shirt making at the Manhattan Trade School for Girls. During her hearing with the commission in 1914, O'Reilly bristled at the remarks of Senator Page (R-VT), who described cooking and housekeeping as "vocational" subjects for high school girls in Vermont. If cooking was a "vocational" subject like engineering or carpentry, she questioned, then would boys also take home economics? "Well, men don't do the cooking in Vermont," Senator Page responded. "Perhaps they ought to," O'Reilly retorted. "And if a boy can sew on a button better than a girl, why, let him sew on his buttons." O'Reilly cautioned the commissioners to not let their notions of tradition dictate the future of vocational education in American public schools. "It is unjust to think that because we have been cooking all our lives we are going to go on and be cooks forever."[12]

Nestor viewed the Smith-Hughes bill as an opportunity to empower working-class girls in American cities through trade education. While drafting their recommendations to Congress, Nestor submitted a resolution from the National WTUL that all industrial programs supported by the Smith-Hughes bill be coeducational. The resolution also stated that trade programs in urban school districts should teach the philosophy of collective bargaining and the history of industry. Nestor argued that Congress should encourage state governments to support "new opportunities for women" in fields like printing, architecture, and engineering with federal aid in addition to supporting garment trade programs for dressmaking and millinery. Nestor said nothing about white-collar work during their proceedings. Fellow commissioners also ignored "commercial" education and focused on the twin investments of agricultural education and industrial training for American students.

Nestor had mixed success convincing her fellow commissioners to invest in the wage-earning potential of urban girls. Commissioners did not agree that Congress should invest in emerging employment opportunities for urban girls. Instead, fellow commissioners argued that the bill should fund vocational programs that represent "the most common occupations" currently employing women and girls in cities. As Commissioner Winslow put it, their goal was to address existing job needs rather than "what men and women might do that they are not doing." Nestor was successful in convincing her colleagues that federal aid for vocational education in urban school districts should prepare boys and girls for wage-earning pursuits only. In their report to Congress, Smith wrote that urban schools could use federal aid to prepare girls for jobs "based upon a knowledge of home economics" such as waitressing, nursing, nutrition, and interior design. He was explicit that funds for "industrial education" in urban school districts must focus on wage-earning trades for boys and girls. The original draft of the Smith-Hughes bill did include funding for home economics teachers and teacher training programs at land-grant state colleges. But Senator Smith and Representative Hughes did not recommend funding for homemaking education in urban school districts when they introduced the bill to Congress the following year.[13]

The exclusion of home economics from urban school budgets sparked immediate outrage from the General Federation of Women's Clubs (GFWC). First organized in Chicago, the GFWC represented more than 3,000 local women's clubs across the country and promoted clubwomen's reform agendas on the national level. At their Biennial Convention in Chicago in 1915, members organized a Home Economics Committee to lobby for a redrafting of the Smith-Hughes bill. Federation leaders argued that clubwomen were responsible for ensuring home economics make it into the final bill. Lucy V. Dorsey, a clubwoman from Pittsburgh, urged state and local club affiliates to lobby for the bill's redrafting. In the GFWC's monthly magazine, Dorsey explained that Senator Hughes had called her at least twice to encourage clubwomen to publicly endorse the Smith-Hughes bill. "Mr. Hughes, who introduced it [the bill], writes me he is dependent largely on the women to secure its passage," she wrote in the spring of 1916. But Dorsey declined her endorsement and encouraged fellow clubwomen to actively oppose the bill unless their interests were represented. "The bill as presented is unsatisfactory," she wrote. This required clubwomen's "active efforts" and "immediate action" to ensure that Congress invest in training urban girls for domesticity.[14]

GFWC members argued that federal support for home economics was essential in city school districts because so many urban girls spent their girlhood employed. Helen Louise Johnson, president of the GFWC, served as chair of the Home Economics Committee in 1916. Johnson argued that America's impending entrance into World War I exacerbated home conditions in American cities by pulling young women into manufacturing jobs. "We cannot afford to have women taken from the home into industry," she wrote. Demand for industrial workers was particularly dangerous for girls, transforming "happy children" into "tired, dull eyed, hopeless, stupid, or vicious young people." City schools needed to instill the skills and values of homemaking *before* working-class girls left school for work. Federal investment in home economics, she argued, was a tool for "safeguarding the home and its interest."[15]

Clubwomen spent two years lobbying Smith and Hughes to redraft the bill so that urban school officials could allocate federal funds for home economics. The GFWC successfully convinced the congressmen to redraft the bill in 1916. Support for the revision also came from Representative Horace Mann Towner (R-IA), whose wife, Harriet Elizabeth Towner, was a prominent figure in the national clubwomen's movement. In an impassioned speech on the Senate floor, Towner argued the importance of preparing urban girls for their "higher vocations" after exiting the workforce. "If you elevate the home in the mind of the girl who thinks too much about becoming a shop girl, or a factory worker, rather than of going to the home and becoming a mother," he argued, "it would elevate the whole scheme of home-making and home-keeping." Towner finished his speech to applause.[16]

President Wilson signed the Smith-Hughes Act into law in March 1917, one month before declaring war on Germany. The revised bill included federal funding for home economics programs at the high school level along with programs in agricultural and industrial trades. Notably, Smith and Hughes attached funding for home economics to a state's budget for industrial education in urban school districts. The Smith-Hughes Act allowed each state to devote up to 20 percent of their budget for industrial education to home economics programs in evening, part-time, or regular day schools for girls. The Smith-Hughes Act, then, not only offered federal support to train girls for homemaking in urban school districts; the bill also implied that girls' training for the home was a specific responsibility of the urban school district.[17]

The Smith-Hughes Act brought government officials into the supervision of public school programs for the first time in American history. The Smith-Hughes Act established a Federal Board for Vocational Education staffed with education reformers who conducted national studies on agricultural, industrial, and home economics education. Federal "supervisors" in these three areas set standards for training vocational teachers at state colleges and wrote course material to nationalize vocational education in local high schools. This program of federal oversight continued until 1963 when the Kennedy administration replaced the Smith-Hughes Act with a new federal vocational education policy that included even greater investments from Congress. Federal support for vocational programs in public high schools expanded after 1963 to a current budget of more than $1 billion annually. In sum, the Smith-Hughes Act marked the beginning of a century-long federal investment in training American high school students for work.[18]

Debates between urban women groups over the purpose of girls' vocational education entered the national stage during the drafting of the Smith-Hughes Act. Nestor kept home economics out of the original Smith-Hughes bill for fear that the inclusion of domestic education would limit opportunities for working-class girls to improve their employment prospects. Clubwomen, in contrast, viewed their eleventh-hour contribution to the Smith-Hughes Act as an investment in better homes and healthier children. World War I lent credence to clubwomen's assertion that the government should invest in educating working-class girls for expert homemaking before they left school to support the wartime economy. In the decade that followed, their allies used Smith-Hughes funding to promote unpaid homemaking as both the assumed vocation and primary citizenship duty of American girls.

Working Girls as "Homemakers of Tomorrow"

The Smith-Hughes Act also created new career opportunities for education reformers in state-level office. To qualify for funding, each state established a State Board for Vocational Education that distributed government aid to vocational programs in local high schools and teacher training programs in state colleges. All forty-eight states established a state board by 1918. State boards hired expert "supervisors" of agriculture, industry, and home economics who coordinated with their counterparts on the Federal Board for Vocational Education. Both federal and state supervisors conducted studies on child labor to suggest vocational programming in secondary education. They developed curricula for local schools and established certification requirements for teachers of agricultural, industrial, and home economics courses. The Smith-Hughes Act of 1917 both expanded the role of the federal government in secondary education and brought the state into the direct supervision of the public school curriculum.[19]

State supervisors in the industrial North used Smith-Hughes funds to bring children of legal working age back into the public school system. Congress allocated a conservative $7 million toward the creation of vocational classes and teacher training programs over a ten-year period. State governments needed to match or exceed each federal dollar for a total investment of at least $14 million by 1927. States with large manufacturing centers—New York, Pennsylvania, and Illinois—received the most funding under the Smith-Hughes Act. Most states in the industrial North invested their limited funded in evening, extension, and part-time "continuation" programs for students who had already left school for work. Over half of all children enrolled in Smith-Hughes programs in Illinois and Massachusetts were part-time students who earned wages during regular school hours. Working children and adults in part-time programs accounted for 90 percent of enrollment in Smith-Hughes programs in New York and 70 percent of enrollment in Pennsylvania.[20]

The Federal Board for Vocational Education encouraged state boards to invest in part-time continuation schools to extend the school lives of working-age children and reduce child labor. In addition to vocational skills, federal officials argued that continuation schools for working children should emphasize good hygiene and citizenship expectations. Illinois's first state supervisor of industry, A. E. Wreidt, worked with Chicago school officials to establish seven continuation programs for working boys between fourteen and sixteen years old during World War I. In the stockyards district, four continuation schools trained boy meat-packers to advance to office jobs for their employers. Autoworkers between the ages of fourteen and eighteen could attend the Automobile Continuation School to strengthen their mechanic skills. Young drafters and carpenters prepared for higher-paid positions in the building trades at the Washburne Continuation School. Other continuation schools collaborated with local unions to train steamfitters, electricians, leatherworkers, clockmakers, and plumbers.[21]

States across the Manufacturing Belt amended their school attendance laws to include mandatory continuation schooling for working children after World War I. Sixteen states passed mandatory continuation school attendance laws for children "of the working paper class" in 1919. Twenty-six states required children of working age to attend continuation school by 1929. Most continuation school laws (including the Illinois law) required that working children attend continuation school for at least one full day or two half days a week. More than 16,000 boys and girls in Chicago attended a part-time continuation school during the 1924–25 school year. Continuation schools usually included vocational training, general education, and "instruction in citizenship." The new continuation school laws both expanded the number of part-time programs and the role of government-funded education in the lives of working-class children. School officials in Chicago invested 75 percent of their Smith-Hughes budget toward continuation schooling for working children in the 1920s. The Federal Board for Vocational Education admitted that some parents found these laws to be "an encroachment upon individual liberties for their children." But federal officials maintained the importance of part-time schooling to promote the "general welfare" of working-class children and ward off "unemployment, poverty, and social unrest."[22]

Part-time continuation schools reinforced racial and gender hierarchies within the urban economy. Continuation schools that offered apprenticeship programs for boys were inaccessible to Black students due to the notorious racial hostility of Chicago's craft unions. In 1930, less than 3 percent of Black men in Chicago found employment in the skilled trades because of discrimination in the union movement. Continuation programs located in or near Black neighborhoods did not collaborate with unions. The South Division Continuation School—located in a dilapidated schoolhouse that briefly housed Flower Tech—offered training in "semi-skilled" trades like auto repair and general machine job. At least one part-time program in a South Side public school catered specifically to professional chauffeurs. Chicago school officials relied on government funding to support de facto segregation in men's industrial trades.[23]

The Illinois State Board for Vocational Education funded continuation schools that taught "vocational home economics" to girls of legal working age. The first state supervisor of home economics, Cora Davis, argued that working girls needed continuation education to prepare for future homemaking. Davis studied household science at the University of Chicago in the 1910s and chaired the Department of Domestic Science at the Illinois State Normal University. Davis echoed the principles of the domestic science movement that Chicago would have safer homes and healthier children if working-class girls learned how to care for children and "cook simple home meals." Chicago had five home economics continuation schools by 1920. The city's largest was the Winchell Continuation School located near Fulton Market in Chicago's meatpacking district. According to Davis, girls who earned wages in this district "went into shops just as soon as the school laws permit." The Winchell Continuation School helped these working girls of today become "home makers of tomorrow." Most of the students at Winchell were second-generation immigrant girls who worked in garment factories. Davis also used government aid to educate their mothers. By 1920, Chicago school officials organized fifteen evening programs that taught cooking and childcare to "foreign women" over eighteen who earned wages during the day. In their inaugural year, nearly 9,000 working girls and women attended these home economics programs each week.[24]

Illinois invested far fewer resources in girls' continuation schooling in the postwar decade. Most wage-earning girls who obeyed continuation school laws did so in part-time "general education" programs offered in neighborhood high schools. These part-time programs offered a version of the "comprehensive" high school championed by Ella Flagg Young in the 1910s. Girls took both academic coursework and "vocational home economics" subjects like cooking, sewing, hygiene, and "home craft." State boards also funded commercial continuation schools that taught penmanship, arithmetic, and typing to working boys and girls. In some cities, commercial programs included home economics lessons for female students studying office work. A recommended lesson plan in Wisconsin stated that girls' commercial education should include "a course on proper food, proper clothing, and personal hygiene." Black girls were unlikely to enroll in Chicago's handful of commercial continuation programs given their discrimination in white-collar fields. Roughly three hundred Black women and girls held office jobs in the entire city of Chicago in 1930. Instead, commercial continuation schools helped white working girls improve their clerical skills and respectability for the marriage market through a combination of white-collar and domestic training.[25]

State-funded continuation schools extended the boundaries of working-class childhood in the 1920s. Initially, state governments like Illinois required continuation schooling for children with legal working papers between ages fourteen and sixteen. States raised this age requirement to seventeen or eighteen by the mid-1920s. Illinois raised the age requirement of their continuation school attendance law to eighteen years old in 1923. In doing so, state governments suggested that child labor—and therefore "childhood"—extended to age eighteen rather than fourteen or sixteen.[26] Raising the age requirement empowered local school officials to bring additional children who legally left school for work back into the school system. Children between fourteen and eighteen who did not attend continuation school for eight hours a week lost their working papers and were required to return to normal day school. In Chicago, truant officers could fine their families between twenty-five and one hundred dollars.[27]

Gendered conceptions of child labor placed additional regulations around girls. Girls who left school to earn wages required continuation schooling. Those who left school for unpaid "service or assistance at home" also required continuation schooling until age eighteen in Illinois. Home economics was the backbone of girls' continuation schooling due to the financial support offered through the Smith-Hughes Act. By the mid-1920s, nearly all of Chicago's Smith-Hughes budget for home economics went toward continuation and evening classes for caretakers and wage earners who had already left the school system. Chicago's investment in home economics for working girls was representative of Smith-Hughes spending across the industrial North. In Massachusetts, 88 percent of girls enrolled in Smith-Hughes home economics programs were part-time students who had already left school legally.[28]

The Smith-Hughes Act created new avenues of directing the labor of urban students and extending their school lives through continuation programs. Local school officials used government aid to invest in the continued learning of working-class children who left the school system for financial and caretaking responsibilities. State supervisors of industry invested in male breadwinning power through trade programs that were largely inaccessible to Black male students. State supervisors of home economics prepared white working girls for unpaid service to their future homes in a decade when most working-class Black women relied on paid household service for their livelihood. Continuation school laws protected working-class children's access and rights to a public education. These government-funded programs also promoted gendered and racialized assumptions about the expected work roles of American citizens.

Equalization for Women

The nation's largest home economics organization, the AHEA, was remarkably silent about the Smith-Hughes Act during World War I. Members were initially hesitant to associate home economics with the vocational education movement. They worried that calling home economics "vocational" belittled the social importance of homemaking in the general education of women and girls. The funding and professional opportunities afforded through the Smith-Hughes Act encouraged AHEA leadership to change their attitude. In 1921, the president of the AHEA, Mary E. Sweeny, urged members to reconsider "what conditions best promote the development of the work." Writing in the *Bulletin of Home Economics*, Sweeny encouraged home economists to meet with "our foremost educators" in government supervision. The Smith-Hughes Act created new "opportunities and responsibilities" for the home economist and offered a favorable "outlook on her profession."[29]

The term "home economics" reflect the AHEA's social commitments and departure from earlier goals of the domestic science movement. By the 1920s, home economists moved away from turn-of-the-century terms like "domestic" and "household" to describe women's contributions to their homes. For college-educated white women, these words suggested traditional and burdensome systems of labor that were often followed by the racially stigmatized word "service." Instead, white home economists on college campuses wrote frequently about the social work of "homemaking" and said very little about the labor of "housekeeping." The word "home" evoked an environment for professional women to cultivate. "Home" suggested social ideals of comfort and family unity. Associating the feminine "home" with the term "economics" also provided these women more social cachet on college campuses by connecting their domestic-facing research to the new field of social studies.[30]

AHEA members pursued supervisory positions on federal and state boards for vocational education after World War I. Anna E. Richardson was appointed as the first supervisor of home economics on the Federal Board for Vocational Education in 1919. Richardson studied domestic science at the University of Chicago and Columbia University before establishing a home economics teacher training program at Agnes Scott Women's College in Georgia. On the federal board, she coordinated with state officials to standardize the training of teachers in land-grant state colleges. Richardson was often careful to distinguish home economics from the vocational education movement despite her role on the Federal Board for Vocational Education. She argued that home economics courses should de-emphasize domestic labor skills and instead focus on teaching girls "the sociological significance of family life."[31]

Labor women also wanted supervisory roles over the girls' curriculum at the state and federal levels. In 1920, the National WTUL sent a petition to the Federal Board for Vocational Education demanding the appointment of "women familiar with the problems of women in industry." Mary Anderson, a former Chicago shoe-stitcher and WTUL member, endorsed the petition. Anderson made history earlier that year when elected the first president of the Women's Bureau of the US Labor Department. Under pressure from Anderson, the Federal Board for Vocational Education appointed one woman, Anna L. Burdick, to serve as a "special agent for girls and women in trades and industry." Labor women complained that Burdick was not qualified for the job. Burdick was a former school official from Iowa tasked with studying job opportunities for working girls in American cities and advising on girls' continuation schools. She had a middle-class background and no labor experience beyond the teaching profession. As

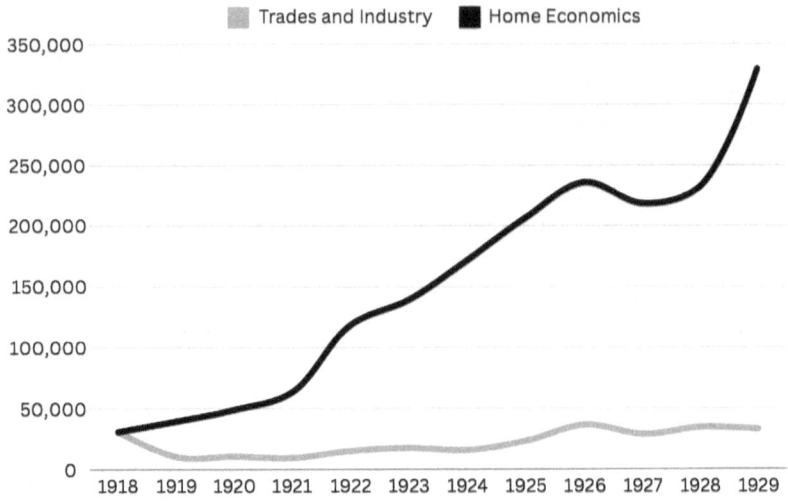

Female Enrollment in Smith-Hughes Funded Programs, 1918–1929

Data from Annual Reports of the Federal Board for
Vocational Education, 1918–1929

Anderson argued, the board also needed to hire working-class women who understood "not only where a girl can get a job but what that job means to the girl." Her request was denied.[32]

Labor activists had some success supervising the use of government funding for girls' trade education at the state level. During World War I, the public school systems of Chicago and New York used Smith-Hughes funds to open continuation programs for dressmakers following pressure from labor women. The New York State Board for Vocational Education funded continuation training for girls in retail and department stores and bought new equipment for the Manhattan Trade School for Girls. State governments invested far fewer resources to girls' trade education, however, and these programs for wage earning suffered from low enrollment and lack of funding. In 1920, less than 7,000 women and girls nationwide enrolled in part-time programs for "trades and industry." More than ten times the number of women and girls enrolled in part-time programs for home economics that year.[33]

Home economists had more success supervising the girls' curriculum in part due to their relationship with teacher training programs at land-grant state colleges. In fact, the AHEA encouraged members to pursue supervisory roles on state boards for vocational education to help professionalize home economics teacher training programs at their colleges. Only thirty-three state colleges had four-year home economics programs before the Smith-Hughes Act. Over the next nine years, the number of four-year home economics programs increased to 651 with support from the Smith-Hughes Act. Home economics departments also expanded on Black college campuses. In 1923, thirteen historically Black colleges received government aid to train home economics teachers. State boards subsidized the salaries of Black teachers in the South to bring home economics education into segregated public schools.[34]

Black home economists, however, were not represented on state boards for vocational education or accepted into the AHEA. Perhaps the most prestigious Black teacher training program that benefited from the Smith-Hughes Act was at Tuskegee University in Alabama. The Alabama State Board for Vocational Education hired a white home economist from Ohio, Ivol Spafford, as state supervisor of home economics. Spafford oversaw requirements for Black teachers trained at Tuskegee, wrote lesson plans for public schools, and controlled the Smith-Hughes purse strings. Government funding supported a new generation of Black home economics teachers in public high schools across the New South. But the leadership opportunities available for home economists under the Smith-Hughes Act mostly benefited white college-educated women.[35]

In the 1920s, nearly all state supervisors of home economics were AHEA members who standardized home economics at both the college and high school levels. AHEA member Adah Hess replaced Cora Davis as state supervisor of home economics for Illinois in 1921. Hess trained home economics teachers at the University of Illinois. She also wrote the syllabus for home economics programs that were eligible for state funding in local high schools. The Lucy Flower Technical School for Girls (Flower Tech) was one of the few all-day schools in Illinois to receive state support as a "home economics school" under Hess's leadership. School architects outfitted the new Flower Tech facility in Garfield Park with cooking labs and display rooms for dressmaking majors to showcase finished garments. The school had a beauty parlor lined with sinks for hairdressing and stations for manicures. Notably, the new Flower Tech was the only high school in America with a functioning childcare clinic. School officials encouraged neighborhood mothers to drop off their babies at the clinic during school hours so girls could practice "mothercraft" through "direct contact with small children." Access to federal and state funds after World War I allowed Flower Tech to modernize as the premier technical school for girls in the Midwest.[36]

The emphasis on "mothercraft" reflected Flower Tech's primary purpose to educate white American girls for gendered work roles. This training sat

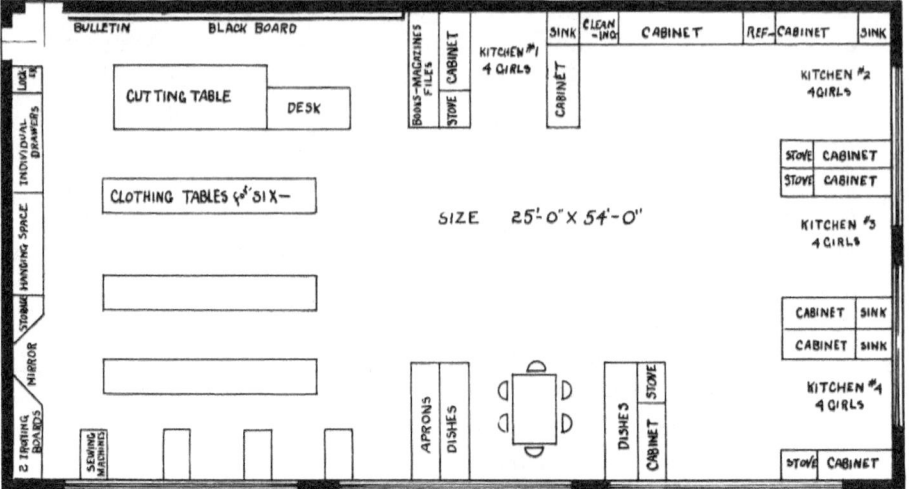

Standardized floorplan for organizing home economics courses in Illinois with space for garment design (*left*), cooking (*right*), and meal serving (*center*) issued by the Illinois supervisor of home economics, 1938 (published in the *State Board for Vocational Education Bulletin*, no. 70)

awkwardly in the curriculum for Black students, who were encouraged by school officials to prepare for both homemaking and domestic wage earning. Doris Clark Cheatam, who enrolled at Flower Tech in 1927, recalled the racism of the school's vocational guidance counselor, who expected Black students to use these school resources to prepare for domestic service despite their plans to go to college. She recalled that many white peers did not question this training in motherhood and became "just housewives" after graduating. Black students continued to push back against the racial assumptions of "vocational home economics" for decades. Flower Tech's assistant superintendent in the 1950s explained to historian Nancy Green that Black girls did not like home economics because they resented "the Aunt Jemima image." Vocational home economics was narrowly defined as homemaking training for European immigrant daughters in urban schools like Flower Tech. For Black students, vocational home economics served a twin function of education for homemaking and preparation for the lowest-paid jobs in the US economy.[37]

In 1921, the AHEA called for a redrafting of the Smith-Hughes Act to provide more job security for white home economists and more federal funding for their public school courses. Louise Stanley, chair of the AHEA's Legislative Committee, spearheaded these lobbying efforts in Congress. Stanley trained as a chemist during the domestic science movement and served as chair of the Department of Home Economics at the University of Missouri. She argued that the Smith-Hughes Act handicapped state boards by preventing supervisors from investing more than 20 percent of their budget for industrial education in home economics. Stanley called for an amendment that would remove this 20 percent cap so that states could split their budgets equally between home economics (girls) and industrial education (boys) in urban school districts. The AHEA also complained that the Smith-Hughes Act allowed state boards to reimburse local schools for the salaries of home economics teachers (states "may") but did not guarantee salary reimbursements (states "must"). Stanley framed the funding disparities as a form of gender discrimination that disadvantaged the only public school subject strictly for girls and taught by women. On the AHEA's behalf, Senator Simeon Fess (R-OH) introduced the Fess Home Economics Amendment (Fess Amendment) to the Sixty-Sixth Congress in 1921.[38]

The Fess Amendment was among a handful of legislative reforms supported by national women's groups in the post-suffrage decade. The suffrage movement ended in 1920 with the ratification of the Nineteenth Amendment, which banned voting discrimination based on sex. White women had the privilege of exercising their right to vote fully because they did not experience race-based voting restrictions at the local level.[39] After 1920, the nation's largest suffrage groups—the National American Woman Suffrage Association (NAWSA) and the National Council of Women Voters (NCWV)—formed the League of Women Voters (LWV) as a nonpartisan group dedicated to political lobbying and educating women on their citizenship rights. The LWV helped keep Progressive Era political issues alive in the postwar decade. Their most notable achievement was the short-lived Sheppard-Towner Act of 1921, the first federal welfare program, which funded healthcare services for mothers and infants until 1929. The LWV also endorsed the Fess Amendment in 1921. Along with the Sheppard-Towner Act, members hoped the Fess Amendment would support the work of motherhood by investing in the next generation of caretakers.[40]

The Fess Amendment received formal endorsements from over thirty national women's groups in 1921. Representatives from many of these groups also made statements on the House floor in support of the AHEA's proposal for more home economics funding. Groups dedicated to the advancement of women in politics and higher education endorsed the bill on the grounds of "equalization" for women. "The National League of Women Voters believe in this policy of equalization of opportunity for girls and boys," argued the LWV's chairwoman. The vice president of the Association of Collegiate Alumnae (ACA) agreed that increasing the funding for home economics education was a matter of "equalization in educational opportunities" for female students: "We believe that every girl ought to have the opportunity of securing this education." These spokeswomen suggested that limiting the funds for home economics was tantamount to sexism.[41]

Groups like the AHEA and LWV, however, did not ask for gender equality in vocational education through the Fess Amendment. Rather, they promoted gender segregation in public education by assuming that only one program—home economics—was important for female students. "Equalization" meant separate but equal resources for girls' education in home economics. "Equalization" meant equal job security for white college-educated home economists only, not Black home economists who were excluded from the AHEA. This vision of equality under the Smith-Hughes Act differed from the goals of women trade unionists like Nestor who wanted equal access to government supervision and programs for girls in trades and industry. The National WTUL was a notable absence on the list of women's groups that endorsed the Fess Amendment in 1921.[42]

Congress did not pass the Fess Amendment in 1921. They did, however, approve a series of other investments in home economics education due to the pressure of politically powerful white women's groups. Congress approved the creation of the US Bureau of Home Economics two years later, a federal agency dedicated to the study and dissemination of home economics education. Louise Stanley was appointed director of the Bureau of Home Economics in 1923 and held that position for the next twenty years. During its forty-year existence, home economists with the bureau published sample course syllabi, recipes, and sewing patterns used by public school students. The establishment of the bureau under Stanley's direction also helped standardize home economics education as a feature of girls' secondary education. According to a national study by the US Bureau of Education, only 17 percent of high school girls took classes with names like "household arts" or "domestic science" before the Smith-Hughes Act. The bureau reported that over 60 percent of American high schools offered programs ubiquitously called "home economics" a decade later.[43]

The activism of AHEA members in vocational supervision helped thousands of white college-educated women chart new career paths for themselves in the 1920s. Ironically, many of these women were able to achieve their reform goals by challenging the very social roles they taught. Leading home economists were mostly unmarried and childless women. Louise Stanley and Anna Richardson never married. Adah Hess lived in Springfield, Illinois, with a female roommate well into her sixties. Less than 9 percent of state supervisors of home economics from this period were or had ever been married themselves. Home economists used their positions of government power to project homemaking expectations onto working-class girls, requiring these students conform to middle-class gender conventions that they themselves rejected.[44]

Americanization Through Home Economics

Members of the AHEA also gained control over girls' public education by linking home economics to Americanization efforts in local school districts. Citizenship training became a formal function of American public education after World War I. Hyper-patriotism on the home front inspired new state laws requiring students to engage in pro-America exercises during school. For example, states adopted a revised version of the Pledge of Allegiance that clarified expected loyalties of first- and second-generation students. Rather than pledging to "*my* Flag," the recitation expanded to specify allegiance to "*the* Flag of the United States of America." By 1925, the state legislature of Illinois required all high school students to take a "civics" class for an hour a week to learn US history and principles of democratic government. Civics was also required in continuation schools for working children in the 1920s. As one Illinois state official explained, the new civics requirement made "good citizens out of our school children."[45]

Education for citizenship reflected the ethnic and political hostilities of the postwar decade. Congress passed a series of immigration restrictions after World War I that placed quotas on non-white immigrants and ejected residents with "un-American" political ideals like anarchy. A series of quota-based immigration reforms culminated in the Johnson-Reed Act of 1924, the most restrictive immigration policy in US history, which issued heavy quotas on immigrants from eastern Europe and banned all immigration from Asia. The Johnson-Reed Act enforced a homogeneous American citizenship by explicitly rejecting entry to immigrants based on ethnicity and race. Postwar immigration policies also promoted middle-class gender expectations for American families. Along with anarchists and communists, the United States ejected "radicals" who challenged the breadwinner-homemaker family model such as polygamists. In the postwar period, American immigration policy promoted a normative vision of American citizenship rooted in whiteness, patriotism, and the middle-class family unit.[46]

New civics requirements in urban public schools taught gendered citizenship expectations to the children of immigrants, who still dominated urban classrooms. In 1920, the US Bureau of Education published a civics syllabus specifically for first- and second-generation children in the "city schools." Mary Woodlock, a middle-class social reformer working in

New York City, developed the syllabus for use across the industrial North. Chicago school officials first introduced the course in a Far South Side elementary school whose students represented nearly twenty nationalities. According to Chicago school officials, these were the children of "low wage earners" who "live in crowded houses" and "hold on to their foreign language and customs." Woodlock's course encouraged teachers to appoint female students as "little housekeepers" in charge of cleaning and decorating their classroom. Girls took turns in this role to learn that women citizens have "an attitude of helpfulness" and "take good care of the pretty things." Male students took turns as classroom "commissioners" placed in charge of the hallways, stairways, and playground. Girls tidied the private classroom spaces. Boys "inspected" public halls and stairways to "report upon their condition." The commissioner roles taught boys that good citizens protect city buildings because property damage "causes loss to every citizen." Girls learned that citizenship rights stemmed from unpaid service to others.[47]

Male school officials used vocational education to prepare the sons of European immigrants for productive breadwinning in urban high schools. In 1926, the Chicago Board of Education (BOE) listed vocational education as a social studies requirement for ninth-grade students along with civics. School officials explained that the city's dedicated trade schools would still "turn out skilled workers." In the neighborhood high schools, however, shop classes were redefined as "cultural subjects" that emphasized how American men "work together in organized society." Ninth-grade boys devoted the first half of the school year to US history and civics and the second half to vocational education and guidance. Other school officials suggested that this new focus of shop class quelled political radicalism among the children of working-class immigrants. As a social study, trade education encouraged "industrial peace" between employers and "immigrant workmen." Ultimately, trade courses prepared working-class boys for the breadwinning responsibilities of male citizenship under American capitalism. As one school official put it, trade classes taught boys to appreciate "the complex economic world in which they must play their specialized parts."[48]

The Chicago BOE also listed home economics as a social study for high school girls after World War I. As state supervisor, Adah Hess argued that home economics prepared girls for citizenship through fostering appreciation for the social role of the American homemaker. Home economics classes taught "home appreciation," "desirable home relationships," and "the relations of the family to society." In a 1927 syllabus for high school courses, Hess advised Illinois teachers to engage girls in discussions on how good homemakers fostered "desirable family relationships" by caring for their husbands and devoted free time to their community through church activities. According to one Chicago school official, the purpose of home economics was "character training" under the new social studies curriculum. Rather than emphasize domestic trades like cooking or sewing, home economics taught girls the right cultural "attitudes" toward the home such as to feel "happy" and be "helpful."[49]

The new Flower Tech curriculum reflected this shift in vocational education toward cultural appreciation for American work roles. In 1917, more than 80 percent of urban high schools included garment design or dressmaking courses as part of their "household arts" programs for girls. By 1927, only 6 percent of female students learned garment skills in four-year public high schools. Instead, more than 90 percent of American high schools included lessons on "selection and cost of textiles" as part of their home economics coursework. Economic changes following World War I contributed to the new emphasis on garment buying rather than making. Mass production of ready-made clothing reduced the number of garments produced by tradeswomen after the war and supported attention to consumption rather than production in the girls' curriculum. Yet the shift also reflects the values of home economists, who argued that the social role of household clothing buyer warranted greater public investment than the paid work of garment producer. Explaining the purpose of the new Smith-Hughes courses, Hess argued: "Teachers know it is much harder to spend money wisely than it is to earn it."[50]

Home economists like Hess suggested that reforming needle trade courses would Americanize the daughters of immigrants by teaching girls to dress and shop appropriately. A 1928 study of home economics in city high schools found that 36 percent had budgets for students to practice shopping under the supervision of trained home economics teachers. In Denver public schools, high school girls learned "intelligent shopping" with the average "clothing budget of a high school girl." Students took inventory of their current wardrobes and received advice from teachers on additional clothing needs. Home economics teachers advised girls on what additional articles to buy with their wages based on factors like "appropriateness" and "becomingness." Courses on buying allowed middle-class home economists to police the purchasing power of working-class girls and assign them grades based on the respectability of their appearance. These lessons also helped working girls learn budgeting skills they would presumably use as good American homemakers. After learning to shop for themselves, girls learned to cloth a family of five based on the budget of their "station in life." Home economists instructed girls to become model citizen women through engaging responsibly with the consumer economy and preserving their respectability for the marriage market.[51]

Advocates of the Fess Amendment explicitly linked home economics to Americanization efforts to curry support from Congress. The LWV endorsed the Fess Amendment in 1921 explicitly for "Americanization through home economics." A representative from the Chicago Woman's Club (CWC) likewise explained the group's support for home economics as "education for citizenship" that encouraged "the betterment of both home and country." These arguments were also leveraged to bring home economics out of the urban school district. Home economists argued that girls in rural high schools also needed to learn "American standards" of homemaking through Smith-Hughes-funded home economics courses. Ohio state supervisor of home economics Edna White reported that all working girls had access to evening or part-time home economics programs in the urban school district of Cleveland through new continuation school laws. "The work in most cities is already well established," she explained in 1921. Yet White had 175 active requests from rural Ohio school districts that desired more government support for home economics. Rural school officials framed these requests as an investment in high school citizenship training. According to women of the farmers' advocacy group, the National Grange, rural school districts also carried "the heavy responsibility of Americanizing the large alien population now finding its way to the farms."[52]

Congress addressed these concerns at the end of the decade through the George-Reed Act of 1929. The act was a supplement to Smith-Hughes that authorized millions of additional dollars for vocational programs in agriculture and home economics specifically. No additional funding was allocated for industrial education in urban school districts where, as White put it, vocational education was "already well established." The George-Reed Act split additional funds evenly between agriculture and home economics and required states to use the money specifically for these two purposes. This provision was a departure from the Smith-Hughes Act, which provided that states "may" use funds for home economics but not "must." In addition, the George-Reed Act supported to work of AHEA members by allowing states to pay the salaries of state supervisors of home economics with federal funds, offering increased job security for the college-educated home economists who oversaw most of the girls' vocational budget. AHEA members celebrated the George-Reed Act as the culmination of over a decade of lobbying. As one member of the Federal Board of Vocational Education declared: "The great value of a Nation of good homes has become a settled conviction."[53]

In the postwar decade, women's groups supported citizenship training in local school districts by arguing that home economics prepared the daughters of immigrants for the socially essential work of American homemaking. Doing so cemented in school curricula the expectation that women's jobs and women's citizenship stemmed from their unpaid labor toward children, husbands, and homes. These were not new ideas in the 1920s. New was women's use of federal and state funding streams to direct girlhood education and labor in the name of patriotism and national improvement. The George-Reed Act of 1929 confirmed this investment in using girls' education to promote "a Nation of good homes." By 1930, all forty-eight states relied on government aid for home economics and all forty-eight states required at least one year of home economics for girls enrolled in a four-year high school.[54]

Race, Labor, and American Womanhood

The success of the home economics movement was a win for women school reformers, who made their local initiatives like childcare and cooking courses a national priority after World War I. The racialized assumptions about gender, labor, and citizenship intrinsic to these courses were nationalized as well. In 1923, the Federal Board for Vocational Education published a study on home economics education for Black women and girls in southern school districts. The study was conducted by Carrie Lyford, a white home economist who taught Black teachers at the Hampton Normal and Agricultural Institute in Virginia. Lyford's report found that many southern state boards for vocational education did not make full use of available funding for home economics, unlike their northern peers. She urged southern state officials to invest in the domestic training of Black girls so they could understand "citizenship" through studying "the average American home." Lyford suggested that rural Black parents had unkempt houses because they did not appreciate "the value of money." Home economists needed to teach their daughters American homemaking values like "wise use of income" and "good taste is dress and in house furnishings." Black girls could use their education to bring "good health habits" into rural Black households. Lyford hoped that Americanizing rural Black girls would be easier because they had American-born parents. Unlike the daughters of European immigrants, Black girls had "few firmly established customs" and no "deep-rooted family traditions to outlive."[55]

That Lyford framed home economics as "Americanization" for African American girls is telling. Doing so implied that all women must prove their worthy citizenship through the standards of their homes. She suggested that the right education—namely, home economics under the leadership of white government-employed home economists—had the power to make

Black women and girls worthy of their full rights to citizenship. Lyford's report reinforced the "semi-citizenship" status of Black women and girls by questioning their full rights to American identity based on cultural assessments of their homes and domestic know-how. Her report suggested that most Black homes (and Black homemakers) were intrinsically less American because they did not meet the standards of women in the home economics movement.[56]

Lyford recommended that state boards for vocational education also use government aid to prepare Black girls for paid domestic service work. At the time of her report, over 40 percent of gainfully employed Black women and girls over the age of ten worked as domestic servants or laundresses. She explicitly called upon "white State Supervisors" to prepare Black girls for occupations "closely related to the home" in which "colored women have shown special adaptability." Doing so was important, she continued, to prepare these students to "take their places in the economic organization of society." Home economics taught second-generation girls that good citizenship was defined by unpaid homemaking. Unpaid homemaking *and* paid housework were the American expectations for Black girls. This distinction provided only the daughters of immigrants with a path to good citizenship.[57]

As a form of citizenship training for girls, home economics offered first- and second-generation immigrants a path to whiteness. Members of groups like the AHEA and GFWC argued that immigrant daughters needed homemaking training in the public schools because of their mothers' ethnic identities. These girls lacked the appropriate cultural exposure to American homemaking skills because of their quasi-white status as immigrant offspring. Home economics encouraged white ethnic girls to assert their white social citizenship status. At least in theory, these courses made immigrant daughters "American" through lessons in American womanhood. Along with access to white-collar skills and jobs, this Americanness was defined in contrast with the expectations of Black women's labor. Government home economists taught white girls that homemaking and breadwinning were discrete jobs held respectively by good (white) American women and men. Educating Black girls for both homemaking *and* breadwinning denied them the social respect and presumptive citizenship rights associated with either role.[58]

In the 1920s, AHEA members exported home economics far beyond the urban school district to Americanize colonial subjects. Congress extended the benefits of the Smith-Hughes Act to the territory of Hawai'i in 1924 as part of a broader effort to acculturate colonized children through American public schooling. Victor Houston, the congressional delegate in Hawai'i, argued that vocational programs would solve "Americanization problems" among the mostly Hawai'ian, Japanese, Chinese, and Portuguese children who attended American public schools on the islands. Home economist and AHEA member Dora S. Lewis served as supervisor of home economics for the islands and oversaw the teacher training program at the University of Hawai'i in Honolulu until 1929. The home economics department at the University of Hawai'i served a racially diverse student body in the 1920s. Yet the Federal Board for Vocational Education approved funding specifically to train "white teachers of home economics" to work in American public schools in Hawai'i.[59]

US school officials in Hawai'i tried to Americanize local families through home economics education for girls. The Smith-Hughes Act funded "Mothers' Classes" for young girls on the islands similar to programs for second-generation immigrants in urban school districts. These "little mothers" learned to care for younger siblings at home on behalf of working parents through lessons in sick day management and nursing. By 1929, nearly half of these "Mothers' Classes" engaged girls as young as eleven in the care of actual infants brought to the school for daycare services. Hawai'ian girls learned to cook in home economics courses and were encouraged to share their new knowledge with mothers at home. They used part of the school day to make household items to bring home with them, like small cabinets for food storage and portable oil ovens made from five-gallon kerosene cans. These courses mirrored earlier school initiatives to Americanize immigrant homes through girlhood labor in cities like Chicago. In the postwar decade, American school officials embraced the same strategy to encourage middle-class standards of childcare, comfort, and cleanliness on the colonized islands of Hawai'i.[60]

White home economists also relied on girls' labor to support the expansion of public education in Hawai'i. Dora Lewis hoped to increase school attendance rates among native children by improving the school lunch program in American elementary schools. Groups of mostly Hawai'ian and Japanese girls provided institutional labor for her lunch program. As part of their home economics curriculum, girls in grades six through eight cooked and served school lunches to their classmates at least once a week. Girls learned to cook nutritious meals, sanitize dishware, and practice the gender expectations of helpfulness. Home economics was not purely educational in this colonial context. Home economics likely saved the government money and kept American public schools running smoothly by enlisting girl workers.[61]

American home economists further blurred the line between child labor and education by training Hawai'ian girls for breadwinning responsibilities.

In 1928, hundreds of women reformers met in Honolulu for the First Pan-Pacific Women's Conference. The conference was chaired by Jane Addams and attended by mainland women interested in "problems of women and children about the Pacific." Louise Stanley traveled to Honolulu on behalf of the AHEA. At the conference, she argued that girls in the Pacific needed home economics for the "double responsibility" of improving home conditions and earning wages on the islands. "Part time jobs are going to be both essential and desirable," she argued. The Hawai'ian supervisor of home economics organized part-time continuation schools for domestic service following the conference. At least one of these government-funded schools in Oahu placed girls out as "housemaids" after their domestic training.[62]

These distinctions in home economics education after World War I reinforced race-based assumptions about labor and citizenship for girls. Educating Black girls for the double burden of breadwinning and homemaking was inherently in conflict with the home economics vision of appropriate work for American women. Home economists relied on girlhood labor to promote public education in the colonized territory of Hawai'i and to Americanize the domestic lives of local families. These variations in the home economics curriculum placed unequal labor burdens on girls and suggested disparate expectations of citizenship.

Conclusion

The vocational education movement nationalized after the Smith-Hughes Act of 1917 with the support of women school reformers. Two branches of these women reformers—working-class labor activists and wealthy white clubwomen—shaped the Smith-Hughes Act and the trajectory of government-funded education for girls for the next half century. Clubwomen in the GFWC not only safeguarded government investment in training girls for homemaking during World War I; their lobbying efforts also ensured that a generation of college-educated white women had supervisory control over the girls' vocational curriculum. Gendering the history of the Smith-Hughes Act demonstrates that girlhood was central to the development of federal education policy in the twentieth century.

The inclusion of home economics in the Smith-Hughes Act allowed white college-educated women to advance their careers by serving on federal and state boards for vocational education. These state actors used government funding to oversee the vocational training of working-class girls. Through continuation schooling, state officials extended the boundaries of childhood to bring young workers back into the school system and direct their education toward respectable employment. In states like Illinois, girls who legally left school to earn wages were required by law to study home economics for at least one day a week. State officials designed continuation schools to increase the wage-earning potential of boys and the homemaking potential of girls. Black girls in particular lacked meaningful investments in their vocational training because school reformers fixated on Americanizing the daughters of immigrants.

The Smith-Hughes Act also nationalized urban anxieties about working-class girls, labor, and American homes. State officials mandated home economics education for high school girls in all forty-eight states and the territory of Hawai'i by 1930. All relied on the Smith-Hughes Act and George-Reed Act to fund vocational programs, particularly in the form of evening and continuation programs for students working outside the school system. Government support for home economics helped Americanize and "whiten" second-generation girls through practice in American homemaking. State supervisors suggested that Black girls could not fully meet the citizenship expectations promoted by the home economics movement because they also required training for wage earning. These racial disparities in girls' domestic education had roots in the nineteenth century. But after World War I, women educators successfully argued that the government should invest in unequitable expectations of domestic labor through "vocational home economics."

Conclusion

Urban women's groups used education to remake the labor, leisure, and domestic lives of working-class girls in industrial cities during the Gilded Age and Progressive Era. Staples of twenty-century schooling—guidance counseling, home economics, attendance laws—were spearheaded by women education reformers to direct urban girls toward housekeeping, motherhood, and decent labor. White women in the settlement house and women's club movements leveraged considerable power over public schools from the outside. Domestic science, vocational counseling, and courses for "little mothers" were brought into Chicago schools by local women's groups with informal relationships to school leadership. Reforming the girls' curriculum created new opportunities in school governance for women to serve as maternal guides for girls and oversee new departments like household arts and vocational guidance. Between 1870 and 1930, women school reformers helped gender public education while expanding white women's access to professional careers in schools, state governments, and federal agencies.

Girl-centered school reform also helped segregate public education by race in the urban North. White women's groups designed programs that only applied (or appealed) to white working-class girls. They suggested that Black girls fell outside the bounds of state child protection by centering white American girls in lobbying efforts to regulate childhood health and labor. Working both outside and inside the school system, women education reformers reinforced Black women's subjugation to service work and argued that Black girls *should* prepare for both homemaking and breadwinning roles. Their successful reforms to the school curriculum ultimately positioned respectable labor for white women as defined by unpaid service to their homes and families. This ideal of feminine labor was explicitly linked to citizenship education in American schools after World War I, furthering the racial divisions promoted by women school reformers on the local level.

These school reformers were often well meaning. Settlement house workers and labor activists hoped to use the growing power of public education to curb serious urban health issues harming working communities. They argued that the public school system had a social responsibility to protect children from dangerous workplaces and equip them with skills to become successful adults under industrial capitalism. These goals were not fully reached through education reform because schools do not exist in vacuums. Reforming how girls trained for work could not reorient the female labor market. Extended school attendance laws did not change the fact that working families relied on their children's labor for their livelihoods. The school reformers highlighted in this book, to use Cristina Groeger's term, fell into an "education trap" of believing school reform could solve complex systemic issues ranging from industrial poverty to worker exploitation to poor residential resources.[1]

Women's school reform was further flawed by relying on the education and labor of individual girls to solve urban social problems. Reformers often contradicted themselves in doing so. They chastised immigrant parents who made their daughters perform domestic chores at home but mandated that girls train for domestic labor in school. They suggested girlhood labor was "education" if conducted under the guidance of middle-class school officials and "labor" when performed in working-class homes. Other contradictions plagued these gendered reforms. Women in the vocational guidance movement argued that working-class girls needed to earn higher wages to avoid the sex trade. They simultaneously accused girls who earned good wages of sexual delinquency and frivolous shopping habits. These ironies reveal how cultural ideas about gender, labor, and the city were in flux throughout the Progressive Era. White women's groups negotiated these tensions through public school reform and placed new burdens on female students in the process.

Girls were not passive recipients of women's attempts to redirect their labor through education reform. Children continued to leave the school system illegally despite tightened attendance laws. Many immigrant daughters secured office work by ignoring the vocational education movement and strengthening their English, math, and typing skills in neighborhood high schools. Black girls resisted teachers and administrators who pushed them toward domestic service work and redefined institutions like Flower Tech in pursuit of academic excellence. These examples remind us that records left behind by reformers and school administrators reveal only a partial history of school reform. Progressive Era initiatives like vocational education did not always align with the interests of local communities or mark a significant shift in the lives of everyday families. In most cases, school reformers failed to reshape working-class girlhood through education reform.

This reform movement, however, had serious consequences for twentieth-century students. White women reformers extended the legal boundaries of childhood through carceral education and mandatory school attendance law. They cemented normative expectations of white American womanhood in physical culture and home economics courses and enforced racial segregation in girls' vocational programs. They established state-funded carceral schools like the Illinois State Training School for Girls that disproportionately confined Black girls and trained them for domestic service to the institution. Women's groups created new public school bureaucracies that pushed mandatory vocational guidance on working-class girls and oversaw how working-class children made their legal transition from school to work. In their effort to remake white working-class girlhood, women education reformers expanded the parental power of school officials over the lives of all urban children.

This women-led school reform movement solidified government investment in girls' unequal homemaking education for the next half century. Officials in all forty-eight states and the territory of Hawai'i required at least one year of home economics for female high school students by 1930. Home economists with the US Bureau of Home Economics published sample course syllabi, recipes, and sewing patterns used by public school students until 1962. The purpose of home economics for white American girls fluctuated to meet shifting expectations of women's citizenship throughout the middle of the twentieth century. During the Great Depression, home economists echoed turn-of-the-century domestic scientists by asserting the public health importance of teaching girls to address rising rates of malnutrition and poor housing conditions caused by the economic crisis. Home economists de-emphasized these public health goals after World War II much like after World War I. In the 1950s, AHEA members responded to postwar consumer culture by focusing coursework on girls' preparation as future household shoppers.[2]

Women labor activists advocated for girls' trade education when World War II placed new manufacturing expectations on working-class women. The Chicago BOE established a second girls-only public school in 1943 that focused exclusively on wage-earning pursuits for female students living in the stockyards district, a neighborhood affectionately called Back of the Yards by 1940. The Ellen Richards Trade School for Girls—named after the domestic scientist and AHEA founder—offered programs in dressmaking, millinery, commercial art, restaurant work, and cosmetology. After the war, however, school officials argued that these programs helped girls find husbands in addition to jobs. The BOE renamed the school Richards Vocational High School for Girls to de-emphasize the previous focus on trade skills. School officials explained that the cosmetology program at Richards

Vocational High School now allowed girls to improve their appearance through learning the latest hairstyles and manicure trends. "Lovely hands add to a lady's charm," explained one school official. The city's second all-girls public school was short-lived. Richards Vocational High School for Girls moved locations at least twice in the following decade before closing. The school reopened in 1988 as a coeducational school now known as Richards Career Academy.[3]

School officials also de-emphasized career training for working-class girls at Flower Tech after World War II. In 1956, school officials replaced "technical" with "vocational" to reflect the centrality of home economics in the curriculum. An administrator at Lucy Flower Vocational School for Girls (Flower Vocational) argued that the name change reflected shifting labor priorities for American women. "Earlier technical education was specialized preparation for a vocation," she wrote. The school no longer offered dedicated training to earn a living. "It offers, instead, a general education with practice in homemaking." Despite the name change, Flower Vocational offered a wider range of technical programs for girls than during the Progressive Era. Notably, Flower Vocational introduced a nursing program that provided practical experience in a nearby hospital to prepare students for nursing school. "Secretarial studies" also expanded in the curriculum after World War II, so much so that school officials adopted a new motto in 1954: "Training today for living in the home or the office tomorrow."[4]

Black students continued to experience racial segregation in the girls' curriculum. Popular vocational programs after World War II, like secretarial studies and cosmetology, prepared students to transition out of the workforce and emphasized social expectations for white American women. Cosmetology was one of the most popular programs for Flower Vocational students. "Beauty culture" was first introduced at Flower Tech in the 1920s to help Black students find work in salons. As explained in chapter 5, however, Black students were unwelcome in beauty culture classes due to racial hostilities in the school. In the decades that followed, cosmetology courses at Richards Vocational and Flower Tech devolved into exercises on personal grooming. Girls practiced styling their own hair, doing their makeup, and giving manicures to their friends. The Illinois State Board for Vocational Education, which funded both schools under the Smith-Hughes Act, summarized the goal of cosmetology at Richards Vocational in 1952: "Girls learn to be beautiful."[5]

Female students continued to circumvent many of these school reforms. Black students resisted pressure from teachers and administrators to pursue home economics for domestic service. In addition to excelling academically, Black girls pushed their way into new vocational programs like nursing after World War II despite racial discrimination from white school officials. Joan Howell Lawson, the daughter of a health technician and domestic servant, attended Flower Tech from 1950 to 1954 and was the first in her family to graduate from high school. She recalled thirty years later how guidance counselors at Flower Tech dissuaded her from pursing nursing because of her race. Vocational guidance counselors helped her white classmates become registered nurses after graduation, arranging for some to receive grants and work in private hospitals. Howell Lawson had to get there on her own. She enrolled at the Cook County School of Nursing after graduation and earned a master's degree in public health from the University of Illinois.[6]

A new generation of women reformers challenged a near century-long tradition of gendered schooling in the 1970s. Agitation against gender discrimination in education writ large led Congress to enact Title IX of the Education Amendments Act of 1972. Title IX prohibited gender discrimination in all federally funded educational activities. After 1972, women's groups demanded that Congress enforce Title IX in local public schools to open male-dominated vocational programs to girls. Vocational opportunities for girls had changed very little since World War I. Nearly all high school girls in Illinois (92 percent) enrolled in home economics in 1972. Girls accounted for 69 percent of students studying secretarial work and 86 percent of students in retail and sales. Boys still dominated trade and industry programs, accounting for 90 percent of shop room students. "Segregated classes are illegal," one feminist wrote in a 1975 letter to Congress. "Enforce the law!"[7]

Congress organized a special committee to investigate "sex stereotyping" in vocational education in 1975. The committee was chaired by its only female member, Shirley Chisholm, the first Black woman elected to Congress in 1968 and the first woman to run for US president on a major party ticket. Chisholm heard testimony from women's groups demanding Congress hold local school administrators accountable for not promoting coeducation in local public schools. Marilyn Steele, an education reformer from Flint, Michigan, testified that vocational guidance counselors should encourage female students to enroll in male-dominated trade programs. Steele argued that states should penalize public school districts for using "textbooks that show men in jobs and mothers with their aprons in the kitchen." Most home economics course material promoted "sex stereotyping" and was a clear violation of Title IX according to Steele. She echoed Progressive Era labor activists like Agnes Nestor in accusing Michigan school officials of promoting gender inequality by denying girls enrollment in trade programs. By not enforcing Title IX, Congress allowed local schools to teach "the socially determined custom, reinforced in our public schools, of preselection of occupation by sex."[8]

Feminist education reformers wanted public schools to reform girls' education to better meet the needs of working-class women in Rust Belt cities. When the Smith-Hughes Act became law in 1917, nearly 77 percent of female workers in urban America were single women and girls who exited the workforce in their early twenties. This was no longer the case a half century later. By the 1970s, 63 percent of female workers were married with children. Women school reformers in the 1970s argued that vocational programs designed to help girls earn temporary "pin money" and prepare for full-time homemaking were woefully out of step with the realities of working-class family life. Nancy Perlman of the Coalition of Labor Union Women also testified before Congress in 1975 on sexism in urban vocational programs. She argued that girls' programs for retail and secretarial work were insufficient for girls who would become breadwinners for their families. "Women work out of economic necessity," she explained. "They are working to put food in their children's mouths and to pay the rent."[9]

Like their Progressive Era counterparts, feminists in the 1970s suggested that reforming girlhood education could improve women's domestic and labor lives for the better. In statements before Congress, Perlman argued that home economics courses should be coeducational so boys learned to pick up their share of household labor. Perlman hoped education reform would inspire new domestic gender norms. She also implied that home economics education could train the next generation of working-class mothers to juggle inequitable labor expectations. Perlman envisioned home economics classes that no longer taught girls to appreciate the joys of full-time homemaking. Instead, girls could learn how a part-time nurse arranges childcare for her three kids when she works a night shift at the hospital.[10]

Second-wave feminists dismantled many of the gendered traditions in American education that Progressive Era women helped put in place. Prestigious trade schools for boys went coed across the industrial North in the 1970s, though not without controversy. In the fall of 1972, 400 female students joined a student body of nearly 5,000 boys in Chicago's largest high school: Albert Grannis Lane Technical High School (Lane Tech). By 1974, girls composed nearly half of incoming freshmen at Lane Tech eager to study engineering, welding, and building trades. Sexism among teachers and students presented obstacles in their access to traditionally-male learning spaces. School administrators questioned whether "girls in mini skirts" would pose dangerous distractions and potentially cause shop room accidents. One alumna in the class of '79 recalled how her shop teacher assigned girls to sort and clean drill bits and hand them out to the boys. Home economics courses continued to cater to female students in neighborhood high schools through the 1990s. Nevertheless, gendered expectations of labor and schooling became less rigid by the end of the twentieth century.[11]

Like Progressive Era school reformers, Title IX education reformers were mostly white women who overlooked the intersectional experiences of female students. Their fight for gender equality in education focused on challenging cultural expectations of white womanhood (full-time homemaking) and expanding access to male-dominated professions. Yet students of color increasingly populated Rust Belt public schools after Title IX. Sixty percent of Chicago public school students were Black in 1970, and a growing minority of Latinx students represented nearly 10 percent of public school enrollment. White girls benefited most from the breakdown of gender barriers through access to elite all-boys schools like Lane Tech. Lane Tech catered to the children of white skilled workers and middle-class professionals on the North Side of Chicago. Less than 15 percent of Lane Tech students were Black in 1972. Lane Tech retained its reputation for academic and technical rigor when white girls from North Side families entered the student body. The coed high school officially announced a new commitment to preparing all students for four-year colleges and careers in technology in the proceeding decades. Today Albert Lane Tech College Prep High School is a highly selective public magnet school that claims more alumni with PhD degrees than any other high school in America.[12]

The post–Title IX history of Lucy Flower Vocational School for Girls unfolded in stark contrast to Lane Tech. Flower Vocational went coed in 1978 without fanfare or controversy. Flower Vocational catered almost exclusively to the daughters of working-class Black families living on the West Side of Chicago in 1978. Flower Vocational had a student body of 1,000 female students at the time, 99 percent of whom were Black. The school maintained a vocational focus throughout the twentieth century while Lane Tech transitioned to a college prep curriculum. School officials suggested that vocational programs were more practical for working-class and minority students, whom they considered unlikely to attend four-year colleges. Programs at Flower Vocational prepared Black boys and girls for work in health services, restaurant work, and business management after 1978. The school boasted multiple student-run businesses by the 1990s including a café called the Flower Pot and a printing office that served neighborhood businesses. The Chicago BOE abruptly closed Flower Vocational in 2003. The former all-girls public school was one of twenty-two neighborhood schools serving Black and Latinx students that school officials shuttered between 2002 and 2004 due to low enrollment or "low performance."[13]

Centering girlhood in the expansion of public education between 1870 and 1930 reveals the importance of gender ideology in the history of American school reform. Shifting gender, labor, and sexual anxieties about the white working girl informed public school policy, course requirements, and government spending on education. Protecting the physical and moral health of girls through education reform supported gender segregation and the marginalization of Black girlhood in public school programs and state safety regulations. A new generation of feminists desegregated education by gender in the 1970s so female students could access more prestigious educational credentials. But this women-led reform movement also buttressed racial inequalities in urban education by centering on the white working girl.

Acknowledgments

I have the pleasure of thanking an incredible group of mentors, scholars, and loved ones who made this book possible. This project began in the Department of History at Loyola University Chicago and benefited from the thoughtful reading and research guidance of Elizabeth Fraterrigo, Elliott Gorn, and Kate Rousmaniere. Timothy Gilfoyle served as an incredible mentor who pushed my thinking on gender and urban history. I thank Elizabeth Tandy Shermer, Michelle Nickerson, Benjamin Johnson, Patricia Mooney-Melvin, Ted Karamanski, and D. Bradford Hunt for their support. Working with colleagues to organize the Loyola Graduate Workers' Union with the Service Employees International Union (SEIU) shaped my investments in labor history. I am grateful for the solidarity of my fellow organizers.

Financial support for this research came from the King V. Hostick Research Scholarship from the Illinois Historical Society and the Arthur J. Schmitt Foundation. Additional support came from the Newberry Library's Scholars-in-Residence program, the Department of History at Loyola University Chicago, and the Department of History at Texas State University. Thank you to the knowledgeable and patient archivists and librarians who assisted me at the Abraham Lincoln Presidential Library and Museum, the Chicago Board of Education Archives, the Chicago History Museum, the Geneva Historical Society, the Illinois State Archives, the Newberry Library, and the University of Illinois at Chicago Special Collections at Richard J. Daley Library. I am indebted to alumnae of Lucy Flower Technical High School for Girls who agreed to share their stories with historian Nancy Green in the 1980s, and to Green for making her oral history collection accessible to researchers at the Chicago History Museum.

I was fortunate to research and write this book alongside an amazing community of scholars. Thank you to Ella Wagner, Cristina Groeger, Carl Ewald, Michelle Bezark, Nicholas Kryczka, Nathalie Barton, Michelle May-Curry, Justin Randolph, and Miranda Sachs for their insights and inspiration. Jessica Pliley generously read this manuscript at a critical stage in its development. This book was made better by fellow members of the History of Education Society, including Charles Dorn, Maxwell Greenberg, Julia Haagar, Benjamin Justice, Jason Mayernick, Kyle Miron, Rachel Rosenberg, and Jonathan Zimmerman. I presented sections of this research at conferences of the Urban History Association over the years, where my arguments were strengthened by the suggestions of discussants and fellow panelists. Thank you to Molly Brookfield, Marta Gutman, Elizabeth Todd-Breland, and Dara Walker. I thank Wendy Gamber and Robyn Muncy for offering their expert feedback and enthusiasm for sections of the manuscript.

Timothy Mennel at the University of Chicago Press supported this project throughout its slow and messy development into a book manuscript. Thank you to my editor Lilia Fernández for her guidance and close reading of the manuscript on behalf of the Historical Studies of Urban America series. I thank the anonymous readers who improved the quality of this manuscript immeasurably with their honest feedback and encouragement.

Lastly, I was sustained by the love of friends and family while writing this book. Thank you to Jonathan Wyrick, Rachel Gregory, Simone McCready Kenny, Sandy Lorentzen, Sofia Macht, Alyx Harch, Shannon Pimmel, Harris Greenwood, Gunnar Poole, Ali Schmidt, Ryan Fox, Chance Bone, and Liz Pleasant. Thank you to my Book Babes in Austin, Texas, for ensuring I read non-history books during this process. I am grateful for the support of my entire extended family, especially Japhet Oram, Maya Lusis, Eric Lusis, and Jake Lusis. Thank you to Susan Glenn and James Gregory for inspiring me to become a historian. Most of all, I thank the brilliant minds of my mother, Renee LeBoeuf, and my late father, Jack Oram, who were exemplary academic role models throughout my life.

Parts of chapter 4 originally appeared in Ruby Oram, "'A Superior Kind of Working Woman': The Contested Meaning of Vocational Education for Girls in Progressive-Era Chicago," *The Journal of the Gilded Age and Progressive Era* 20, no. 3 (2021): 392–410, doi:10.1017/S153778142100013X. © 2021 Cambridge University Press. Reprinted with permission.

Archive Abbreviations

ALPLM   Abraham Lincoln President Library and Museum
CBEA   Chicago Board of Education Archives
CHM   Chicago History Museum
GHS   Geneva Historical Society
ISA   Illinois State Archives
UIC   University of Illinois Chicago

Notes

INTRODUCTION

1. Ellen Henrotin, "Industrial School at Park Ridge," *Illinois Club Bulletin* 1, no. 1 (October 1909): 10.

2. Helen Cusack published her 23-part series under the alias "Nell Nelson" between July 30 and August 27, 1888, in the *Chicago Times* and the *New York World*. Her series was compiled into a best-selling book two months later. See Nell Nelson, *The White Slave Girls of Chicago* (Barkley Publishing, 1888). For a digital resource on the series, see Rebecca Parker, "Nell Nelson: *City Slave Girls*," http://nelson.newtfire.org.

3. Lynn Gordon, "Women and the Anti–Child Labor Movement in Illinois, 1890–1920," *Social Service Review* 51 (June 1977): 228–48; Meredith Tax, *The Rising of the Women: Feminist Solidarity and Class Conflict, 1880–1917* (Monthly Review Press, 1980), 66–90; Lara Vapnek, *Breadwinners: Working Women and Economic Independence, 1865–1920* (University of Illinois Press, 2009), 55–65; Eric W. Liguori, "Nell Nelson and *The Chicago Times* 'City Slave Girls' Series: Beginning a National Crusade for Labor Reform in the Late 1800s," *Journal of Management History* 18, no. 1 (2012): 61–81.

4. Cusack, "City Slave Girls," *Chicago Times*, August 26, 1888, 19.

5. Cusack, "City Slave Girls," *Chicago Times*, August 4, 1888; Department of the Interior, Census Office, "Table XXXVI—Occupations," *Statistics of the Population of the United States at the Tenth Census (June 1, 1880)* (US Government Printing Office, 1883), 870; US Department of Commerce, "Table 30," *A Social-Economic Grouping of the Gainful Workers of the United States, 1930* (US Government Printing Office, 1938), 66–67. On women in the waged workforce, see Lynn Y. Weiner, *From Working Girl to Working Mother: The Female Labor Force in the United States, 1820–1980* (University of North Carolina Press, 1985); Joanne Meyerowitz, *Women Adrift: Female Wage Workers in Chicago, 1880–1930* (University of Chicago Press, 1988); Wendy Gamber, *The Female Economy: The Millinery and Dressmaking Trades, 1860–1930* (University of Illinois Press, 1997); Nan Enstad, *Ladies of Labor, Girls of Adventure: Working Women, Popular Culture, and Labor Politics at the Turn of the Twentieth Century* (Columbia University Press, 1999); Alice Kessler-Harris, *Out to Work: A History of Wage-Earning Women in the United States* (Oxford University Press, 2003).

6. On "new" immigration to Chicago, see Eric L. Hirsch, *Urban Revolt: Ethnic Politics in the Nineteenth-Century Chicago Labor Movement* (University of California Press, 1990); Dominic A. Pacyga, *Polish Immigrants and Industrial Chicago: Workers on the*

South Side, 1880–1922 (University of Chicago Press, 1991); John T. McGreevy, *Parish Boundaries: The Catholic Encounters with Race in the Twentieth-Century Urban North* (University of Chicago Press, 1996); Richard Schneirov, *Labor and Urban Politics: Class Conflict and the Origins of Modern Liberalism in Chicago, 1864–97* (University of Illinois Press, 1998); Carl Smith, *Urban Disorder and the Shape of Belief: The Great Chicago Fire, the Haymarket Bomb, and the Model Town of Pullman* (University of Chicago Press, 1995); Thomas A. Guglielmo, *White on Arrival: Italians, Race, Color, and Power in Chicago, 1890–1945* (Oxford University Press, 2003); Andrew J. Diamond, *Chicago on the Make: Power and Inequality in a Modern City* (University of California Press, 2017). On immigrants and public education, see Bernard J. Weiss, *American Education and the European Immigrant, 1840–1940* (University of Illinois Press, 1982); Alan Wieder, *Immigration, the Public School, and the 20th Century American Ethos: The Jewish Immigrant as a Case Study* (University Press of America, 1985); Stephen Brumberg, *Going to America, Going to School: The Jewish Immigrant Public School Encounter in Turn-of-the-Century New York City* (Praeger, 1986); Paula Fass, *Outside In: Minorities and the Transformation of American Education* (Oxford University Press, 1989); Stephanie Nicole Richardson, *History of Immigrant Female Students in Chicago Public Schools, 1900–1950* (Peter Lang, 2004); Melissa Klapper, *Small Strangers: The Experience of Immigrant Children in America, 1880–1920* (Ivan R. Dee, 2007).

7. "Summary of School Statistics," *Forty-Sixth Annual Report of the Board of Education (BOE) For the Year Ending June 30, 1900* (Hack & Anderson Printers, 1901), 168, Chicago Board of Education Archives (CBEA), Chicago, IL; "Overcrowded Schools," *Chicago Tribune*, September 6, 1888, 8. On the development of urban education in this period, see Lawrence Cremin, *The Transformation of the School: Progressivism in American Education, 1867–1957* (Vintage, 1964); Lawrence Cremin, *American Education: The Metropolitan Experience, 1876–1980* (HarperCollins, 1988); Michael B. Katz, *Class, Bureaucracy, and Schools: The Illusion of Educational Change in America* (Praeger, 1971); David Tyack, *The One Best System: A History of American Urban Education* (Harvard University Press, 1974); William J. Reese, *Power and the Promise of School Reform: Grassroots Movements During the Progressive Era* (Routledge & Kegan Paul, 1986); Jeffrey Mirel, *The Rise and Fall of an Urban School System: Detroit, 1907–81* (University of Michigan Press, 1993).

8. On urban school reform and social control, see Julia Wrigley, *Class Politics and Public Schools: Chicago, 1900–1950* (Rutgers University Press, 1982); David Hogan, *Class and Reform: School and Society in Chicago, 1880–1930* (University of Pennsylvania Press, 1985); Michael B. Katz, *The Irony of Early School Reform: Educational Innovation in Mid-Nineteenth Century Massachusetts* (Harvard University Press, 1968); Michael B. Katz, *Improving Poor People: The Welfare State, the "Underclass," and Urban Schools as History* (Princeton University Press, 1995); Cristina Viviana Groeger, *The Education Trap: Schools and the Remaking of Inequality in Boston* (Harvard University Press, 2021); Erika M. Kitzmiller, *The Roots of Educational Inequality: Philadelphia's Germantown High School, 1907–2014* (University of Pennsylvania Press, 2022); Agustina S. Paglayan, *Raised to Obey: The Rise and Spread of Mass Education* (Princeton University Press, 2024).

9. St. Clair Drake and Horace R. Cayton, *Black Metropolis: A Study of Negro Life in a Northern City* (Harcourt, 1945), 9 (table 2); Moira Elizabeth Hinderer, "Making African-American Childhood: Chicago, 1915–1945" (PhD diss., University of Chicago, 2007), 5; James R. Grossman, *Land of Hope: Chicago, Black Southerners, and the Great Migration* (University of Chicago Press, 1989).

10. Drake and Cayton, *Black Metropolis*, 12; William Cronon, *Nature's Metropolis: Chicago and the Great West* (W. W. Norton, 1991); Smith, *Urban Disorder and the Shape of Belief*; Harold L. Platt, *Shock Cities: The Environmental Transformation and Reform of Manchester and Chicago* (University of Chicago Press, 2005); Michael Willrich, *City of Courts: Socializing Justice in Progressive Era Chicago* (Cambridge University Press, 2003).

11. On racism in the settlement house movement, see Elisabeth Lasch-Quinn, *Black Neighbors: Race and the Limits of Reform in the Settlement House Movement, 1890–1945* (University of North Carolina Press, 1993). On the settlement house movement, see Mina Julia Carson, *Settlement Folk: Social Thought and the American Settlement Movement, 1885–1930* (University of Chicago Press, 1990); Rivka Shpak Lissak, *Pluralism and Progressives: Hull House and the New Immigrants, 1890–1919* (University of Chicago Press, 1990); Robyn Muncy, *Creating a Female Dominion in American Reform, 1890–1935* (Oxford University Press, 1991); Dolores Hayden, *The Grand Domestic Revolution: A History of Feminist Designs for American Homes, Neighborhoods, and Cities* (MIT Press, 1992); Linda Gordon, *Pitied but Not Entitled: Single Mothers and the History of Welfare, 1890–1935* (Harvard University Press, 1995); Kathryn Kish Sklar, *Florence Kelley and the Nation's Work: The Rise of Women's Political Culture, 1830–1900* (Yale University Press, 1995); Sarah Deutsch, *Women and the City: Gender, Space, and Power in Boston, 1870–1940* (Oxford University Press, 2000); Camilla Stivers, *Bureau Men, Settlement Women: Constructing Public Administration in the Progressive Era* (University Press of Kansas, 2000); Maureen Flanagan, *Seeing with Their Hearts: Chicago Women and the Vision of the Good City, 1871–1933* (Princeton University Press, 2002); Louise W. Knight, *Citizen: Jane Addams and the Struggle for Democracy* (University of Chicago Press, 2005); Anna R. Igra, *Wives Without Husbands: Marriage, Desertion, and Welfare in New York, 1900–1935* (University of North Carolina Press, 2006); Anya Jabour, *Sophonisba Breckinridge: Championing Women's Activism in Modern America* (University of Illinois Press, 2019).

12. See Elizabeth Anne Payne, *Reform, Labor, and Feminism: Margaret Dreier Robins and the Women's Trade Union League* (University of Illinois Press, 1988); Tax, *The Rising of the Women*; Flanagan, *Seeing with Their Hearts*; Jabour, *Sophonisba Breckinridge*; Sklar, *Florence Kelley and the Nation's Work*; Muncy, *Creating a Female Dominion in American Reform*; Knight, *Citizen*.

13. This book builds on the work of Jane Bernard Powers, who analyzes the contributions of urban women's groups to school reform in *The "Girl Question" in Education: Vocational Education for Young Women in the Progressive Era* (Routledge, 1992). Also see Jackie M. Blount, "Ella Flagg Young and the Gender Politics of *Democracy and Education*," *Journal of the Gilded Age and Progressive Era* 16, no. 4 (2017): 409–23.

14. Quotes from Tyack, *The One Best System*; David Gamson, *The Importance of Being Urban: Designing the Progressive School District, 1890–1940* (University of Chicago Press, 2019); Sklar, *Florence Kelley and the Nation's Work*.

15. On the relationship between public education and juvenile carcerality, see Tera Eva Agyepong, *The Criminalization of Black Children: Race, Gender, and Delinquency in Chicago's Juvenile Justice System, 1899–1945* (University of North Carolina Press, 2018); Judith Kafka, "Growing Up Together: Brooklyn's Truant School and the Carceral and Educational State, 1857–1924," *Journal of Urban History* 49 (2003): 974–94. On policing girlhood in carceral schools, see Barbara M. Brenzel, *Daughters of the State: A Social Portrait of the First Reform School for Girls in North America, 1856–1905* (MIT Press, 1983); Joan Gittens, *Poor Relations: The Children of the State of Illinois, 1818–1990*

(University of Illinois Press, 1994); Mary E. Odem, *Delinquent Daughters: Protecting and Policing Adolescent Female Sexuality in the United States, 1885–1920* (University of North Carolina Press, 1995); Ruth Alexander, *The Girl Problem: Female Sexual Delinquency in New York, 1900–1930* (Cornell University Press, 1995); Anne Meis Knupfer, *Reform and Resistance: Gender, Delinquency, and America's First Juvenile Court* (Routledge, 2001); Michael Rembis, *Defining Deviance: Sex, Science, and Delinquent Girls, 1890–1960* (University of Illinois Press, 2011). On the growing power of the state in Progressive Era schooling, see Gamson, *The Importance of Being Urban*; Tracy L. Steffes, *School, Society, and State: A New Education to Govern Modern America, 1890–1940* (University of Chicago Press, 2012).

16. On maternalism and women's reform in the Progressive Era, see Paula Baker, "The Domestication of Politics: Women and American Political Society, 1780–1920," *American Historical Review* 89 (June 1984): 620–47; Seth Koven and Sonya Michel, "Womanly Duties: Maternalist Politics and the Origins of Welfare States in France, Germany, Great Britain, and the United States, 1880–1920," *American Historical Review* 95 (October 1990): 1076–108; Flanagan, *Seeing with Their Hearts*; Deutsch, *Women and the City*; Elizabeth Clapp, *Mothers of All Children: Women Reformers and the Rise of Juvenile Courts in Progressive Era America* (Pennsylvania State University Press, 1998); Gwendolyn Mink, *The Wages of Motherhood: Inequality in the Welfare State, 1917–1942* (Cornell University Press, 1996); Muncy, *Creating a Female Dominion in American Reform*; Cynthia Edmonds-Cady, "Mobilizing Motherhood: Race, Class, and the Uses of Maternalism in the Welfare Rights Movement," *Women's Studies Quarterly* 37, nos. 3/4 (2009): 206–22. On Black women and maternal reform, see Anne Meis Knupfer, *Toward a Tenderer Humanity and a Nobler Womanhood: African-American Women's Clubs in Turn-of-the-Century Chicago* (New York University Press, 1996); Wanda A. Hendricks, *Gender, Race, and Politics in the Midwest: Black Club Women in Illinois* (Indiana University Press, 1998); Cheryl D. Hicks, *Talk with You Like a Woman: African American Women, Justice, and Reform in New York, 1890–1935* (University of North Carolina Press, 2010); Lisa G. Materson, *For the Freedom of Her Race: Black Women and Electoral Politics in Illinois, 1877–1932* (University of North Carolina Press, 2010); Marcia Chatelain, *South Side Girls: Growing Up in the Great Migration* (Duke University Press, 2015).

17. Muncy, *Creating a Female Dominion in American Reform*.

18. Julia Grant, *The Boy Problem: Educating Boys in Urban America, 1870–1970* (John Hopkins University Press, 2014), 5. For histories of gender and school reform in the Progressive Era, see Geraldine Clifford, "Marry, Stitch, Die or Do Worse," in *Work, Youth, and Schooling: Historical Perspectives on Vocationalism in American Education*, ed. Harvey A. Kantor and David B. Tyack (Stanford University Press, 1982), 233–68; David Tyack and Elizabeth Hansot, *Learning Together: A History of Coeducation in American Public Schools* (Russell Sage Foundation, 1990); John Rury, *Education and Women's Work: Female Schooling and the Division of Labor in Urban America, 1870–1930* (SUNY Press, 1990); Powers, *The "Girl Question" in Education*; Karen Graves, *Girls' Schooling During the Progressive Era: From Female Scholar to Domesticated Citizen* (Routledge, 1998).

19. On the invention of childhood, see Anthony M. Platt, *The Child Savers: The Invention of Delinquency* (University of Chicago Press, 1969); Viviana A. Zelizer, *Pricing the Priceless Child: The Changing Social Value of Children* (Princeton University Press, 1985); Elliott West and Paula Petrik, *Small Worlds: Children and Adolescents in America*,

1850–1950 (University of Kansas Press, 1992); David Nasaw, *Going Out: The Rise and Fall of Public Amusements* (Basic Books, 1993); Daniel Thomas Cook, *The Commodification of Childhood: The Children's Clothing Industry and the Rise of the Child Consumer* (Duke University Press, 2004); Karen Sanchez Eppler, *Dependent States: The Child's Part in Nineteenth-Century America Culture* (University of Chicago Press, 2005); James Marten, *Children and Youth During the Gilded Age and Progressive Era* (New York University Press, 2014); Jennifer S. Light, *States of Childhood: From the Junior Republic to the American Republic, 1895–1945* (MIT Press, 2020); Crystal Lynn Webster, *Beyond the Boundaries of Childhood: African American Children in the Antebellum North* (University of North Carolina Press, 2021); Miranda Sachs, *An Age to Work: Working-Class Childhood in Third Republic Paris* (Oxford University Press, 2023).

20. On race and childhood, see Webster, *Beyond the Boundaries of Childhood*; Agyepong, *The Criminalization of Black Children*; Jennifer Ritterhouse, *Growing Up Jim Crow: How Black and White Southern Children Learned Race* (University of North Carolina Press, 2006); Geoff K. Ward, *The Black Child-Savers: Racial Democracy and Juvenile Justice* (University of Chicago Press, 2012); Corinne T. Field and LaKisha Michelle Simmons, eds., *The Global History of Black Girlhood* (University of Illinois Press, 2022).

21. On the category of girlhood, see Claudia Mitchell, "Mapping Girlhood Studies: The Journal, the Academic Field, and the Prospects," *Journal of Social Policy Studies* 11, no. 1 (2013): 103–18; Jane Hunter, *How Young Ladies Became Girls: The Victorian Origins of American Girlhood* (Yale University Press, 2003); Claudia Mitchell, *Girlhood and the Politics of Place* (Berghahn Books, 2016); Nicholas L. Syrett, *American Child Bride: A History of Minors and Marriage in the United States* (University of North Carolina Press, 2016); LaKisha Michelle Simmons, *Crescent City Girls: The Lives of Young Black Women in Segregated New Orleans* (University of North Carolina Press, 2015); Field and Simmons, *The Global History of Black Girlhood*.

22. For social histories of young single working girls in Progressive Era American cities, see Kathy Peiss, *Cheap Amusements: Working Women and Leisure in Turn-of-the-Century New York* (Temple University Press, 1986); Elizabeth Ewen, *Immigrant Women in the Land of Dollars: Life and Culture on the Lower East Side, 1890–1925* (Monthly Review Press, 1985); Meyerowitz, *Women Adrift*; Enstad, *Ladies of Labor, Girls of Adventure*; Hicks, *Talk with You Like a Woman*; Sharon Wood, *The Freedom of the Streets: Work, Citizenship, and Sexuality in a Gilded Age City* (University of North Carolina Press, 2005); Simmons, *Crescent City Girls*; Simone Cinotto, *Making Italian America: Consumer Culture and the Production of Ethnic Identities* (Fordham University Press, 2014).

23. The Nancy Green Papers (1983–1992) were donated to the Chicago History Museum in 1996. The collection includes recorded interviews, interview notes, and surveys from Green's ninety-six interviews with Flower Tech alumnae from 1983 to 1984.

24. The names of girls referenced in juvenile court and carceral school records have been altered for privacy.

25. See Danielle Dreilinger, *The Secret History of Home Economics: How Trailblazing Women Harnessed the Power of Home and Changed the Way We Live* (W. W. Norton, 2021); Sarah Stage and Virginia B. Vincenti, eds., *Rethinking Home Economics: Women and the History of a Profession* (Cornell University Press, 1997); Sharon Y. Nickols and Gwen Kay, *Remaking Home Economics: Resourcefulness and Innovation in Changing Times* (University of Georgia Press, 2015); Rima Apple, *Perfect Motherhood: Science and Childrearing in*

America (Rutgers University Press, 2006); Megan J. Elias, *Stir It Up: Home Economics in American Culture* (University of Pennsylvania Press, 2010); Carolyn M. Goldstein, *Creating Consumers: Home Economists in Twentieth-Century America* (University of North Carolina Press, 2014).

26. Kitzmiller, *The Roots of Educational Inequality*.

CHAPTER ONE

1. "Girls in Wild Riot," *Chicago Tribune*, March 11, 1895, 1; "No Sham Riot This," *Chicago Tribune*, March 29, 1895, 1; Testimony of Mamie Davis, March 20, 1895, Secretary of State, Governors Reports Index: State Board of Commissioners of Public Charities, Home for Juvenile Female Offenders, 115/17A/F4, Illinois State Archives (ISA), Springfield, IL.

2. See Alexander W. Pisciotta, *Benevolent Repression: Social Control and the American Reformatory-Prison Movement* (New York University Press, 1994). On gender and carceral institution building in this period, see Estelle Freedman, *Their Sisters' Keepers: Women's Prison Reform in America, 1830–1930* (University of Michigan Press, 1981); Nicole Hahn Rafter, *Partial Justice: Women, Prisons, and Social Control* (Northeastern University Press, 1985); Emily Hainze, "Wayward Reading: Women's Crime and Incarceration in the United States, 1890–1935" (PhD diss., Columbia University, 2017). On childhood and carcerality, see Anthony M. Platt, *The Child Savers: The Invention of Delinquency* (University of Chicago Press, 1969); Paul Boyer, *Urban Masses and Moral Order in America, 1829–1920* (Harvard University Press, 1992); Tera Eva Agyepong, *The Criminalization of Black Children: Race, Gender, and Delinquency in Chicago's Juvenile Justice System, 1899–1945* (University of North Carolina Press, 2018).

3. Studies of the first carceral institutions for women and girls in the urban North highlight the racial disparities in this movement. Examples of carceral institutions that initially only accepted white inmates include the first carceral school for girls in America, the Lancaster Industrial School for Girls in Massachusetts, and the first state women's prison in America, the Indiana State Women's Prison. See Barbara M. Brenzel, *Daughters of the State: A Social Portrait of the First Reform School for Girls in North America, 1856–1905* (MIT Press, 1983); The Indiana Women's Prison History Project, *Who Would Believe a Prisoner? Indiana Women's Carceral Institutions, 1848–1920*, ed. Michelle Daniel Jones and Elizabeth Nelson (New Press, 2023).

4. Mary E. Odem, *Delinquent Daughters: Protecting and Policing Adolescent Female Sexuality in the United States, 1885–1920* (University of North Carolina Press, 1995), 8–37; Ruth Alexander, *The Girl Problem: Female Sexual Delinquency in New York, 1900–1930* (Cornell University Press, 1995); Anne Meis Knupfer, *Reform and Resistance: Gender, Delinquency, and America's First Juvenile Court* (Routledge, 2001); Lisa Pasko, "Damaged Daughters: The History of Girls' Sexuality and the Juvenile Justice System," *Journal of Criminal Law and Criminology* (Summer 2010): 1099–130; Michael Rembis, *Defining Deviance: Sex, Science, and Delinquent Girls, 1890–1960* (University of Illinois Press, 2011); Nicole Perry, *Policing Sex in the Sunflower State: The Story of the Kansas State Industrial Farm for Women* (University of Kansas Press, 2021).

5. For histories of domestic service, see Daniel E. Sutherland, *Americans and Their Servants: Domestic Service in the United States from 1800–1920* (Louisiana State University Press, 1981); Linda Martin and Kerry Segrave, *The Servant Problem: Domestic*

Workers in North America (McFarland, 1985); Elizabeth Clark-Lewis, *Living In, Living Out: African American Domestics in Washington, D.C., 1910–1940* (Smithsonian Institution Press, 1994); Vanessa H. May, *Unprotected Labor: Household Workers, Politics, and Middle-Class Reform in New York, 1870–1940* (University of North Carolina Press, 2010); Andrew Urban, *Brokering Servitude: Migration and the Politics of Domestic Labor During the Long Nineteenth Century* (New York University Press, 2018); Faye E. Dudden, "Experts and Servants: The National Council on Household Employment and the Decline of Domestic Service in the Twentieth Century," *Journal of Social History* 20, no. 2 (1986): 269, part II. On the continued use of mandatory education as a tool of "reform," see Sabina E. Vaught, *Compulsory: Education and the Dispossession of Young in a Prison School* (University of Minnesota Press, 2017).

6. For scholarship on race, gender, and criminality, see Kali Nicole Gross, *Colored Amazons: Crime, Violence, and Black Women in the City of Brotherly Love, 1880–1910* (Duke University Press, 2006); Cheryl D. Hicks, *Talk with You Like a Woman: African American Women, Justice, and Reform in New York, 1890–1935* (University of North Carolina Press, 2010); Khalil Gibran Muhammad, *The Condemnation of Blackness: Race, Crime and the Making of Modern Urban America* (Harvard University Press, 2010); Sarah Haley, *No Mercy Here: Gender, Punishment, and the Making of Jim Crow Modernity* (University of North Carolina Press, 2016); Agyepong, *The Criminalization of Black Children*.

7. Maureen Flanagan, *Seeing with Their Hearts: Chicago Women and the Vision of the Good City, 1871–1933* (Princeton University Press, 2002), 1.

8. Montrose, "Girls Industrial School: An Appeal for Help," *Chicago Tribune*, November 23, 1878, 10.

9. Eliza Archard, "What About the Girls?" *The Radical*, August 1867, 715.

10. Archard, "What About the Girls?" 715. On the "worthy poor" and "child saving" efforts, see Platt, *The Child Savers*; Boyer, *Urban Masses and Moral Order in America*; Joan Gittens, *Poor Relations: The Children of the State of Illinois, 1818–1990* (University of Illinois Press, 1994); Linda Gordon, *Heroes of Their Own Lives: The Politics and History of Family Violence* (University of Illinois Press, 2002); Kenneth Cmiel, *A Home of Another Kind: One Chicago Orphanage and the Tangle of Child Welfare* (University of Chicago Press, 1995).

11. "Girls' Industrial School: Meeting of the Managers," *Chicago Tribune*, June 2, 1877, 8; Helen M. Beveridge, "President's Report," *Third Annual Report of the Illinois Industrial School for Girls* (Rand, McNally & Co., 1880), 8, ALPLM; Arlien Johnson, "Public Policy and Private Charities: A Study of Legislation in the United State and of Administration in Illinois," (PhD diss., University of Chicago, 1931), 96.

12. Marcia Chatelain, *South Side Girls: Growing Up in the Great Migration* (Duke University Press, 2015), 27–28.

13. "Industrial School," *Chicago Tribune*, October 2, 1879, 9.

14. "Charities—Girls' Industrial Schools," *Annotated Statutes of the State of Illinois, in Force January 1, 1880*, vol. 1, edited by Herbert Starr and Russell Curtis (Law Book Publishers, 1885), 436; "Abstracts of the Official Reports of the School Officers of the States," *Executive Document of the House of Representatives for the Second Session of the Forty-Sixth Congress, 1879–1880*, vol. 2: *Education* (US Government Printing Office, 1880), 54.

15. Mr. and Mrs. McKinnis, "Suggestions as to Executive Power of Supervision of Illinois Industrial School for Girls in Evanston," September 24, 1895, Secretary of State, Executive Department Records, Misc. Manuscripts, Dependent Children, 1886, 115/17A/D6, ISA; "Charities—Girls' Industrial Schools," 436; "The Illinois Industrial School for Girls," *Chicago Tribune*, October 4, 1886, 1.

16. The Illinois Manual Training School for Boys first opened in Norwood Park, Illinois, and relocated in 1890 to Glenwood, where it was renamed the Glenwood Manual Training School. See "Dedicated the School," *Chicago Tribune*, September 28, 1890, 9; "Making Good Men of Bad Boys," *Chicago Tribune*, June 30, 1892, 3; H. MacQueary, "Schools for Dependent, Delinquent and Truant Children in Illinois," *American Journal of Sociology*, July 1930, 13; David S. Tanenhaus, "Between Dependency and Liberty: The Conundrum of Children's Rights in the Gilded Age," *Law and History Review* (2005): 351–85. This extension of girlhood mirrored age of consent laws in the period. See Odem, *Delinquent Daughters*, 8–37.

17. "Abstracts of the Official Reports of the School Officers of the States," 54. Also see Homer Folks, "The Care of Destitute, Neglected, and Delinquent Children (Lyon Company Printers, 1900), 125–26; "Industrial School for Girls," *National Magazine*, July 1857, 57; *Twenty-First Biennial Report of the Board of State Commissioners of Public Charities of the State of Illinois, 1909* (Illinois State Printers, 1911), 381–423; Platt, *The Child Savers*; Michael B. Katz, *In the Shadow of the Poorhouse: A Social History of Welfare in America* (Basic Books, 1986); Gittens, *Poor Relations*; Victoria Lynn Getis, "A Disciplined Society: The Juvenile Court Reform, and the Social Sciences in Chicago, 1890–1930" (PhD diss., University of Michigan, 1994); Margaret K. Rosenheim, Franklin E. Ziming, David S. Tanenhaus, and Bernardine Dohrn, eds., *A Century of Juvenile Justice* (University of Chicago Press, 2002); Arnold Binder, Gilbert Geis, and Dickson Bruce, eds., *Juvenile Delinquency: Historical, Cultural, and Legal Perspectives* (Routledge, 2001); Geoff K. Ward, *The Black Child-Savers: Racial Democracy and Juvenile Justice* (University of Chicago Press, 2012); Agyepong, *The Criminalization of Black Children*.

18. Huntington, *The Kitchen Garden*, 12; Beveridge, *Annual Report of the Illinois Industrial School for Girls* (1880), 8, ALPLM; Boyer, *Urban Masses and Moral Order in America*.

19. Lara Vapnek, *Breadwinners: Working Women and Economic Independence, 1865–1920* (University of Illinois Press, 2009), 34–35; Joanne Meyerowitz, *Women Adrift: Female Wage Workers in Chicago, 1880–1930* (University of Chicago Press, 1988), 5; US Census, "Population, Comparative Occupation Statistics for the United States, 1870 to 1930: Part II—A Comparable Series of Statistics Presenting a Distribution of the Nation's Labor Force, by Occupation, Sex, and Age," https://www.census.gov/content/dam/Census/library/publications/1943/demo/occ-1870-1930-ch2.pdf.

20. Lucy Maynard Salmon, *Domestic Service* (Macmillan, 1897), 146–48 (table III); Helen Cusack, "City Slave Girls," part 4, *Chicago Tribune*, August 2, 1888, 1–2; Louise Montgomery, *The American Girl in the Stockyards District* (University of Chicago Press, 1913), 52–53. For more on the stigma surrounding domestic labor among working girls, see Sutherland, *Americans and Their Servants*; Martin and Segrave, *The Servant Problem*; Christine Stansell, *City of Women: Sex and Class in New York, 1789–1860* (University of Illinois Press, 1987), 155–68; May, *Unprotected Labor*.

21. "Letters from the People: Qualifications of Servants," *Chicago Tribune*, July 15, 1876, 3.

22. Harriet J. Willard, *Familiar Lessons for Little Girls: For Industrial Schools and for Homes*, vol. 1. (Geo. Sherwood & Co., 1880), 45, ALPLM; Willard, *Familiar Lessons for Little Girls*, vol. 2 (Geo. Sherwood & Co., 1882), 9, 17, 31, ALPLM.

23. Emily Huntington, *The Kitchen Garden; or, Object Lessons of House Work* (J. W. Schermerhorn & Co., 1893); "Kitchen-Gardens: Teaching the Young Idea in Chicago How to Keep House," *Chicago Tribune*, November 7, 1883, 8; Willard, *Familiar Lessons for Little Girls*, vol. 1, 54, ALPLM.

24. "The Kitchen Garden: What Is Being Done Throughout the United States," *New York Times*, November 25, 1880, 8; Mary McClees, "Kitchen-Garden Schools: Under the Auspices of the NWCTU," *Christian Union*, July 2, 1883, 32; "Cooking in the Public Schools: The Kitchen Garden Association Wants a Chance to Teach It There," *Chicago Tribune*, May 30, 1888, 1.

25. "How to Keep House: What the Kitchen Garden Association Is Doing," *Chicago Tribune*, April 29, 1885, 8; "Little Housekeepers: How They Are Taught Their Duties," *Chicago Tribune*, March 27, 1885, 8; "The Kitchen Garden Association," *Chicago Tribune*, March 15, 1883, 8. "Cooking in the Public Schools," 1; May, *Unprotected Labor*, 2; Annie Hungerford White, "Training Schools for Women," *Journal of Industrial Education*, August 1891, 12.

26. "Chicago's Kitchen Garden," *Chicago Tribune*, May 24, 1891, 6; McClees, "Kitchen-Garden Schools."

27. "Letters from the People: Qualifications of Servants," 3.

28. "Letters from the People: Reducing Servants' Wages," *Chicago Tribune*, July 2, 1876, 6.

29. Susan Strasser, *Never Done: A History of American Housework* (Pantheon, 1982), 203–23; Mrs. D. A. Lincoln, *The Boston School Kitchen Text-Book: Lessons in Cooking for Use of Classes in Public and Industrial Schools* (Roberts Brothers, 1887), xxi, ALPLM; "To Make More Servants: Woman's Club Takes Up Problem of Household Help," *Chicago Tribune*, November 18, 1898, 9.

30. Correspondence from George Burchard to Gov. Altgeld, September 8, 1895; Mrs. Gertrude M. Singleton to Gov. Altgeld, September 8, 1895; Mrs. Shacklefold to Gov. Altgeld, n.d.; correspondence from L. Wellman to Gov. Altgeld, September 8, 1895: Secretary of State, Executive Department Records, Misc. Manuscripts, Dependent Children, 1886 (115/17A/D6), ISA. Johnson, "Public Policy and Private Charities," 140; MacQueary, "Schools for Dependent, Delinquent and Truant Children in Illinois," 13; *First Biennial Report of the State Guardians for Girls* (1893), 25, ALPLM.

31. "Industrial Schools for Girls," *Sixth Biennial Report of the Board of State Commissioners of Public Charities of the State of Illinois, November 1880* (State Printer and Binders, 1880), 104; *First Biennial Report of the State Guardians for Girls* (1893), 25, ALPLM.

32. See Gross, *Colored Amazons*; Hicks, *Talk with You Like a Woman*; Muhammad, *The Condemnation of Blackness*; Agyepong, *The Criminalization of Black Children*, 11. In the American West and Southwest, Mexican Americans and Asian Americans were the target of urban criminalization. See Miroslava Chávez-García, *States of Delinquency: Race and Delinquency in the Making of California's Juvenile Justice System* (University of

California Press, 2012); Kelly Lytle Hernández, *City of Inmates: Conquest, Rebellion, and the Rise of Human Caging in Los Angeles, 1771–1965* (University of North Carolina Press, 2017); "Charge of Commitment," *First Biennial Report of the State Guardians for Girls*, 10.

33. Rebecca M. McLennen, *The Crisis of Imprisonment: Protest, Politics, and the Making of the American Penal State, 1776–1941* (Cambridge University Press, 2008), 88.

34. Testimony of Mrs. Charlotte C. Holt, questioned by Miss Julia Lathrop, Board of State Commissioners of Public Charities, March 15, 1895, ISA.

35. Knupfer, *Reform and Resistance*, 199 (table 12); Ben B. Lindsey, "Under the Committee on Juvenile Courts and Probation," *The Survey* 14 (August 1905): 1030; Laura S. Abrams, "Guardians of Virtue: The Social Reformers and the 'Girl Problem,' 1890–1920," *Social Service Review* 74, no. 3 (2000): 439.

36. Brenzel, *Daughters of the State*; Ophelia Amigh, *Biennial Report of the Illinois State Training School for Girls, 1902–1904* (Phillips Brothers, State Printers, 1904), box 121.5, GHS. The Illinois State Training School officially closed in 1978 and was bulldozed shortly after to make room for the Fox Run housing subdivision.

37. Testimony of Margaret R. Wickens, questioned by Dr. B. Boerne Bettman, March 16, 1895, Secretary of State, Governors Reports, Index: State Board of Commissioners of Public Charities, Home for Juvenile Female Offenders, 115/17A/F4, ISA; Wickens, "Report of the Superintendent," *First Biennial Report of the State Guardians for Girls* 7–9, ISA.

38. "Trustees' Report," *First Biennial Report of the State Guardians for Girls*, 6, ISA.

39. Ophelia Amigh, *Biennial Report of the Illinois State Training School for Girls, 1894–1896* (Ed. F. Hartman, State Printer, 1896), 10; correspondence from A. O. Schneider to Gov. Altgeld, December 8, 1896; correspondence from Ophelia Amigh to Gov. Altgeld, December 12, 1896; correspondence from O. L. Amigh to Charlotte Holt, September 14, 1896, Secretary of State, Governors Reports, Index: State Board of Commissioners of Public Charities, Home for Juvenile Female Offenders, 115/17A/F4, ISA.

40. On the history of "mother blame," see Linda Gordon, *Pitied but Not Entitled: Single Mothers and the History of Welfare, 1890–1935* (Harvard University Press, 1995); Gordon, *Heroes of Their Own Lives*; Molly Ladd-Taylor, *Mother-World: Women, Child Welfare, and the State, 1890–1930* (University of Illinois Press, 1995); Molly Ladd-Taylor and Lauri Umansky, eds., *"Bad" Mothers: The Politics of Blame in Twentieth-Century America* (New York University Press, 1998); Gwendolyn Mink, *Welfare's End* (Cornell University Press, 1998); Dorothy Roberts, *Torn Apart: How the Child Welfare System Destroys Black Families—and How Abolition Can Build a Safer World* (Basic Books, 2022).

41. Ellen M. Henrotin, Year: 1900; Census Place: Chicago Ward 24, Cook, Illinois; Page: 17; Enumeration District: 0710; FHL microfilm: 1240273; Ophelia M. Aniegh (Amigh), Year: 1900; Census Place: Geneva, Kane, Illinois; Roll: 312; Page: 24; Enumeration District: 0108; FHL microfilm: 1240312.

42. Correspondence from Rev. George Hoover to Gov. Altgeld, October 8, 1895; correspondence from Richard Werner to Gov. Altgeld, October 16, 1895. Secretary of State, Executive Department Records, Misc. Manuscripts, Dependent Children, 1886 (115/17A/D6), ISA; "Domestics: Absolutely Necessary to Successful Housekeeping,"

Chicago Tribune, October 20, 1872, 7; Helen M. Beveridge, *Annual Report of the Illinois Industrial School for Girls* (Rand, McNally & Co., 1881), 6, ALPLM.

43. Correspondence from Rev. George Hoover to Gov. Altgeld, October 8, 1895; correspondence from Richard Werner to Gov. Altgeld, October 16, 1895. Secretary of State, Executive Department Records, Misc. Manuscripts, Dependent Children, 1886 (115/17A/D6), ISA; Beveridge, *Annual Report of the Illinois Industrial School for Girls* (1881), 6, ALPLM.

44. Anne E. Bowler, Chrysanthi S. Leon, and Terry G Lilley, "What Shall We Do with the Young Prostitute? Reform Her or Neglect Her? Domestication as Reform at the New York State Reformatory for Women at Bedford, 1901–1913," *Journal of Social History* (Winter 2013): 458–81.

45. Principal Charlotte Dye, *Biennial Report of the Illinois State Training School for Girls, 1904–1906* (Phillip Brothers, State Printers, 1904), 7, 13–15; "Suggestions for Employers," *Biennial Report of the Illinois State Training School for Girls, 1904–1906*, 23–26, box 121.5, GHS.

46. "The Truth About the Removal of Mrs. Ophelia L. Amigh," *Geneva Republican*, July 22, 1911, box 121, GHS; "Letters," *Biennial Report of the State Training School for Girls, 1906–1908, 1908–1910*, box 121.1, GHS.

47. "Articles of Indenture," *Biennial Report of the State Training School for Girls 1902–1904*, box 121.5, 22, GHS; "Report of Parole Department," *Biennial Report of the State Training School for Girls* (October 1, 1914), 12, GHS; Ellen Henrotin, "Industrial School at Park Ridge," *Illinois Club Bulletin* 1, no. 1 (October 1909): 10.

48. US Census, *Thirty-Third Statistical Abstract of the United States, 1910* (Government Printing Office, 1911), table 18, p. 52; Linda Marie Fritschner, "Servants or Ladies: The Differential Implementation of a Federal Mandate," *School Review* 85, no. 2 (1977): 287–96; Cynthia M. Blair, *I've Got to Make My Livin': Black Women's Sex Work in Turn-of-the-Century Chicago* (University of Chicago Press, 2010); Urban, *Brokering Servitude*.

49. Marguerite Stockman Dickson, *Vocational Guidance for Girls* (Rand McNally, 1919), 44–46, 185. On the racialization of domestic service work in this period, see Danielle Phillips, "Cleaning Race: Irish Immigrant and Southern Black Domestic Workers in the Northeast United States, 1865–1930," in *U.S. Women's History: Untangling the Threads of Sisterhood*, ed. Leslie Brown, Jacqueline Castledine, and Anne Valk (Rutgers University Press, 2017), 13–31; Melissa E. Wooten and Enobong H. Branch, "Defining Appropriate Labor: Race, Gender, and Idealization of Black Women in Domestic Service," *Race, Gender & Class* 19, nos. 3/4 (2012): 292–308; Enobong Hannah Branch and Melissa E. Wooten, "Suited for Service: Racialized Rationalizations for the Ideal Domestic Servant from the Nineteenth to the Early Twentieth Century," *Social Science History* 36, no. 2 (2012): 169–89; Danielle Taylor Phillips, "Moving with the Women: Tracing Racialization, Migration, and Domestic Workers in the Archive," *Signs* 38, no. 2 (2013): 379–404.

50. Clark-Lewis, *Living In, Living Out*, 105.

51. Jane Addams, *A New Conscience and an Ancient Evil* (Macmillan, 1909), 168–69, 176.

52. Addams, *A New Conscience*, 168–69, 176.

53. Johnson, "Public Policy and Private Charities"; Ellen Henrotin, *Annual Report of the Illinois Industrial School for Girls, 1908–1909*, 16, ALPLM.

54. "The Employment of Colored Women in Chicago from a Study Made by the Chicago School of Civics and Philanthropy," *The Crisis* 1 (January 1911): 24–25; Gross, *Colored Amazons*; Tera Eva Agyepong, "Race, the Construction of Dangerous Sexualities, and Juvenile Justice," in *Intimate States: Gender, Sexuality, and Governance in Modern US History*, edited by Margot Canaday, Nancy F. Cott, and Robert O. Self (University of Chicago Press, 2021), 134.

55. Carrie S. O'Conner, *Biennial Report of the State Training School for Girls, 1912–1914*, box 121.5, GHS.

56. Agyepong, "Race, the Construction of Dangerous Sexualities, and Juvenile Justice," 134; O'Conner, *Biennial Report of the State Training School for Girls, 1912–1914*, box 121.5, GHS.

57. For more on the Amanda Smith Industrial School, see Anne Meis Knupfer, *Toward a Tenderer Humanity and a Nobler Womanhood African-American Women's Clubs in Turn-of-the-Century Chicago* (New York University Press, 1996), 76–81; Chatelain, *South Side Girls*. For another example of Black-run carceral school alternatives, see Lindsey Elizabeth Jones, "How to Play in the Right Way: Recreation and Respectability at the Virginia Industrial School for Colored Girls, 1915–1940," in *The Global History of Black Girlhood*, ed. Field and Simmons, 82–97.

58. "Girls Perish in Fire at Amanda Smith School," *Chicago Defender*, November 30, 1918, 1; Agyepong, *The Criminalization of Black Children*, 74.

59. Mrs. R. T. Bryton, "Illinois Industrial School for Girls," *Chicago Tribune*, January 14, 1886, 3.

CHAPTER TWO

1. Louise Montgomery, *The American Girl in the Stockyards District* (University of Chicago Press, 1913), 69–70.

2. Elizabeth Anderson, *Agents of Reform: Child Labor and the Origins of the Welfare State* (Princeton University Press, 2021), 237; Montgomery, *The American Girl in the Stockyards District*, 3; Lara Vapnek, *Breadwinners: Working Women and Economic Independence, 1865–1920* (University of Illinois Press, 2009), 34–35; "Manufacturing, Wholesale Trade, Transportation, Building and Real Estate," *Report of the Department of Health of the City of Chicago for the Year 1891* (P. F. Pettibone & Co., 1892), 74–77; "Work and Wages of Men, Women, and Children," *Bulletin of the Department of Labor*, no. 8, vol. 2 (US Government Printing Office, 1987), 248–49.

3. On child labor reform in the Progressive Era, see Anderson, *Agents of Reform*; Walter Trattner, *Crusade for the Children: A History of the National Child Labor Committee and Child Labor Reform in America* (University of Chicago Press, 1970); Kriste Lindenmeyer, *"A Right to Childhood": The U.S. Children's Bureau and Child Welfare, 1912–46* (University of Illinois Press, 1997); James D. Schmidt, *Industrial Violence and the Legal Origins of Child Labor* (Cambridge University Press, 2010); John A. Filter, *Child Labor in America: The Epic Legal Struggle to Protect Children* (University of Kansas Press, 2018); Betsy Wood, *Upon the Altar of Work: Child Labor and the Rise of a New American Sectionalism* (University of Illinois Press, 2020).

4. Shelley Sallee, *The Whiteness of Child Labor Reform in the New South* (University of Georgia Press, 2004). Wood, *Upon the Altar of Work*.

5. On the history of health and physical education in public schools, see Janey Golden, Richard A. Meckel, and Heather Munro Prescott, eds., *Children and Youth in Sickness and in Health* (Greenwood Press, 2004); Richard A. Meckel, *Classrooms and Clinics: Urban Schools and the Protection and Promotion of Child Health, 1870–1930* (Rutgers University Press, 2013); Lindenmeyer, *"A Right to Childhood"*; Martha H. Verbrugge, *Active Bodies: A History of Women's Physical Education in Twentieth-Century America* (Oxford University Press, 2021); Kellie Burns and Helen Proctor, eds., *The Curriculum of the Body and the School as Clinic: Histories of Public Health and Schooling* (Routledge, 2023); Harvey Green, *Fit for America* (Pantheon, 1986); Tim Armstrong, ed., *American Bodies: Cultural Histories of the Physique* (New York University Press, 1996); Sharon L. Walsh, *Eugenics and Physical Culture Performance in the Progressive Era* (Springer, 2020).

6. "City Slave Girls: Definite Plans for the Amelioration of the Conditions of the Factory Serfs," *Chicago Times*, October 24, 1888, 5; "They Must Go to School: Women Insist on the Enforcement of the Compulsory Law," *Chicago Tribune*, November 29, 1888, 1; "Mrs. Col. Parker to the Council: An Address on Compulsory Education," *Chicago Tribune*, December 18, 1888, 3; Meredith Tax, *The Rising of the Women: Feminist Solidarity and Class Conflict, 1880–1917* (Monthly Review Press, 1980), 66–89.

7. "School Board Members: Think Some of Them at Least Should Be a Woman," *Chicago Tribune*, May 26, 1887, 11; "Women on the School Board: Educational as Well as Property Interests Should Be Taken Care Of," *Chicago Tribune*, June 6, 1887, 8A; "Women on the School Board," *Chicago Tribune*, May 29, 1887, 2; "Women Her Theme: Mrs. Charles Henrotin Talks of the Federation Policy," *Chicago Tribune*, May 27, 1894; "The Board Of Education: An Argument in Favor of Appointing Women to That Body," *Chicago Tribune*, May 6, 1888, 30; Julia Wrigley, *Class Politics and Public Schools: Chicago, 1900–1950* (Rutgers University Press, 1982); David Hogan, *Class and Reform: School and Society in Chicago, 1880–1930* (University of Pennsylvania Press, 1985).

8. "Women and the Public Schools: Why the Two New Assistant Superintendents Should Be of the Gentler Sex," *Chicago Tribune*, June 27, 1887, 6; "The Board of Education: More School Sites Wanted," *Chicago Tribune*, June 2, 1887, 3. On Chicago women in school governance, see Maureen Flanagan, *Seeing with Their Hearts: Chicago Women and the Vision of the Good City, 1871–1933* (Princeton University Press, 2002), 59–72; Lana Ruegamer, "'The Paradise of Exceptional Women': Chicago Women Reformers, 1863–1893" (PhD diss., Indiana University, 1982), 167. On maternalism and municipal reform, see Paula Baker, "The Domestication of Politics": Women and American Political Society, 1780–1920," *American Historical Review* 89 (June 1984): 620–47; Seth Koven and Sonya Michel, "Womanly Duties: Maternalist Politics and the Origins of Welfare States in France, Germany, Great Britain, and the United States, 1880–1920," *American Historical Review* 95 (October 1990): 1076–108; Gwendolyn Mink, "Schooling for Motherhood: Woman's Role and 'American' Culture in the Curriculum," in *The Wages of Motherhood: Inequality in the Welfare State, 1917–1942* (Cornell University Press, 1995), 77–96; Sarah Deutsch, *Women and the City: Gender, Space, and Power in Boston, 1870–1940* (Oxford University Press, 2000); Elizabeth Clapp, *Mothers of All Children: Women Reformers and the Rise of Juvenile Courts in Progressive Era America* (Pennsylvania State University Press, 1998); Robyn Muncy, *Creating a Female Dominion in American Reform, 1890–1935* (Oxford University Press, 1991); Cynthia Edmonds-Cady, "Mobilizing Motherhood: Race, Class, and the Uses of Maternalism in the Welfare Rights Movement," *Women's Studies Quarterly*

37, nos. 3/4 (2009): 206–22; Maureen Flanagan, *Constructing the Patriarchal City: Gender and the Built Environments of London, Dublin, Toronto, and Chicago, 1870s into the 1940s* (Temple University Press, 2018).

9. The Edwards Law also established a legal framework for Americanizing immigrant children through mandated school attendance. The law stated that children must attend any school, public or parochial, so long as that school was taught in the English language. The BOE printed 55,000 pamphlets describing the new law that were distributed to students in public and parochial schools throughout Chicago. Students were instructed to deliver the pamphlets to their parents, which were published in nine different languages including German, Italian, Swedish, Polish, and Yiddish. See Florence Kelley, "The Illinois Child-Labor Law," *American Journal of Sociology* 3, no. 4 (January 1898): 490; Stephen J. Provasnik, "Compulsory Schooling, from Idea to Institution: A Case Study of the Development of Compulsory Attendance in Illinois, 1857–1907" (PhD diss., University of Chicago, 1999), 238, 267; Peter Rousma De Boer, "A History of the Early Compulsory School Attendance Legislation in the State of Illinois" (PhD diss., University of Chicago, 1968).

10. See Eileen Boris, *Home to Work: Motherhood and the Politics of Industrial Homework in the United States* (Cambridge University Press, 1994); Nancy Woloch, *A Class by Herself: Protective Laws for Women Workers, 1890s–1990s* (Princeton University Press, 2015).

11. Kathryn Kish Sklar, *Florence Kelley and the Nation's Work: The Rise of Women's Political Culture, 1830–1900* (Yale University Press, 1995), 142.

12. On the settlement house movement, see Flanagan, *Seeing with Their Hearts*; Clapp, *Mothers of All Children*; Muncy, *Creating a Female Dominion in American Reform*; Camilla Stivers, *Bureau Men, Settlement Women: Constructing Public Administration in the Progressive Era* (University Press of Kansas, 2000). On Black settlement house women, see Anne Meis Knupfer, *Toward a Tenderer Humanity and a Nobler Womanhood: African-American Women's Clubs in Turn-of-the-Century Chicago* (New York University Press, 1996); Cheryl D. Hicks, *Talk with You Like a Woman*, esp. chap. 3.

13. Florence Kelley, "First Annual Report of the Factory Inspector of Illinois (1893)," reprinted in Edith Abbott and Sophonisba Breckinridge, *Truancy and Non-Attendance in the Chicago School* (University of Chicago Press, 1917), appendix III, 405.

14. Florence Kelley, "Second Annual Report of the Factory Inspector of Illinois, 1893," 21–22, UIC Special Collections.

15. Julia Grant, *The Boy Problem: Educating Boys in Urban America, 1870–1970* (John Hopkins University Press, 2014), 74. Also see Cara A. Finnegan, "Appropriating the Healthy Child," in *Making Photography Matter: A Viewer's History from the Civil War to the Great Depression* (University of Illinois Press), 81–124.

16. B. J. Baldwin, "History of Child Labor Reform in Alabama," *Annals of the American Academy of Political and Social Science* (July 1911): 111; Sallee, *The Whiteness of Child Labor Reform in the New South*; Geoff K. Ward, *The Black Child-Savers: Racial Democracy and Juvenile Justice* (University of Chicago Press, 2012); Laura F. Edwards, "The Problem of Dependency: African Americans, Labor Relations, and the Law in the Nineteenth-Century South," *Agricultural History* (Spring 1998): 313–40.

17. Kelley, "First Annual Report of the Factory Inspector of Illinois (1893)," in *Truancy and Non-Attendance in the Chicago Schools*, appendix III, 406; Florence Kelley, "Scholarship for Working Children," in *The Child Workers of the Nation: Proceedings of the Fifth Annual Conference, Chicago, Illinois, January 21–23, 1909* (Child Labor Committee, 1909), 103.

18. Degenerative theory was popularized by sociologist Robert Dugdale's 1877 study of a "degenerate family," *The Jukes*. See Nicole Hahn Rafter, *Creating Born Criminals* (University of Illinois Press, 1997); James W. Trent Jr., *Inventing the Feeble Mind: A History of Mental Retardation in the United States* (Oxford University Press, 1995).

19. Patricia Vertinsky, "Exercise, Physical Capability, and the Eternally Wounded Woman in Late Nineteenth Century North America," *Journal of Sport History* (Spring 1987): 17. Also see Carroll Smith-Rosenberg, *Disorderly Conduct: Visions of Gender in Victorian America* (Knopf, 1985); Kelley, "Second Annual Report of the Factory Inspector of Illinois, 1893," 21–22, UIC Special Collections.

20. On the American eugenics movement, see Molly Ladd-Taylor, *Fixing the Poor: Eugenic Sterilization and Child Welfare in the Twentieth Century* (John Hopkins University Press, 2017); Nancy Ordover, *American Eugenics: Race, Queer Anatomy, and the Science of Nationalism* (University of Minnesota Press, 2003); Wendy Kline, *Building a Better Race: Gender, Sexuality, and Eugenics from the Turn of the Century to the Baby Boom* (University of California Press, 2005); Alexandra Minna Stern, *Eugenic Nation: Faults and Frontiers of Better Breeding in Modern America* (University of California Press, 2015); Ann Gibson Winfield, *Eugenics and Education in America: Institutionalized Racism and the Implications of History, Ideology, and Memory* (Peter Lang, 2007); Edwin Black, *War Against the Weak: Eugenics and America's Campaign to Create a Master Race* (Dialog Press, 2012); Adam Cohen, *Imbeciles: The Supreme Court, American Eugenics, and the Sterilization of Carrie Buck* (Penguin Press, 2016).

21. Michele Mitchell, *Righteous Propagation: African Americans and the Politics of Racial Destiny After Reconstruction* (Chapel Hill: University of North Carolina Press, 2004), 90–91.

22. Florence Kelley, quoted in Woloch, *A Class by Herself*, 40–42; Lauren MacIvor Thompson, "'The Reasonable (Wo)man': Physicians, Freedom of Contract, and Women's Rights, 1870–1930," *Law and History Review* 32, no. 4 (November 2018): 798; Suellen Hoy, "Chicago Working Women's Struggle for a Shorter Day, 1908–1911," *Journal of the Illinois State Historical Society* (1998–) 107, no. 1 (Spring 2014): 9–44.

23. Pike and Drier quoted in Nancy Schrom Dye, *As Equals and as Sisters: Feminism, the Labor Movement, and the Women's Trade Union League of New York* (University of Missouri Press, 1980), 145, 142. Also see Elizabeth Anne Payne, *Reform, Labor, and Feminism: Margaret Dreier Robins and the Women's Trade Union League* (University of Illinois Press, 1988); Thomas C. Leonard, "Protecting Family and Race: The Progressive Case for Regulating Women's Work," *American Journal of Sociology and Economics* 64, no. 3 (July 2005): 757–90; Susan Lehrer, *Origins of Protective Labor Legislation for Women, 1905–1925* (SUNY Press, 1987); Julie Novkov, *Constituting Workers, Protecting Women: Gender, Law, and Labor in the Progressive Era and New Deal Year* (University of Michigan Press, 2001); Woloch, *A Class by Herself*.

24. Montgomery, *The American Girl in the Stockyards District*, 30, 56.

25. On enslavement and medical ideology of Black bodies, see Rana A. Hogarth, *Medicalizing Blackness: Making Racial Difference in the Atlantic World, 1780–1840* (University of North Carolina Press, 2017); Dawn P. Harris, *Punishing the Black Body: Marking Social and Racial Structures in Barbados and Jamaica* (University of Georgia Press, 2017). On the body and Black womanhood, see Sabrina Strings, *Fearing the Black Body: The Racial Origins of Fat Phobia* (New York University Press, 2019); Kali Nicole Gross, *Colored Amazons: Crime, Violence, and Black Women in the City of Brotherly Love, 1880–1910* (Duke University Press, 2006).

26. Janet Greenlees, "Workplace Health and Gender Among Cotton Workers in America and Britain, 1880s–1940s," *International Review of Social History* (December 2016): 459–85.

27. "Women See Girls Work," *Chicago Tribune*, November 27, 1901, 4.

28. *Eleventh and Twelfth Annual Reports of the Factory Inspectors of Illinois, 1903 and 1904* (Illinois State Printers, 1906), xvi, Florence Kelley Papers, UIC Special Collections; "The Child Labor Law," *Fiftieth Annual Report of the BOE for the Year Ending June 30, 1904* (BOE, 1905), 43, CBEA; "Child Labor Certificates," *Fifty-First Annual Report of the BOE for the Year Ending June 30, 1905* (BOE, 1906), 176, CBEA.

29. Abbott and Breckinridge, *Truancy and Non-Attendance in the Public Schools*, 445; Florence Kelley, "Burdens Are Unreasonable," in *Unreasonable Industrial Burdens on Women and Children—Effect on Education* (1912), 165, box 1, folder 12. Florence Kelley Papers, UIC Special Collections.

30. See Trattner, *Crusade for the Children*; Lindenmeyer, *"A Right to Childhood"*; Wood, *Upon the Altar of Work*; Anderson, *Agents of Reform*.

31. Kelley, "First Annual Report of the Factory Inspector of Illinois (1893)," in *Truancy and Non-Attendance in the Chicago Schools*, appendix III, 406; Kelley, "Scholarship for Working Children," in *The Child Workers of the Nation: Proceedings of the Fifth Annual Conference, Chicago, Illinois, January 21–23, 1909* (Child Labor Committee, 1909), 103; Sklar, *Florence Kelley and the Nation's Work*, 237–64; Patricia Carter, "Guiding the Working-Class Girl: Henrietta Rodman's Curriculum for the New Woman, 1913," *Frontiers: A Journal of Women Studies* (2017): 133.

32. Abbott and Breckinridge, *Truancy and Non-Attendance in the Chicago Schools*, 297.

33. Pearl Spencer, interview with Elizabeth Balanoff, June 8, 1976, Labor Oral History Project, 4, 16, 19, Roosevelt University, Chicago, IL; Sophie Kosciolowski, interview with Elizabeth Butters, January 5, 1971, Labor Oral History Project, 58, Roosevelt University, Chicago, IL.

34. "Finds a Certificate Mill," *Chicago Tribune*, February 14, 1907, 1; Frances Barnes, "Children Want Work: Inspector Says No," *Chicago Tribune*, July 19, 1908, D4. See Susan J. Pearson, "Age Ought to Be a Fact: The Campaign Against Child Labor and the Rise of the Birth Certificate," *Journal of American History* (2015): 1144–65; Susan J. Pearson, *The Birth Certificate: An American History* (University of North Carolina Press, 2021).

35. Harriet Van Der Vaart, "The Consumers' League of Illinois," in *National Consumers' League, Sixth Annual Report* (1905) 52; "Day Full of Troubles: Board Overwhelmed by Visitors and Swamped by Pleas for Labor Certificates," *Chicago Tribune*, September 9, 1903, 3.

36. W. S. Christopher, "Report on Child Study," *Forty-Fifth Annual Report of the BOE for the Year Ending June 23, 1899* (John F. Higgins Printer, 1900), 27–41, 52, 74, CBEA; Daniel P. MacMillan, "The Physical and Mental Examination of Public School Pupils in Chicago," *Charities and the Commons*, December 22, 1906, 3–8.

37. See Golden, Meckel, and Prescott, *Children and Youth in Sickness and in Health*; Meckel, *Classrooms and Clinics*; Burns and Proctor, *The Curriculum of the Body and the School as Clinic*; A. R. Ruis, "'The Penny Lunch Has Spread Faster than the Measles': Children's Health and the Debate over School Lunches in New York City, 1908–1930," *History of Education Quarterly* 55, no. 2 (2015): 190–217.

38. Bernarr A. Macfadden, *Macfadden's Encyclopedia of Physical Culture*, vol. 1 (Physical Culture Publishing, 1899), 3; Davis S. Churchill, "Making Broad Shoulders: Body-Building and Physical Culture in Chicago, 1890–1920," *History of Education Quarterly* (August 2008): 356; Green, *Fit for America*; Armstrong, *American Bodies*; Walsh, *Eugenics and Physical Culture Performance in the Progressive Era*.

39. Bernarr A. Macfadden, *The Virile Powers of Superb Manhood: How Developed, How Lost: How Regained* (Physical Culture Publishing, 1900), 11–12, 14; R. Marie Griffith, "Apostles of Abstinence: Fasting and Masculinity During the Progressive Era," *American Quarterly* (December 2000): 614, 619.

40. Mark Seltzer, *Bodies and Machines* (Routledge, 1992); J. Michael Duvall, "Processes of Elimination: Progressive-Era Hygiene Ideology, Waste, and Upton Sinclair's *The Jungle*," *American Studies* (Fall 2002): 29–56; Alan Hyde, "The Fatigued Body: On the Progressive History of the Body as Machine," in *Bodies of Law* (Princeton University Press, 1997).

41. Christian Meier, "Report of the Committee on Physical Culture," *Forty-Sixth Annual Report of the BOE for the Year Ending June 30, 1900* (Hack & Anderson Printers, 1901), 155, CBEA; "Physical Culture," *Forty-Seventh Annual Report of the BOE for the Year Ending June 30, 1901* (BOE, 1902), 65, CBEA; Macfadden, *Macfadden's Encyclopedia of Physical Culture*, 3; Churchill, "Making Broad Shoulders," 363; Armstrong, *American Bodies*; Ella Flagg Young, "Value of Physical Education," *Sixtieth Annual Report of the BOE for the Year Ending June 30, 1914* (BOE, 1915), 167, CBEA; Dr. Jessie Newkirk quoted in "Athletics for Girls Strenuous in West," *New York Times*, May 3, 1914; Ella Flagg Young, "Physical Education," *Superintendent's Report, 1910–1911*, 97–98.

42. "Cult of Good Dress," *Chicago Tribune*, January 5, 1895, 6; "Women and the Dress," *Chicago Tribune*, October 14, 1888, 25; "Women in Physical Culture," *Chicago Tribune*, April 17, 1904, 12.

43. Lucille E. Hill, *Athletics and Outdoor Sports for Women* (Macmillan, 1903); Hill, "Basket Ball for Girls Denounced as Dangerous," *Chicago Tribune*, October 12, 1903, 13; "Too Much Athletics Not Good for Girls," *Chicago Tribune*, March 16, 1903, 3; "Think in Curves and Be Beautiful," *Chicago Tribune*, October 23, 1907, 3. Also see Roberta J. Park, "Physiology and Anatomy Are Destiny!?: Brains, Bodies and Exercise in Nineteenth Century American Thought," *Journal of Sport History* (Spring 1991): 31–63; Smith-Rosenberg, *Disorderly Conduct*.

44. See Grant, *The Boy Problem*; Trent, *Inventing the Feeble Mind*.

45. Daniel P. MacMillan, "Reports of the Departments on Their Special Subjects: Child Study and Educational Research," *Fifty-Eighth Annual Report of the BOE for the*

Year Ending June 20, 1912 (BOE, 1913), 214–15, CBEA; Montgomery, *The American Girl in the Stockyards District*, 65.

46. Chicago Board of Education, "Medical Inspection of Pupils" (sec. 97), *Rules of the Education Department of the Board of Education of the City of Chicago, Adopted May 19, 1910*, 11; Civil Service Commission, "Medical Inspection of School Children," *Reports on the Investigation into Organization and Administration, Department of Health, City of Chicago* (W. J. Hartman Co. Printers, 1915), 33.

47. During the 1914–15 school year, 694 boys and 293 girls were placed in special education classrooms for "subnormal" children. See "Table 1—Enrollment," *Sixty-First Annual Report of the BOE for the Year Ending June 30, 1915* (BOE, 1916), 154; MacMillan, "Reports of the Departments on Their Special Subjects: Child Study and Educational Research," 214–15; "Child Study," *Sixtieth Annual Report of the BOE, 1914*, 158, CBEA; Grant, *The Boy Problem*, 93–117. For more on how educational professionals classified "subnormal" children, see Leonard P. Ayres, *Laggards in Our Schools: A Study of Retardation and Elimination in City School Systems* (Russell Sage Foundation, 1909); Esther Ladewick, *Scholarship for Children of Working Age*, Social Service Monographs, no. 7 (University of Chicago Press, 1929), 81.

48. "Child Study," *Sixtieth Annual Report of the BOE, 1914*, 160, CBEA. Also see "Report of the Superintendent," *Sixty-Fourth Annual Report of the BOE for the Year Ending June 30, 1918* (BOE, 1918), 190, CBEA.

49. Alice Kessler-Harris, *Out to Work: A History of Wage-Earning Women in the United States* (Oxford University Press, 2003); Montgomery, *The American Girl in the Stockyards District*, 29, 55–57.

50. "School Hygiene Lecturer Warns Girls' Mothers: Average Chicago Young Woman Unfit for Maternity, Dr. Caroline Hedger Says," *Chicago Tribune*, October 21, 1913, 13; Caroline Hedger, *The School Children of the Stockyards District* (US Government Printing Office, 1913). This program was followed a few years later with Ella Flagg Young's controversial and short-lived effort to institute the nation's first sex education program in Chicago public schools. See Courtney Q. Shah, *Sex Ed, Segregated: The Quest for Sexual Knowledge in Progressive-Era America* (University of Rochester, 2015); Jeffrey P. Morgan, "Modernism Gone Mad: Sex Education Comes to Chicago, 1913," *Journal of American History* (September 1996): 481–513. For more on sex and health education reforms in this period, see Robin E. Jensen, *Dirty Words: The Rhetoric of Public Sex Education, 1870–1924* (University of Illinois Press, 2010); Jonathan Zimmerman, *Too Hot to Handle: A Global History of Sex Education* (Princeton University Press, 2015).

51. Mary Woodlock and Sadie Meisbord, "Hygiene and English," *New York Teachers Monographs: Details of Grade Work* 12, no. 4 (December 1910): 97–103; "School Hygiene Lecturer Warns Girls' Mothers."

52. "School Hygiene Lecturer Warns Girls' Mothers"; "Says Fault of Race Suicide Lies with Men, Not Women," *Chicago Tribune*, May 14, 1908, 3; Ladd-Taylor, *Fixing the Poor*.

53. Jane Addams, *Twenty Years at Hull House* (Macmillan, 1927), 442–43; "Dancing Classes," *Hull-House Year Book, 1906–1907*, 27–28; "Athletic Contests," *Hull-House Year Book, 1906–1907*, 30–31, digitized by Internet Archive; Knupfer, *Toward a Tenderer Humanity and a Nobler Womanhood*, 100. Also see George Eisen, "Sport, Recreation and Gender: Jewish Immigrant Women in Turn-of-the-Century America (1880–1920),"

Journal of Sport History (Spring 1991): 108–9; Kathleen E. McCrone, "Class, Gender, and English Women's Sport, c. 1890–1914," *Journal of Sport History* (Spring 1991): 159–82; Linda J. Borish, "Athletic Activities of Various Kinds: Physical Health and Sport Programs for Jewish American Women," *Journal of Sport History* (Summer 1999): 240–70; Ava Purkiss, *Fit Citizens: A History of Black Women's Exercise from Post-Reconstruction to Postwar America* (University of North Carolina Press, 2023).

54. See Annelise Orleck, *Common Sense and a Little Fire: Women and Working-Class Politics in the United States, 1900–1965* (University of North Carolina Press, 1995); Roy Rosenzweig, *Eight Hours for What We Will: Workers and Leisure in an Industrial City, 1870–1920* (Cambridge University Press, 1983); Elliott Gorn, *The Manly Art: Bare-Knuckle Prize Fighting in America* (Cornell University Press, 1986). On gender, class, and leisure see Kathy Peiss, *Cheap Amusements: Working Women and Leisure in Turn-of-the-Century New York* (Temple University Press, 1986); Nan Enstad, *Ladies of Labor, Girls of Adventure: Working Women, Popular Culture, and Labor Politics at the Turn of the Twentieth Century* (Columbia University Press, 1999).

55. Graham Taylor, "Girls' Gym," *Chicago Commons: A Social Center for Civic Co-Operation*, December 1904, 25–26.

56. "Exercise Habit for Girl Worker: Qualities Making for Health," *Chicago Tribune*, December 12, 1909, E5; Florence Kelley, "Part-Time Schools," *Child Labor Bulletin* 1 (June 1912): 111, Florence Kelley Papers, UIC Special Collections.

57. Elias Tobenkin, "Little Women, Wonders of the Slums, Take Up Life's Burdens Early," *Chicago Tribune*, September 27, 1908, 10; "'Little Mothers' of Down Town Chicago," *Chicago Tribune*, August 2, 1903, A3. Reports of "little motherhood" were common throughout the industrial North. See David Nasaw, "The Little Mothers," in *Children of the City: At Work and at Play* (Oxford University Press, 1985), 110–24.

58. "'Little Mothers' of Down Town Chicago."

59. Tobenkin, "Little Women, Wonders of the Slums, Take Up Life's Burdens Early."

60. Fannie Shapiro, quoted in Stephanie Nicole Richardson, *History of Immigrant Female Students in Chicago Public Schools, 1900–1950* (Peter Lang, 2004), 64–65.

61. Abbott and Breckinridge, *Truancy and Non-Attendance in the Public Schools*, 134–35; "Cause of Absence," *Fifty-Second Annual Report of the BOE for the Year Ending June 30, 1906* (BOE, 1907), 197, CBEA.

62. "Has New 'Truancy' Problem: Supt. Bodine Finds Many Children Seeking Work in Vain," *Chicago Tribune*, May 9, 1908, 1; Abbott and Breckinridge, *Truancy and Non-Attendance in the Public Schools*, 446.

63. "Has New 'Truancy' Problem"; "'Little Mothers' of Down Town Chicago." Reports of "little motherhood" were common throughout the industrial North. See Nasaw, "The Little Mothers," 110–24.

64. "Has New 'Truancy' Problem"; "'Little Mothers' of Down Town Chicago."

CHAPTER THREE

1. Florence Kelley, *The Practical Housekeeping Center* (pamphlet, 1909), box 1, folder 20, Florence Kelley Papers, UIC Special Collections; Florence Kelley, *Some Ethical Gains Through Legislation* (Macmillan, 1905), Florence Kelley Papers, UIC Special

Collections, 182; Kathryn Kish Sklar, *Florence Kelley and the Nation's Work: The Rise of Women's Political Culture, 1830–1900* (Yale University Press, 1995).

2. On the origins of domestic education in urban schools, see Dolores Hayden, *The Grand Domestic Revolution: A History of Feminist Designs for American Homes, Neighborhoods, and Cities* (MIT Press, 1992); Geraldine Clifford, "Marry, Stitch, Die or Do Worse," in *Work, Youth, and Schooling: Historical Perspectives on Vocationalism in American Education*, ed. Harvey A. Kantor and David B. Tyack (Stanford University Press, 1982), 233–68; Karen Graves, *Girls' Schooling During the Progressive Era: From Female Scholar to Domesticated Citizen* (Routledge, 1998).

3. On the domestic science movement, see Hayden, *The Grand Domestic Revolution*; Margaret W. Rossiter, *Women Scientists in America: Struggles and Strategies to 1940* (Johns Hopkins University Press, 1982); Gwendolyn Mink, "Schooling for Motherhood," in *The Wages of Motherhood: Inequality in the Welfare State, 1917–1942* (Cornell University Press, 1995), 77–98; Sarah Stage and Virginia B. Vincenti, eds., *Rethinking Home Economics: Women and the History of a Profession* (Cornell University Press, 1997); Maresi Nerad, *The Academic Kitchen: A Social History of Gender Stratification at the University of California, Berkeley* (SUNY Press, 1999); Ellen Fitzpatrick, *Endless Crusade: Women Social Scientists and Progressive Reform* (Oxford University Press, 1990); Lynn Dorothy Gordon, *Gender and Higher Education in the Progressive Era* (Yale University Press, 1990); Kim Tolley, *The Science Education of American Girls: A Historical Perspective* (Routledge, 2003). The domestic science movement was the precursor to national "home economics" movement, which is discussed in greater detail in chapter 6.

4. On the manual training movement, see David Tyack, *The One Best System: A History of American Urban Education* (Harvard University Press, 1974); Kantor and Tyack, *Work, Youth, and Schooling*; Harvey A. Kantor, *Learning to Earn: School, Work, and Vocational Reform in California, 1880–1930* (University of Wisconsin Press, 1988); Herbert M. Kliebard, *Schooled to Work: Vocationalism and the American Curriculum, 1876–1946* (Teachers College Press, 1999); Glenn P. Lauzon, ed., *Educating a Working Society: Vocationalism in Twentieth-Century American Schools* (Information Age, 2019). On gender and manual training, see Jane Bernard Powers, *The "Girl Question" in Education: Vocational Education for Young Women in the Progressive Era* (Routledge, 1992); Graves, *Girls' Schooling During the Progressive Era*; Rury, *Education and Women's Work*; David Tyack and Elizabeth Hansot, *Learning Together: A History of Coeducation in American Public Schools* (Russell Sage Foundation, 1990); Julia Grant, *The Boy Problem: Educating Boys in Urban America, 1870–1970* (John Hopkins University Press, 2014).

5. Nancy Tomes, *The Gospel of Germs: Men, Women, and the Microbe in American Life* (Harvard University Press, 1999); Daniel Eli Burnstein, *Next to Godliness: Confronting Dirt and Despair in Progressive Era New York City* (University of Illinois Press, 2006).

6. Margaret W. Rossiter, "'Women's Work' in Science, 1880–1910," *Isis* 71, no. 3 (September 1980): 394; Ellen Richards, quoted in Tomes, *The Gospel of Germs*, 135, 137–38; "Dr. Mary Green Talks of Kitchens," *Chicago Tribune*, October 6, 1894, 13; "Pure Food Interest Increases: Dr. Mary Green Lectures on Soups and How to Prepare Them," *Chicago Tribune*, October 9, 1894, 4; Kerreen Rieger, "All but the Kitchen Sink: On the Significance of Domestic Science and the Silence of Social Theory," *Theory and Society* (July 1987): 497–526; Caroline Lieffers, "'The Present Time Is Eminently Scientific':

The Science of Cookery in Nineteenth-Century Britain," *Journal of Social History* (Summer 2012): 936–59.

7. On how women used domestic science to access professional careers, see Danielle Dreilinger, *The Secret History of Home Economics: How Trailblazing Women Harnessed the Power of Home and Changed the Way We Live* (W. W. Norton, 2021); Stage and Vincenti, *Rethinking Home Economics*.

8. "Domestic Science," *Woman's Era* 1, no. 1 (March 24, 1894): 6; "Free Domestic Science School," *Chicago Defender*, September 20, 1919, 4; "Associated Clubs Cooking Class," *Chicago Defender*, July 30, 1910, 1, accessed through Digital Commonwealth. The term "politics of respectability" belongs to Evelyn Brooks Higginbotham, *Righteous Discontent: The Women's Movement in the Black Baptist Church, 1880–1920* (Harvard University Press, 1993). Also see Michele Mitchell, *Righteous Propagation: African Americans and the Politics of Racial Destiny After Reconstruction* (University of North Carolina Press, 2004).

9. "Cooking in the Public Schools: The Kitchen Garden Association Wants a Chance to Teach It There," *Chicago Tribune*, May 30, 1888, 1; "Science in Households: Women Hold a Discussion on Domestic Economies," *Chicago Tribune*, October 15, 1891, 6; Joseph M. Di Cola and David Stone, *Chicago's 1893 World's Fair* (Arcadia, 2012), 8; Ellen S. Richards, *Plain Words About Food: The Rumford Kitchen Leaflets* (Rockwell and Churchill Press, 1899). For more on the Rumford Kitchen, see Hayden, *The Grand Domestic Revolution*, 151; Tomes, *The Gospel of Germs*, 136; Edward C. Kirkland, "'Scientific Eating': New Englanders Prepare and Promote a Reform, 1873–1907," *Proceedings of the Massachusetts Historical Society* 86 (1974): 28–52; Hamilton Cravens, "Establishing the Science of Nutrition at the USDA: Ellen Swallow Richards and Her Allies," *Agricultural History* 64, no. 2 (1990): 122–33.

10. "National Household Economic Association, Officers and By-Laws," *A Report of the Fifth Annual Meeting*, Nashville, TN, October 27, 1897; "Some Features of Domestic Science: Pickles and Dress Before the National Household Economic Association," *Chicago Tribune*, February 28, 1895, 3; Laura S. Wilkinson, "Household Economics," in *The Congress of Women: Held in the Woman's Building, World's Columbian Exposition, Chicago, U.S.A., 1893, with Portraits, Biographies and Addresses*, ed. Mary Kavanaugh Oldham Eagle (International Publishing, 1894), 233.

11. Richard Sennett, *Families Against the City: Middle Class Homes of Industrial Chicago, 1872–1890* (Harvard University Press, 1984); Tomes, *The Gospel of Germs*; Hayden, *The Grand Domestic Revolution*.

12. On gender and domesticity, see Nancy F. Cott, *The Bonds of Womanhood* (Yale University Press, 1977); Gerda Lerner, *The Creation of Patriarchy* (Oxford University Press, 1986); Glenna Matthews, *Just a Housewife: The Rise and Fall of Domesticity in America* (Oxford University Press, 1987); Scott C. Martin, *Devil of the Domestic Sphere: Temperance, Gender, and Middle-Class Ideology, 1800–1860* (Northern Illinois University Press, 2008); Susan Strasser, *Never Done: A History of American Housework* (Pantheon, 1982); Phyllis Palmer, *Domesticity and Dirt: Housewives and Domestic Servants in the United States, 1920–1945* (Temple University Press, 1989).

13. "Art in Housekeeping: Theory and Practice at the University of Chicago," *Chicago Tribune*, June 9, 1894, 16; Marion Talbot, "Home Sanitary Inspection," *Christian Union*, April 30, 1885, 12; Hayden, *The Grand Domestic Revolution*, 151; Nina Collins,

"Domestic Science at Bradley Polytechnic Institute and the University of Chicago," *Journal of the Illinois State Historical Society* (Autumn 2002): 289–90.

14. Linda M. Perkins, "Bound to Them by a Common Sorrow: African American Women, Higher Education, and Collective Advancement," *Journal of African American History* (Fall 2015): 727; Jacqueline Anne Rouse, "Out of the Shadow of Tuskegee: Margaret Murray Washington, Social Activism, and Race Vindication," *Journal of Negro History* (1996): 31–46; Martha H. Patterson, "Margaret Murray Washington, Pauline Hopkins, and the New Negro Woman," in *Beyond the Gibson Girl: Reimagining the American New Woman, 1895–1915* (University of Illinois Press, 2005), 50–79; Sheena Harris, "Margaret Murray Washington: A Southern Reformer and the Black Women's Club Movement," in *Alabama Women: Their Lives and Times*, ed. Susan Youngblood Ashmore and Lisa Lindquist Dorr (University of Georgia Press, 2017), 129–44. Also see Dreilinger, *The Secret History of Home Economics*.

15. "Art in Housekeeping," 16; Talbot, "Home Sanitary Inspection," 12; Hayden, *The Grand Domestic Revolution*, 151; Collins, "Domestic Science at Bradley Polytechnic Institute and the University of Chicago," 289–90; "Sanitary Science," *Programme of Courses in Sociology and Anthropology, 1894–1895* (University of Chicago Press, 1894), 4; "Classes In," *Chicago Commons* 1, no. 6 (September 1896): 13, digitized by the University of Illinois; "Women Being Taught How to Cook," *Chicago Tribune*, January 3, 1895, 9; Herman Hegner, "Education at Chicago Commons," *Outlook*, August 31, 1895, 344; Sharon Haar, *City as Campus: Urbanism and Higher Education in Chicago* (University of Minnesota Press, 2011); "Provident Hospital's Lady Bountiful: Miss Lulu Stubbs," *Chicago Defender*, August 8, 1914, 1; "Dr. A. Wilberforce Williams Talks on Preventive Measures, First Aid Remedies, Hygienics, and Sanitation," *Chicago Defender*, March 4, 1916, 8.

16. Hayden, *The Grand Domestic Revolution*; Andrea Renner, "A Nation That Bathes Together: New York City's Progressive Era Public Baths," *Journal of the Society of Architectural Historians* (2008): 504–31; Anna Leigh Todd, "Public Health and Personal Hygiene in Progressive-Era Philadelphia." *Pennsylvania Legacies* 19, no. 1 (2019): 3–5. On domestic life in urban tenements, see Donna R. Gabaccia, *From Sicily to Elizabeth Street: Housing and Social Change Among Italian Immigrants, 1880–1930* (SUNY Press, 1984); Margaret Garb, "Health, Morality, and Housing: The 'Tenement Problem' in Chicago," *American Journal of Public Health* (September 2003): 1420–30; Andrew Dolkart, *Biography of a Tenement House in New York City: An Architectural History of 97 Orchard Street* (Center for America Places, 2006); Zachary J. Violette, *The Decorated Tenement: How Immigrant Builders and Architects Transformed the Slum in the Gilded Age* (University of Minnesota Press, 2019).

17. Florence Kelley, "The Sweating System," in *Bureau of Statistics of Labor of Illinois, Seventh Biennial Report, 1892* (HK Rokker, 1893); Eileen Boris, *Home to Work: Motherhood and the Politics of Industrial Homework in the United States* (Cambridge University Press, 1994), 49–80; Elizabeth Anne Payne, *Reform, Labor, and Feminism: Margaret Dreier Robins and the Women's Trade Union League* (University of Illinois Press, 1988), 128; Kathryn Kish Sklar, *Florence Kelley and the Nation's Work: The Rise of Women's Political Culture, 1830–1900* (Yale University Press, 1995).

18. On the history of women's domestic burdens, see Ruth Schwartz Cowan, *More Work for Mother: The Ironies of Household Technology from the Open Hearth to the Microwave* (Basic Books, 1983); Strasser, *Never Done*; Burnstein, *Next to Godliness*.

19. See Knupfer, *Toward a Tenderer Humanity and a Nobler Womanhood*, 27; Mitchell, *Righteous Propagation*; Gordon, *Pitied but Not Entitled*; Ladd-Taylor and Umansky, *"Bad" Mothers*.

20. "Sewing for the Poor," *Harper's Bazaar*, April 2, 1892, 267; Laury MacHenry, "Talks with the Doctor: About Children's Clothing," *Ladies' Home Journal*, February 1890, 15; Eleanor Kirk, "The Home End of the Temperance Question: The Overworked Mother," *Christian Union*, November 14, 1891, 931.

21. "Clothing the Needy," *Chicago Tribune*, December 21, 1884, 9. Most sewing schools were supported by Presbyterian, Episcopalian, and Baptist congregations. At least one was supported by a Jewish synagogue on the West Side of the city. See "Sewing-Schools," *Chicago Tribune*, March 30, 1881, 8.

22. "The Sewing School," *Chicago Tribune*, September 5, 1886, 7; "Free Sewing Schools for Chicago's Poor," *Chicago Tribune*, January 20, 1895, 34; "The Sewing-School Association," *Chicago Tribune*, June 27, 1883, 8; "To Clothe and Educate the Poor," *Chicago Tribune*, January 7, 1892, 12; "Work of One Church's Women," *Chicago Tribune*, February 25, 1894, 14; "Women Being Taught How to Cook," *Chicago Tribune*, January 3, 1895, 9; "The Sewing-School Association," *Chicago Tribune*, June 27, 1883, 8.

23. "To Teach Girls to Sew," *Chicago Tribune*, November 7, 1891, 10; Lucy Flower, "Voice of the People," *Chicago Tribune*, February 18, 1893, 13, 10; Mrs. J. M. Flower, "Present Needs of Chicago Schools," *Chicago Tribune*, January 31, 1892. For more on the reform career of Lucy Flower (1837–1921), see Harriet S. Farwell, *Lucy Louisa Flower, 1837–1920: Her Contribution to Education and Child Welfare in Chicago* (printed privately, 1924).

24. "To Teach Girls to Sew," 10; Flower, "Voice of the People," 13, 10; Flower, "Present Needs of Chicago Schools"; "The Public Sewing Schools," *Chicago Tribune*, November 29, 1891, 12; Mrs. J. M. Flower, "They Want to Teach Needlework," *Chicago Tribune*, November 28, 1891, 12; "Board of Education Proceedings," *Chicago Tribune*, December 10, 1891, 5.

25. "The Faddists and Their Fads," *Chicago Tribune*, February 12, 1893, 28. For more on the "School Fad" controversy, see Julia Wrigley, *Class Politics and the Chicago Public Schools: Chicago, 1900–1950* (Rutgers University Press, 1982); Patricia M. Amburgy, "Fads, Frills, and Basic Subjects: Special Studies and Social Conflict in Chicago in 1893," *Studies in Art Education* 43, no. 2 (2002): 109–23.

26. "Another Fad—Sewing in the Public Schools," *Chicago Tribune*, January 21, 1892, 10; Amburgy, "Fads, Frills, and Basic Subjects," 110; Jackie M. Blount, *Fit to Teach: Same-Sex Desire, Gender, and School Work in the Twentieth Century* (SUNY Press, 2005).

27. The former Tilden Elementary School was located at Elizabeth and Randolph Streets on the West Side of Chicago. Over the next decade, Crane founded and helped pay teacher salaries for at least six of the city's manual training centers. See "Big Offer to Schools," *Chicago Tribune*, May 23, 1905, 7; "How Educational Problems Have Been Solved in Chicago Schools," *Chicago Tribune*, September 1, 1912, G2. The former Hammond Elementary School was located at the southwest corner of Cermak Road and California Avenue. See "For the Work with Muscle," *Chicago Tribune*, December 7, 1895, 3; Hollis W. Field, "The Multimillionaires of Chicago, IL: R. T. Crane," *Chicago Tribune*, June 9, 1907, E1.

28. "Constructive Work and Manual Training," *Forty-Fifth Annual Report of the BOE, 1899*, 137, CBEA; Albert G. Lane, "Ratio of Boys," *Forty-Fourth Annual Report of the BOE for the Year Ending June 30, 1898* (John F. Higgins, 1898), 82, CBEA; John Blake, "Manual Training in the School," *Chicago Tribune*, January 12, 1895, 14; Julia Grant, "A 'Real Boy' and Not a Sissy: Gender, Childhood, and Masculinity, 1890–1940," *Journal of Social History* (2004): 829–51. On cultural perceptions of manliness in this era, see Gail Bederman, *Manliness and Civilization: A Cultural History of Gender and Race in the United States, 1880–1917* (University of Chicago Press, 1995); Michael Kimmel, *Manhood in America: A Cultural History* (Oxford University Press, 1996); Kristin L. Hoganson, *Fighting for American Manhood: How Gender Politics Provoked the Spanish-American and Philippine-American Wars* (Yale University Press, 1998); Dana D. Nelson, *National Manhood: Capitalist Citizenship and the Imagined Fraternity of White Men* (Duke University Press, 1998); Martin Summers, *Manliness and Its Discontents: The Black Middle Class and the Transformation of Masculinity, 1900–1930* (University of North Carolina Press, 2004); E. Anthony Rotundo, *American Manhood: Transformations in Masculinity from the Revolution to the Modern Era* (Basic Books, 2008); Kevin P. Murphy, *Political Manhood: Red Bloods, Mollycoddles, and the Politics of Progressive Era Reform* (Columbia University Press, 2008).

29. Lucy Flower, "Present Needs of Chicago Schools: Mrs. J. M. Flower Discusses the Educational Problem," *Chicago Tribune*, January 31, 1892, 30; "Sewing in the Public Schools: Arguments on Both Sides at a Meeting of Women," *Chicago Tribune*, January 30, 1892, 3; "Illinois Notes," *Chicago Tribune*, February 17, 1893; Flower, "Voice of the People," 13; "Constructive Work and Manual Training," 137, CBEA; Lane, "Ratio of Boys," 82, CBEA.

30. Florence Kelley, "Trade and Technical Education of Girls," *The Chautauquan*, December 26, 1897, 309–11; Kelley, *Some Ethical Gains Through Legislation* 182.

31. Robert Archey Woods and Albert J. Kennedy, *Young Working Girls: A Summary of Evidence from Two Thousand Social Workers* (Houghton Mifflin, 1913), 3; "Solving the Problem," *Chicago Tribune*, November 1, 1891, 33; *Practical Housekeeping Center* (pamphlet, 1909), folder 20, box 1, Florence Kelley Papers, UIC Special Collections; Haar, *City as Campus*, 30.

32. "For Tots as Cooks," *Chicago Tribune*, January 15, 1898, 4; *Forty-Fourth Annual Report of the BOE, 1898*, 58, CBEA. Also see "Manual Training for Girls," *Chicago Tribune*, September 30, 1897, 8; "Domestic Science in Chicago Schools," *Pratt Institute Monthly* (October 1897): 143.

33. "Domestic Science," *Forty-Fourth Annual Report of the BOE, 1898*, 56, CBEA; "Cooking in Public Schools," *Washington Post*, December 19, 1897, 26; "For Tots as Cooks," 4; *Forty-Fourth Annual Report of the BOE, 1898*, 58, CBEA. Also see "Manual Training for Girls," "Domestic Science in Chicago Schools," 143.

34. Evelyn Frake to the BOE, reprinted in "Domestic Science," *Forty-Fourth Annual Report of the BOE, 1898*, 57, CBEA; "Supt. Lewis' Statement," *Twenty-Second Biennial Report of the Superintendent of Public Instruction of the State of Illinois, 1896–1898* (Phillips Bros State Printers, 1898), CVIII.

35. Frake to the BOE, reprinted in "Domestic Science," *Forty-Fourth Annual Report of the BOE, 1898*, 57, CBEA; "Fails to Cut Off a 'Fad': Board of Education Frowns on Walleck's Attack on Domestic Science," *Chicago Tribune*, August 25, 1898, 5; "Test in

Domestic Science," *Chicago Tribune*, August 27, 1898, 10; "Want a Course in Cooking," *Chicago Tribune*, November 21, 1899, 8; "School Methods to Be Unchanged," *Chicago Tribune*, July 14, 1905, 5.

36. Mr. Henry S. Tibbits to Supt. A. G. Lane, reprinted in "Domestic Science," *Forty-Fourth Annual Report of the BOE, 1898*, 58, CBEA; "Summary of School Statistics," *Forty-Sixth Annual Report of the BOE, 1900*, CBEA; "Overcrowded Schools," *Chicago Tribune*, September 6, 1888, 8.

37. "How Educational Problems Have Been Solved in Chicago," G2; "Constructive Work and Manual Training," 137; Lane, "Ratio of Boys," 82; Blake, "Manual Training in the School," 14.

38. "How Domestic Science Is Prolonging the Life of Man," *Chicago Tribune*, April 5, 1903, A5; A. R. Sabin, "District Superintendent's Report," *Forty-Sixth Annual Report of the Superintendent of Schools for the Year Ending June 30, 1900* (Hack and Anderson, 1901), 226, CBEA.

39. Robert M. Smith, "Manual Training and Household Arts," *Fifty-Fifth Annual Report of the BOE for the Year Ending June 30, 1910* (BOE, 1911), 145, CBEA; Smith, "Manual Training and Household Arts," *Fifty-Third Annual Report of the BOE for the Year Ending June 30, 1907* (BOE, 1907), 175, CBEA. Also see Dale Allen Gyure, *The Chicago Schoolhouse: High School Architecture and Educational Reform, 1856–2006* (University of Chicago Press, 2011).

40. Mary Snow, "Household Arts Roundtable," in *Proceedings of the Meeting of the Western Drawing and Manual Training Association*, vol. 17 (Oak Leaves Company, 1910), 122; Snow, "Report of the Household Arts Department," 110; "Know All Home Arts," *Chicago Daily Tribune*, September 7, 1904, 1; Vocational Work in High Schools," *Sixtieth Annual Report of the BOE, 1914*, 332, 337, CBEA.

41. "Household Arts Craze," *Chicago Tribune*, October 4, 1903, 12; "Child Cooks to Try: Small Daughters in 15,000 Families Plan Experiment," *Chicago Tribune*, October 23, 1904, 1; "How Domestic Science Is Prolonging the Life of Man," A5; "What the Public School Is Doing for the Chicago Girl," *Chicago Daily Tribune*, January 26, 1908, E4.

42. See section II of the NHEA's Constitution, appendix, in *Household Economics*, ed. Helen Campbell (C. P. Putnam's Sons, 1897), 268; Strasser, *Never Done*, 203–23; Mrs. D. A. Lincoln, *The Boston School Kitchen Text-Book: Lessons in Cooking for Use of Classes in Public and Industrial Schools* (Roberts Brothers, 1887), xxi, ALPLM; "To Make More Servants: Woman's Club Takes Up Problem of Household Help," *Chicago Tribune*, November 18, 1898, 9.

43. Fannie Barrier Williams, "Domestic Science," *Chicago Tribune*, October 13, 1903, 13; Williams, "The Problem of Employment for Negro Women," in *The New Woman of Color: The Collected Writings of Fannie Barrier Williams, 1893–1918*, ed. Mary Jo Deegan (Northern Illinois University Press, 2002), 55–57. See Danielle Phillips and Deborah Gray White, "Cleaning Race: Irish Immigrant and Southern Black Domestic Workers in the Northeast United States, 1865–1930," in *U.S. Women's History: Untangling the Threads of Sisterhood*, ed. Leslie Brown, Jacqueline Castledine, and Anne Valk (Rutgers University Press, 2017), 22.

44. Maurice Le Basquet, "The New Profession of Home Making," *Bulletin of the American School of Home Economics* (Armour Institute, 1906), 43; Helen Louise Johnson, "Ethics of Hotel Life," *Lake Placid Conference on Home Economics, Proceedings of the Sixth Annual Conference, September 19–24* (1904), 53.

45. Frake to the BOE, reprinted in "Domestic Science," *Forty-Fourth Annual Report of the BOE, 1898*, 57, CBEA; "Fails to Cut Off a 'Fad,'" 5; "Test in Domestic Science," 10; "Want a Course in Cooking," 8; "School Methods to Be Unchanged," 5; Snow, "Household Arts Roundtable," 122; Snow, "Report of the Household Arts Department," 110; "Know All Home Arts," 1.

46. Ella Flagg Young, *Isolation in the School* (University of Chicago Press, 1901), 94–95; "Board of Education Against Segregation in Public Schools," *Chicago Defender*, December 28, 1912, 1. Also see Joan K. Smith, *Ella Flagg Young: Portrait of a Leader* (Educational Studies Press, 1979); Ellen Condliffe Lagemann, "Experimenting with Education: John Dewey and Ella Flagg Young at the University of Chicago," *American Journal of Education* (May 1996): 171–85; Jackie M. Blount, "Ella Flagg Young and the Gender Politics of *Democracy and Education*," *Journal of the Gilded Age and Progressive Era* 16, no. 4 (2017): 409–23; Ella Flagg Young, "The Lucy L. Flower Technical School," *Fifty-Ninth Annual Report of the BOE for the Year Ending June 30, 1913* (BOE, 1913), 268, CBEA; Jackie M. Blount, *Destined to Rule the Schools: Women and the Superintendency, 1873–1995* (SUNY Press, 1998); Anna Durst, *Women Educators in the Progressive Era: The Women Behind Dewey's Laboratory School* (Palgrave Macmillan, 2016).

47. "Urges Schooling for Girl Workers," *Chicago Tribune*, September 28, 1909, 22; Ella Flagg Young, "All Girls to Sew in School: Supt. Young Plans Extension of Cooking Courses Also," *Chicago Daily Tribune*, October 2, 1909, 3.

48. These schools included schools on the Far West Side like Lloyd Elementary at Armitage and Cicero Avenues and May Elementary in East Garfield Park as well as Far South Side schools in Auburn Gresham and Calumet Heights (Gresham, Ryder, and Warren Elementary). See Mary Snow, "Report of the Household Arts Department," *Fifty-Eighth Annual Report of the BOE, 1912*, 162, CBEA; Snow, "Correlation of Household Arts with Other Subjects in the Curriculum," *Proceedings of the Meeting of the Western Drawing and Manual Training Association*, 107, digitized by Google.

49. Cooking and sewing instructors earned less than two-thirds the salary of standard subject teachers in 1904. Under Young's leadership, the average salaries of a household arts and standard subject teacher were the same ($1,125). See "Report of the Superintendent," *Fiftieth Annual Report of the BOE, 1904*, 81, 124, CBEA; James Miles and J. L. Jacobs, Civil Service Commission, *Report on the Budget of Educational Estimates and Expenditures* (John F. Higgins, 1914), 38–39, digitized by Library of Congress.

50. Mary Snow, "Household Arts," *Fifty-Sixth Annual Report of the BOE, 1912*, 162, CBEA; Richard R. Shaw and Brian F. Swartz, *Legendary Locals of Bangor, Maine* (Arcadia, 2015), 51; Snow, "Training for Motherhood," *Fifty-Eighth Annual Report of the BOE, 1912*, 16, CBEA; Ella Flagg Young, "Course of Study," *Fifty-Sixth Annual Report of the BOE, 1912*, 84, CBEA.

51. "Report of the Fifth Annual Meeting," *National Household Economic Association* (1897), 18, accessed through HathiTrust.org; Helen Sayr Gray, "Domestic Science in the Schools and Colleges," *North American Review* (1909): 205–7. Ella Flagg Young explains

this choice in "How Educational Problems Have Been Solved in Chicago Schools," *Chicago Tribune*, September 1, 1912, G2.

52. "Foxy Excuse of Parent Don't Fool Superintendent," *Chicago Defender*, February 6, 1915, 4; "Great Need for More Kindergartens," *Chicago Defender*, October 5, 1912, 1; "Color Issue in Schools," *Chicago Tribune*, October 2, 1902, 5; "Jim Crow School in Chicago," *Chicago Defender*, November 12, 1910, 1; Chicago Commission on Race Relations, *The Negro in Chicago: A Study of Race Relations and a Race Riot* (University of Chicago Press, 1922), 270.

53. Benjamin Richards Andrews, "Upper-Grade Industrial Course—Chicago Public Schools," *United States Bureau of Education*, Bulletin No. 37 (US Government Printing Offices, 1915), 64–66; "Truant Divisions," *Proceedings of the BOE, City of Chicago, July 2, 1912, to June 25, 1913* (BOE, 1913), 931, CBEA; Chicago Commission on Race Relations, *The Negro in Chicago*, 271.

54. "Not Enough Children in City Says Dr. J. B. M'Fatrich," *Chicago Tribune*, November 26, 1911, 4; Snow, "Training for Motherhood," 16; Caroline Hedger, *The School Children of the Stockyards District* (Government Printing Office, 1913); "Prepare to Open Ghetto Nursery," *Chicago Tribune*, December 28, 1907, 4; Child Federation of Philadelphia, *Little Mother's League: Description of Organization and Equipment and Twenty Lessons* (pamphlet, 1919), digitized by Internet Archive.

55. "'Little Mothers' of Down Town Chicago," *Chicago Tribune*, August 2, 1903, A3.

56. Snow, "Training for Motherhood," 9.

57. See report from Crystal Falls, Michigan, in Lelah Mae Crabbs and Mabel Lawrence Miller, *A Survey of Public School Courses in Child Care for Girls* (Merrill-Palmer School, 1927), 35; Child Federation of Philadelphia, *Little Mother's League*, 1. The Little Mothers' Aid Society of New York City provided similar training for girls who worked as the primary caretaker for their young siblings. See "Home of the Little Mothers," *New York Times*, January 8, 1899, 20; "Work for Little Mothers," *New York Times*, March 4, 1900, 8; "'Little Mothers' Get Early Education in Proper Care of Babies," *Chicago Tribune*, August 18, 1911, 3.

58. "Social Uplift," *The Crisis* 8, no. 6 (October 1914): 267; Felix J. Koch, "Little Mothers of Tomorrow," *The Crisis*, May 1917, 289.

59. See healthgrams and handouts in *Report of the Department of Health of the City of Chicago for the Years 1907, 1908, 1909, 1910* (City of Chicago, 1911); Snow, "Training for Motherhood," 9. Also see the Child Federation of Philadelphia, *Little Mothers' Leagues*.

CHAPTER FOUR

1. Agnes Nestor, *Woman's Labor Leader: An Autobiography* (Bellevue Books, 1954), 145.

2. On women and Progressive Era education reform, see Jane Bernard Powers, *The "Girl Question" in Education: Vocational Education for Young Women in the Progressive Era* (Routledge, 1992); Maureen Flanagan, *Seeing with Their Hearts: Chicago Women and the Vision of the Good City, 1871–1933* (Princeton University Press, 2002); Alan R. Sadovnik and Susan F. Semel, eds., *Founding Mothers and Others: Women Educational Leaders During the Progressive Era* (Palgrave Macmillan, 2002); Kate Rousmaniere, *Citizen Teacher: The Life and Leadership of Margaret Haley* (SUNY Press, 2005);

Rebecca S. Montgomery, *Celeste Parrish and Educational Reform in the Progressive-Era South* (Louisiana State University Press, 2018); Lynn Dorothy Gordon, *Gender and Higher Education in the Progressive Era* (Yale University Press, 1990).

3. On the vocational education movement, see Harvey A. Kantor and David B. Tyack, eds., *Work, Youth, and Schooling: Historical Perspectives on Vocationalism in American Education* (Stanford University Press, 1982); Arthur F. McClure, James Riley Chrisman, and Perry Mock, *Education for Work: The Historical Evolution of Vocational and Distributive Education in America* (Associated University Presses, 1985); Harvey A. Kantor, *Learning to Earn: School, Work, and Vocational Reform in California, 1880–1930* (University of Wisconsin Press, 1988); Herbert M. Kliebard, *Schooled to Work: Vocationalism and the American Curriculum, 1876–1946* (Teachers College Press, 1999); Warner Grubb and Marvin Lazerson, *The Education Gospel: The Economic Power of Schooling* (Harvard University Press, 2004); Glenn P. Lauzon, *Educating a Working Society: Vocationalism in Twentieth-Century American Schools* (Information Age, 2019). On vocational education for girls specifically, see Powers, *The "Girl Question" in Education*; Karen Graves, *Girls' Schooling During the Progressive Era: From Female Scholar to Domesticated Citizen* (Routledge, 1998); Clifford, "Marry, Stitch, Die or Do Worse," in *Work, Youth, and Schooling*, ed. Kantor and Tyack; John Rury, *Education and Women's Work: Female Schooling and the Division of Labor in Urban America, 1870–1930* (SUNY Press, 1990).

4. Wendy Gamber, *The Female Economy: The Millinery and Dress Trades, 1860–1930* (University of Illinois Press, 1997); Clifford, "Marry, Stitch, Die or Do Worse."

5. "Give Diploma in Two Years: Authorities Arrange Special High School Course," *Chicago Tribune*, June 21, 1910, 1; Kantor, *Learning to Earn*; Kliebard, *Schooled to Work*; Lauzon, *Educating a Working Society*.

6. Stephen Provasnik, "Disentangling the Triumph of Vocationalism from the Institutionalization of Vocational Education: A Reexamination of the Douglas Commission Report," in *Educating a Working Society*, ed. Lauzon, 75–94; Joseph F. Kett, "'Theory Run Mad': John Dewey and 'Real' Vocational Education," *Journal of the Gilded Age and Progressive Era* 16, no. 4 (2017): 500–514.

7. Organizations represented on the NSPIE included the National Association of Manufacturers, the Progressive (Bull Moose) Party, and the US Chamber of Commerce. Today the organization is called the Association for Career and Technical Education. See Robert Ripley Clough, "The National Society for the Promotion of Industrial Education: Case Study of a Reform Organization, 1906–1917" (PhD diss., University of Wisconsin, 1957); Debora Culpepper, "The Development of Tracking and Its Historical Impact on Minority Students" (PhD diss., Walden University, 2011), 83.

8. "Must Train for Industrial Race; United States Will Lose to Germany If Its Boys Are Not Better Taught," *Chicago Tribune*, January 22, 1908, 16; "Getting Data for Trade Schools," *Chicago Tribune*, December 10, 1907, 8; Theodore Roosevelt, "Industrial Education," *Journal of Education* 67, no. 8 (1908): 201.

9. Jane Addams, "Address," in *National Society for the Promotion of Industrial Education*, Bulletin No. 1, *Proceedings of the Organization Meetings* (January 1907): 43, 39.

10. The other founding members of the Women's Sub-Committee were Sarah Louise Arnold, Emily Greene Balch, Sophonisba Breckinridge, Susan Kingsbury, Florence

Marshall, and Mary Schneck Woolman. Florence Marshall, "Sub-Committee on Industrial Education for Women," in *National Society for the Promotion of Industrial Education*, Bulletin No. 4, *Industrial Training for Women*, October 1907, 1–59; "Is It True That the American Home Is Rapidly Deteriorating, as Some Educators Say?" *New York Times*, November 3, 1907, SM9.

11. For histories of the WTUL, see Nancy Schrom Dye, *As Equals and as Sisters: Feminism, the Labor Movement, and the Women's Trade Union League of New York* (University of Missouri Press, 1980); Alice H. Cook, Val R. Lorwin, and Arlene Kaplan Daniels, *The Most Difficult Revolution: Women and Trade Unions* (Cornell University Press, 1992); Susan Amsterdam, "The National Women's Trade Union League," *Social Service Review* 56, no. 2 (1982): 259–72; Susan Lehrer, *Origins of Protective Labor Legislation for Women, 1905–1925* (SUNY Press, 1987); Elizabeth Anne Payne, *Reform, Labor, and Feminism: Margaret Dreier Robins and the Women's Trade Union League* (University of Illinois Press, 1988); Women's Bureau, US Department of Labor, *Toward Better Working Conditions for Women: Methods and Politics of the National Women's Trade Union League*, Bulletin 252 (1953), 38, Agnes Nestor Papers, box 1, folder 1, CHM. Also see Felice Batlan, *Women and Justice for the Poor: A History of Legal Aid, 1863–1945* (Cambridge University Press, 2015), 37; "Report of Committee on Education," *Report of Proceedings of the Second Biennial Convention of the National Women's Trade Union League of America, Chicago, Sept. 25 to Oct. 1, 1909*, 53–54; Rose Schneiderman, "Fourth Biennial Outlines Educational Work: Industrial Education," *Life and Labor* (August 1913): 236.

12. Nestor, *Woman's Labor Leader*, 43, 83–84, 143; "To Be Taught Laws—No Certificate Without Knowledge of Laws," *Life and Labor* (1914): 34. For more on Agnes Nestor's philosophy of vocational education, see Nestor, "Statement of Mr. Charles H. Verrill, Chief Editor of the Bureau of Labor Statistics," *Report of the Commission on Vocational Aid to Vocational Education*, vol. 2: *Hearings Before Commission* (US Government Printing Office, 1914), 108; General Correspondence, letter from Cleo Murtland to Agnes Nestor, February 18, 1914, box 1, folder 7, Agnes Nestor Papers, CHM.

13. Margaret Dreier Robins, "Industrial Education for Women," in *National Society for the Promotion of Industrial Education Bulletin*, No. 10, *Proceedings, Third Annual Meeting, Milwaukee, Wis.* (NSPIE, 1910), 81; Henry S. Pritchett, "The Aims of the National Society for the Promotion of Industrial Education," in *National Society for the Promotion of Industrial Education Bulletin*, No. 7 (NSPIE, 1908), 8; Rose Schneiderman, "Educational Work: Industrial Education," *Life and Labor* (August 1913): 236–37.

14. Richard T. Crane, owner of a Chicago brass company, paid to install vocational equipment in several schoolhouses and even covered the salaries of early vocational teachers. Similar expenses paid by members of the wealthy McCormick family. See "Big Offer to Schools," *Chicago Tribune*, May 23, 1905, 7; "How Educational Problems Have Been Solved in Chicago Schools," *Chicago Tribune*, September 1, 1912, G2. For more on labor hostility to vocational programs in Chicago, see Julia Wrigley, *Class Politics and Public Schools: Chicago, 1900–1950* (Rutgers University Press, 1982), 48–90.

15. Fannie Casseday Dundan, "The Commercial High School as a Public Asset," *Journal of Education* 74 (September 1911): 259; *Fifty-Ninth Annual Report of the BOE, 1913*, 254–55, 153, CBEA; "Choice of Work," *Fifty-Second Annual Report of the BOE, 1906*, 154, CBEA; "Asks Fair Play in Schools: Cooley Shows Necessity of Revising Present System," *Chicago Tribune*, December 2, 1908, 8.

16. Crane Tech was privately run by the Chicago Commercial Club from 1882–1903 and originally named the English High and Manual Training School. It was incorporated into the Chicago Public School system in 1903, relocated to 2245 West Jackson Boulevard, and renamed after Chicago businessmen Richard T. Crane. Lane Tech, named after the former superintendent of schools, Albert G. Lane, was located at Sedgwick and Division Streets on the North Side of Chicago until relocated farther north to 2501 West Addison Street in 1933.

17. Edwin G. Cooley, "Manual Training and Household Arts," *Fifty-Fifth Annual Report of the BOE for the Year Ending June 30, 1909* (BOE, 1909), 145, CBEA.

18. Theodore Roosevelt, *The Works of Theodore Roosevelt: Citizenship, Politics, and the Elemental Virtues* (Charles Scribner's Sons, 1925), 487; Kevin P. Murphy, *Political Manhood: Red Bloods, Mollycoddles, and the Politics of Progressive Era Reform* (Columbia University Press, 2008), 1–2. On manliness and civilized behavior, see Michael Kimmel, *American Manhood: A Cultural History* (Oxford University Press, 1996); Gail Bederman, *Manliness and Civilization: A Cultural History of Gender and Race in the United States, 1880–1917* (University of Chicago Press, 1995). On manliness and class, see Elliott Gorn, *The Manly Art: Bare-Knuckle Prize Fighting in America* (Cornell University Press, 1986); Gregory L. Kaster, "Labour's True Man: Organized Workingmen and the Language of Manliness in the USA, 1827–1877," *Gender and History* 13 (2001): 24–67. Also see Mark C. Carnes, *Secret Ritual and Manhood in Victorian America* (Yale University Press, 1989); John Tosh, *A Man's Place: Masculinity and the Middle-Class Home in Victorian England* (Yale University Press, 1999).

19. "'Lamblike' Boys?" *Chicago Tribune*, May 3, 1908, 3.

20. "Benton L. Fisher Wins Honors at Crane Technical School," *Chicago Defender*, June 28, 1913, 1; "Parent Must Send Children to School," *Chicago Defender*, September 12, 1914, 1; "Helpful Lectures in Public Schools," *Chicago Defender*, October 12, 1912, 8; "Public School Pupils to Excel Graduate Record," *Chicago Defender*, July 11, 1914, 1.

21. Gamber, *The Female Economy*; Dye, *As Equals and as Sisters*; Cook, Lorwin, and Daniels, *The Most Difficult Revolution*.

22. Cynthia M. Blair, *I've Got to Make My Livin': Black Women's Sex Work in Turn-of-the-Century Chicago* (University of Chicago Press, 2010), 21–22.

23. Lisa M. Fine, *The Souls of the Skyscraper: Female Clerical Workers in Chicago, 1870–1930* (Temple University Press, 1990), 58; Susan Hartman Strom, *Beyond the Typewriter: Gender, Class, and the Origins of Modern Office Work, 1900–1930* (University of Illinois Press, 1992); Cristina Viviana Groeger, *The Education Trap: Schools and the Remaking of Inequality in Boston* (Harvard University Press, 2021).

24. Fine, *The Souls of the Skyscraper*, 30 (table 1). Also see Julie Berebitsky, *Sex and the Office: A History of Gender, Power, and Desire* (Yale University Press, 2012); Angel Kwolek-Folland, *Engendering Business: Men and Women in the Corporate Office, 1870–1930* (John Hopkins University Press, 1998).

25. "To Teach Girls Trades: Chicago to Establish Technical High School Like Those for Boys," *New York Times*, 1908, 1; "Ask Girls' Rights in Trade Courses," *Chicago Tribune*, January 10, 1909, 3; "University Girl Upholds Toilers," *Chicago Tribune*, October 7, 1906, 5. On the Chicago Woman's Club, see Lana Ruegamer, "'The Paradise

of Exceptional Women': Chicago Women Reformers, 1863–1893" (PhD diss., Indiana University, 1982); Flanagan, *Seeing with Their Hearts*.

26. The trade schools in Boston and New York were founded by women affiliated with the Boston-based Women's Educational and Industrial Union (WEIU). See Chas. F. Pidgin, Massachusetts Bureau of Statistics of Labor, *Industrial Education of Working Girls* (Wright & Potter State Printers, 1905), 35–37, Newberry Library, Chicago, IL; Mary Schenck Woolman, *The Making of a Trade School* (Whitcomb & Barrows, 1910), 12–13; Robyn Muncy, *Creating a Female Dominion in American Reform, 1890–1935* (Oxford University Press, 1991); Batlan, *Women and Justice for the Poor*, 37.

27. Lynn Y. Weiner, *From Working Girl to Working Mother: The Female Labor Force in the United States, 1820–1980* (University of North Carolina Press, 1985), 6; Florence M. Marshall, "The Industrial Training of Women," *Annals of American Academy of Political and Social Science* 33 (January 1909): 124–26; Florence M. Marshall, "What the Value of the Years from Fourteen to Sixteen Might Be to Girls," *Report of the Massachusetts Commission on Industrial Education*, 74–79; Mary Schenck Woolman, "Trade and Vocational Education for Girls," *Journal of Education* (December 1912): 696; Mary Schenck Woolman, *The Making of a Girls Trade School* (Columbia University Teachers' College, 1909), 32; Alice Kessler-Harris, *Out to Work: A History of Wage-Earning Women in the United States* (Oxford University Press, 2003), 174.

28. Weiner, *From Working Girl to Working Mother*.

29. Sophonisba Breckinridge, quoted in "University Girl Upholds Toilers," *Chicago Tribune*, October 7, 1906. See Hayden, *The Grand Domestic Revolution*; Flanagan, *Seeing with Their Hearts*; Marta Gutman, *A City for Children: Women, Architecture, and the Charitable Landscapes of Oakland, 1850–1950* (University of Chicago Press, 2014); Anya Jabour, *Sophonisba Breckinridge: Championing Women's Activism in Modern America* (University of Illinois Press, 2019).

30. Suellen Hoy, "Chicago Working Women's Struggle for a Shorter Day, 1908–1911," *Journal of the Illinois State Historical Society* 107, no. 1 (2014): 9–44; Lehrer, *Origins of Protective Labor Legislation for Women*; Dye, *As Equals and as Sisters*; Elizabeth Anne Payne, *Reform, Labor, and Feminism: Margaret Dreier Robins and the Women's Trade Union League* (University of Illinois Press, 1988); Nancy Woloch, *A Class by Herself: Protective Laws for Women Workers, 1890s–1990s* (Princeton University Press, 2015); Julie Novkov, *Constituting Workers, Protecting Women: Gender, Law, and Labor in the Progressive Era and New Deal Year* (University of Michigan Press, 2001).

31. "Statement of Leonora O'Reilly, National Women's Trade Union League," *Report of the Commission on Vocational Aid to Vocational Education*, vol. 2: *Hearings Before Commission* (US Government Printing Office, 1914), 195.

32. Margaret Dreier Robins, "Industrial Education for Women," in *National Society for the Promotion of Industrial Education Bulletin*, No. 10: *Proceedings, Third Annual Meeting, Milwaukee, Wis.* (NSPIE, 1910), 78.

33. "Annual Report of the Compulsory Education Department," *Forty-Seventh Annual Report of the BOE, 1901*, 45, CBEA; "Ratio of Boys," *Forty-Third Annual Report of the BOE for the Year Ending June 30, 1897* (John F. Higgins Printer, 1897), 66, CBEA; "Ratio of Boys," *Forty-Fourth Annual Report of the BOE, 1898*, 82, CBEA; Cooley, "Map Out New School Program," *Chicago Daily Tribune*, May 22, 1902, 2. For more on the prominence of girls in Progressive Era high schools, see Joel Perlmann, *Ethnic*

Differences: Schooling and Social Structure Among the Irish, Italians, Jews, and Blacks in an American City, 1880–1935 (Cambridge University Press, 1989); Graves, *Girls' Schooling During the Progressive Era*.

34. David Tyack and Elizabeth Hansot, *Learning Together: A History of Coeducation in American Public Schools* (Russell Sage Foundation, 1990), 113; John Dewey quoted in Steven Rockefeller, *John Dewey: Religious Faith and Democratic Humanism* (Columbia University Press, 1994), 256; "Urges 3 Schools Solely for Girls," *Chicago Tribune*, November 15, 1908, 3; "Urges Schooling for Girl Workers," *Chicago Tribune*, September 28, 1909, 22; Ella Flagg Young, "All Girls to Sew in School: Supt. Young Plans Extension of Cooking Courses Also," *Chicago Tribune*, October 2, 1909, 3.

35. "No Sex in School or Pupils' Minds: New Local Coeducational Argument Advanced by Mrs. Ella Flagg Young—Answers Jane Addams," *Chicago Tribune*, October 8, 1908, 6.

36. "Urges Schooling for Girl Workers: Mrs. Young Says Boys Have Advantage in Technical High and Other Courses," *Chicago Tribune*, September 28, 1909, 22; Ella Flagg Young, "Superintendent's Report," *Fifty-Ninth Report of the BOE, 1913*, 116, CBEA; Ella Flagg Young, *Ethics in the School* (University of Chicago Press, 1902), 24, 28.

37. "Two Year High School Course," *Chicago Tribune*, January 3, 1911, 10; "Tables VIII–IX: Membership of High School Classes," *Annual Report of 1913*, 319–21, CBEA.

38. "The Composite High School," *Fifty-Ninth Report of the BOE, 1913*, 254, 258, CBEA.

39. Mary Snow, "Household Arts," *Fifty-Eighth Annual Report of the BOE, 1912*, 62, CBEA; Richard R. Shaw and Brian F. Swartz, *Legendary Locals of Bangor, Maine* (Arcadia, 2015), 51; Snow, "Training for Motherhood," *Fifty-Eighth Annual Report of the BOE, 1912*, 16, CBEA. Young also created a four-year manual training program for boys and a four-year household arts program for girls intended to prepare students to teach vocational subjects in Chicago public high schools. "Give Diploma in Two Years," 1; "Two Year High School Course," *Chicago Tribune*, January 3, 1911, 10; "Tables VIII–IX: Membership of High School Classes," *Fifty-Ninth Annual Report of the BOE, 1913*, 319–21, CBEA; "Text Books Used in High Schools," Board of Education, City of Chicago, 1916, 53; "Training for Motherhood," *Fifty-Eighth Annual Report of the BOE, 1912*, 16, CBEA.

40. "Tables VIII–IX: Membership of High School Classes," *Fifty-Ninth Annual Report of the BOE, 1913*, 319–21, CBEA; Nancy Green, interview notes on Nell Willmot Mills, May 9, 1984, box 1, folder "Interviews 1917–1939, White," Nancy Green Papers, CHM; "Vocational Work in High Schools," *Sixtieth Annual Report of the BOE, 1914*, 337, CBEA; Chicago Commission on Race Relations, *The Negro in Chicago: A Study of Race Relations and a Race Riot* (University of Chicago Press, 1922), 270.

41. Blair, *I've Got to Make My Livin'*, 21–22; Chicago Commission on Race Relations, "High School Work," in *The Negro in Chicago*, 269.

42. Ruth Schonle Cavan and Jordan True Cavan, "Education and the Business Girl," *Journal of Educational Sociology* 3 (October 1929): 83; Strom, *Beyond the Typewriter*, 297, 383; Fine, *The Souls of the Skyscraper*.

43. Annelise Orleck, *Common Sense and a Little Fire: Women and Working-Class Politics in the United States, 1900–1965* (University of North Carolina Press, 1995); Meredith Tax, *The Rising of Women: Feminist Solidarity and Class Conflict, 1880–1917* (Monthly

Review Press, 1980); Gus Tyler, *Look for the Union Label: A History of the International Ladies' Garment Workers' Union* (Routledge, 1995).

44. "What's to Be Done with the $50,000?" *Chicago Tribune*, January 19, 1911, 3; Chicago Woman's Club, *Thirty-Second Annual Announcement of the Chicago Woman's Club, 1908–1909* (Libby & Sherwood, 1909), 49. On women's groups involvement with the 1910–11 Chicago garment strikes, see "Strikers Parade; More Aid Given," *Chicago Tribune*, November 14, 1910, 4; Katharine Coman, "Chicago at the Front," *Life and Labor* (January 1911): 15. Also see Mari Jo Buhle, "Socialist Women and the 'Girl Strikers,' Chicago, 1910," *Signs* 1, no. 4 (1976): 1039–51; Flanagan, *Seeing with Their Hearts*, 112–13; Susan Roth Breitzer, "Uneasy Alliances: Hull House, the Garment Workers Strikes, and the Jews of Chicago," *Indiana Magazine of History* (March 2010): 40–70.

45. Ella Flagg Young, "Technical Training for Girls," *Fifty-Seventh Annual Report of the BOE for the Year Ending June 30, 1911* (BOE, 1911), 92, CBEA; "Chicago to Teach Trades for Girls Beginning in June," *Chicago Tribune*, April 28, 1911, 1. Lucy Flower Technical High School for Girls operated out of a small schoolhouse at Twenty-Sixth Street and Wabash Avenue until 1926, when it was relocated to a new facility at 3545 West Fulton Boulevard in the Garfield Park neighborhood of Chicago. The school went coed in 1978, which it remained until its official closing in 2004. The building is now home to Al Raby High School and was added to the National Register of Historic Places in 2017. See Ruby Oram, "The Lucy Flower Technical High School for Girls, Chicago, IL" (Property SG100000960), National Register of Historic Places Nomination Form, June 1, 2017.

46. Ella Flagg Young, "Lucy L. Flower Technical High School," *Fifty-Ninth Annual Report of the BOE, 1913*, 266–67, CBEA; Dora Wells, "The Lucy Flower Technical High School," *School Review* (November 1914): 613. The Chicago BOE opened a second all-girls public school after World War II, the Ellen Richards Trade School for Girls, which is discussed in the conclusion.

47. Young, "Lucy L. Flower Technical School," 268; Dora Wells, "A School Built Around the Girl," *Journal of Education*, November 1931, 374; Wells, "The Lucy Flower Technical High School," 611–15; "Miss Dora Wells Selected as Girls' Trade School Head," *Chicago Tribune*, May 12, 1911, 7.

48. "Chicago's Vocational Schools," *The Carpenter*, January 1913, 21–22; "The Apprentice Schools," *Fifty-Ninth Annual Report of the BOE, 1913*, 252–53, CBEA; "Report of the Trade Schools Committee," April 1917, 1–3, Club Minutes, box 25, Chicago Woman's Club Records, CHM; "Plan for Girls' School: Committee Head Would Use Money for Trade Institution," *New York Times*, March 10, 1914, 10.

49. "Fears Craze for Teaching Crafts: Mrs. Ella Flagg Young Sees Peril in Turning Schools into Mere Workshops," *Chicago Tribune*, December 4, 1912, 2; Wells, "The Lucy Flower Technical High School," 615.

50. Henriette Greenebaum Frank and Amalie Hofer Jerome, eds., *Annals of the Chicago Woman's Club for the First Forty Years of Its Organization, 1876–1916* (Chicago Woman's Club, 1916), 305–6; Women's Bureau, US Department of Labor, *Toward Better Working Conditions for Women: Methods and Politics of the National Women's Trade Union League*, Bulletin 252, 1953, 36, Agnes Nestor Papers, box 1, folder 1, CHM; "Common Welfare," *The Survey* 34, no. 12 (June 19, 1915): 263; Karen Bastorello, *A Power*

Among Them: Bessie Abramowitz Hillman and the Making of the Amalgamated Clothing Workers of America (University of Illinois Press, 2008), 52.

51. Louise Montgomery, *The American Girl in the Stockyards District* (University of Chicago Press, 1913), 64; Powers, *The "Girl Question" in Education*, 113–20; "Table VII: High Schools—1912–1913," *Fifty-Ninth Annual Report of the BOE, 1913*, 318, CBEA; "Chicago to Teach Trades for Girls Beginning in June," 1.

52. Gilda Mazzola Fabits, interview with Nancy Green, November 2, 1983, Nancy Green Papers, CHM; Green, interview notes on Marie Lucas Teske, December 13, 1983, Nancy Green Papers, CHM; interview notes on June Ashworth Logalbo, n.d., folder "Interviews 1917–1939, White," Nancy Green Papers, CHM; Celestine Ellis Jeffries, recorded interview with Green, September 14, 1983, Nancy Green Papers, CHM; Green, interview notes on Anna Quetrochi, n.d., box 1, folder "Interviews 1917–1939, White," Nancy Green Papers, CHM; and Jean Yates Zuber, recorded interview with Green, November 10, 1983, Nancy Green Papers, CHM.

53. Mabel Wheeler was the daughter of Lloyd Garrison Wheeler Sr. (1848–1909). Nancy Green, interview notes on Mabel Wheeler Mason, August 10, 1985, box 1, folder "Interviews 1922–1975, Black," Nancy Green Papers, CHM; Nancy Green, "Remembering Lucy Flower Tech: Black Students in an All-Girl School," *Chicago Magazine* 14, no. 3 (Fall 1985): 46–57.

54. "Mrs. Marie Clay Hudlin and Daughter Both Attend High School," *Chicago Defender*, October 16, 1915, 4; "Miss Irene Hudlin's Debut a Social Triumph," *Chicago Defender*, September 9, 1916, 5; Miss Thomas Finishes Lucy Flower School with Honors," *Chicago Defender*, February 9, 1918; Nancy Green, interview notes on Leanita McClain, n.d., Nancy Green Papers, CHM; Green, interview notes on Jessie Allen McSwain, February 2, 1985, box 1, folder "Interviews 1922–1975, Black," Nancy Green Papers, CHM. For headshot examples, see "Among the First Ten," *Chicago Defender*, October 7, 1939, 18; "Likes Nursing Field," *Chicago Defender*, January 28, 1939, 14. See Michael Homel, *Down from Equality: Black Chicagoans and the Public Schools, 1920–1941* (University of Illinois Press, 1984).

55. Jeanne Michael, self-completed survey on Flower Tech, n.d., box 1, folder "Interviews 1917–1939, White," Nancy Green Papers, CHM; Green, interview notes on Mary Brooks Staver, August 31, 1983, "Interviews 1917–1939, White," Nancy Green Papers, CHM; 1940 US Census, Chicago, Cook, Illinois; Roll: m-t0627-00986; Page: 13A; Enumeration District: 103-2037. Digital Image s.v. "Mary Brooks," Ancestry.com; Sophia A. Theilgaard, "The Lucy Flower Technical High School for Girls" (unpublished diss., 1938), box 1, folder "Lucy Flower," Nancy Green Papers, CHM. See Susan Porter Benson, *Counter Cultures: Saleswomen, Managers, and Customers in American Department Stores, 1890–1940* (University of Illinois Press, 1986).

56. Green, interview notes on Willetta Yates Greer, September 13, 1983, box 1, folder "Interviews 1922–1975, Black," Nancy Green Papers, CHM.

57. "Vice Forces Lucy Flower Girls' School to Move," *Chicago Tribune*, March 7, 1915, 1. Green found that former students and teachers believed the move was deliberate during her oral history interviews. See Green, "Remembering Lucy Flower Tech," 48; "Still 'Jim Crow' Pupils at Wendell Phillips High School," *Chicago Defender*, February 27, 1915, 3. On the history of the Flower Tech building in Garfield Park, see Oram, "The Lucy Flower Technical High School for Girls, Chicago, IL."

58. Mildred Tolliver Hoskins, recorded interview with Nancy Green, February 4, 1985, Nancy Green Papers, CHM; Green, interview notes on Joan Howell Lawson, n.d., Nancy Green Papers, CHM; Marcia Chatelain, *South Side Girls: Growing Up in the Great Migration* (Duke University Press, 2015), 99.

CHAPTER FIVE

1. Chicago Vice Commission, "Outline of Study," in *The Social Evil in Chicago: A Study of Existing Conditions* (Chicago Vice Commission, 1911), 13–20, 42, 63; Eric Anderson, "Prostitution and Social Justice: Chicago, 1910–1915," Social Service Review (June 1974): 204.

2. "Tell About Vice, Suggest Remedy," *Chicago Tribune*, February 9, 1909, 9. On white slavery hysteria, see Jessica Pliley, *Policing Sexuality: The Mann Act and the Making of the FBI* (Harvard University Press, 2014); Ashley Baggett and Carole A. Bentley, "Alleged Crusaders and Self-Fooled Reformers: The Rise and Fall of White Slavery Hysteria in the 1910s," in *Historical Sex Work: New Contributions from History and Archaeology*, ed. Kristen R. Fellows, Angela J. Smith, and Anna M. Munns (University of Florida Press, 2020), 76–93. On sex work and reform in the Progressive Era, see Barbara Meil Hobson, *Uneasy Virtue: The Politics of Prostitution and the American Reform Tradition* (Basic Books, 1987); Marilynn Wood Hill, *Their Sisters' Keepers: Prostitution in New York City, 1830–1870* (University of California Press, 1993); Timothy Gilfoyle, *City of Eros: New York City, Prostitution, and the Commercialization of Sex, 1790–1920* (W. W. Norton, 1994); Larry Whiteaker, *Seduction, Prostitution, and Moral Reform in New York, 1830–1860* (Garland, 1997); Cynthia M. Blair, *I've Got to Make My Livin': Black Women's Sex Work in Turn-of-the-Century Chicago* (University of Chicago Press, 2010).

3. On the vocational guidance movement in urban school districts, see Herbert M. Kliebard, "Vocational Education as Symbolic Action: Connecting Schooling with the Workplace," *American Educational Research Journal* 27 (Spring 1990): 9–26. See Mark Pope, William C. Briddick, and Fatima Wilson, "The Historical Importance of Social Justice in the Founding of the National Career Development Association," *Career Development Quarterly* 61, no. 4 (December 2013): 368–73; Peter A. Sola, "Vocational Guidance: Integrating School and Society in Chicago 1912–16," *Vocational Aspect of Education* 28, no. 71 (December 1976): 117–23; Harvey Kantor, "Choosing a Vocation: The Origins and Transformation of Vocational Guidance in California, 1910–1930," *History of Education Quarterly* 26, no. 3 (1986): 351–75; Tristram Hooley, Ronald Sultana, and Rie Thomsen, *Career Guidance for Social Justice: Contesting Neoliberalism* (Routledge, 2017); Mark L. Savickas, "Meyer Bloomfield: Organizer of the Vocational Guidance Movement (1907–1917)," *Career Development Quarterly* 57, no. 3 (March 2009): 259–73.

4. On girls and Progressive Era consumer culture, see William Leach, *Land of Desire: Merchants, Power, and the Rise of a New American Culture* (Vintage, 1993); Nan Enstad, *Ladies of Labor, Girls of Adventure: Working Women, Popular Culture, and Labor Politics at the Turn of the Twentieth Century* (Columbia University Press, 1999); Kathy Peiss, *Cheap Amusements: Working Women and Leisure in Turn-of-the-Century New York* (Temple University Press, 1986); Cheryl D. Hicks, *Talk with You Like a Woman: African American Women, Justice, and Reform in New York, 1890–1935* (University of North Carolina Press, 2010); Simone Cinotto, *Making Italian America: Consumer Culture and*

the Production of Ethnic Identities (Fordham University Press, 2014); Elizabeth Ewen, *Immigrant Women in the Land of Dollars: Life and Culture on the Lower East Side, 1890–1925* (Monthly Review Press, 1985).

5. "The Wasted Years: Fourteen to Sixteen," *A Report on Vocational Training in Chicago and in Other Cities* (City Club of Chicago, 1912), 33, CBEA; Sophonisba Breckinridge and Edith Abbott, *The Delinquent Child and the Home* (Russell Sage Foundation, 1912), 17; Charles Patrick Neill, Bureau of Labor Statistics, "Juvenile Delinquency and Its Relation to Employment," in *Summary of the Report on Condition of Woman and Child Wage Earners in the United States: Bulletin of the United States Bureau of Labor Statistics*, no. 175 (US Government Printing Office, 1915), 282, available at FRASER Online Archive.

6. Frank Parsons, *Choosing a Vocation* (Houghton Mifflin, 1909), 4, 96–97; John Howard Breneman, "Vocational Guidance" (thesis, University of Montana, 1918).

7. The Vocational Supervision League was renamed the Scholarship and Guidance Association in 1942, which it remains today. See Scholarship and Guidance Association Records, University of Illinois at Chicago (UIC) Special Collections, Richard J. Daley Library, Chicago, IL. On Abbott, Breckinridge, and the Chicago School of Civics and Philanthropy, see Sharon Haar, *City as Campus: Urbanism and Higher Education in Chicago* (University of Minnesota Press, 2011); Anya Jabour, *Sophonisba Breckinridge: Championing Women's Activism in Modern America* (University of Illinois Press, 2019).

8. "See Peril to Girl of 14 Who Leaves School to Work," *Chicago Tribune*, February 19, 1912, 1.

9. NLPCW later became the Committee on the Protection of Women. See Hicks, *Talk with You Like a Woman*, 165; Victoria Earle Matthews, "Some of the Dangers Confronting Southern Girls in the North" (1898), quoted in Hicks, *Talk with You Like a Woman*, 185; "Sorority Helps Girls Pick Work," *Chicago Defender*, May 15, 1926, 5; "A Contribution to Democracy," *Bulletin of National Urban League* 8, no. 1 (January 1919): 6.

10. Blair, *I've Got to Make My Livin'*, 28–30; Joanne Meyerowitz, *Women Adrift: Female Wage Workers in Chicago, 1880–1930* (University of Chicago Press, 1988), 4. Also see Gilfoyle, *City of Eros*; Sharon Wood, *The Freedom of the Streets: Work, Citizenship, and Sexuality in a Gilded Age City* (University of North Carolina Press, 2005); Hicks, *Talk with You Like a Woman*.

11. *Report of the Senate Vice Committee* (Allied Printing Trades Council, 1916), 33–37; Chicago Vice Commission, *The Social Evil in Chicago*, 82.

12. Christopher Diffee, "Sex and the City: The White Slavery Scare and Social Governance in the Progressive Era," *American Quarterly* (June 2005): 411–37; Pliley, *Policing Sexuality*. Also see Hobson, *Uneasy Virtue*; Hill, *Their Sisters' Keepers*; Whiteaker, *Seduction, Prostitution, and Moral Reform*; Mary E. Odem, *Delinquent Daughters: Protecting and Policing Adolescent Female Sexuality in the United States, 1885–1920* (University of North Carolina Press, 1995).

13. Jane Addams, *The Spirit of Young and the City Streets* (Macmillan, 1909), 111–12; Jane Addams, *A New Conscience and an Ancient Evil* (Macmillan, 1909), 214–15. See Janet Beer and Katherine Joslin, "Diseases of the Body Politic: White Slavery in Jane Addams' 'A New Conscience and an Ancient Evil' and Selected Short Stories by Charlotte Perkins Gilman," *Journal of American Studies* 33, no. 1 (1999): 1–18.

14. "See Peril to Girl of 14 Who Leaves School to Work," 1.

15. Anne Davis, "Preliminary Report on Opportunities of Employment in Chicago Open to Girls Under Sixteen," in *Finding Employment for Children Who Leave the Grade Schools to Go to Work* (Hollister Press, 1911), 35, 38. Anne S. Davis became a national leader in the vocational guidance movement. She would later serve as president of the National Vocational Guidance Bureau, consult for the Illinois State Department of Labor, and lobby for federal child labor regulation with the US Children's Bureau. "Calls 'Compulsory Americanization' Tinkering and Stuff," *Chicago Tribune*, June 6, 1918, 10.

16. Sophonisba P. Breckinridge and Edith Abbott, "A Plea for Employment Supervision in the City Schools," in *Finding Employment for Children Who Leave the Grade Schools to Go to Work*, 12–13.

17. Breckinridge and Abbott, "A Plea for Employment Supervision in the City Schools," 17.

18. Breckinridge and Abbott, "A Plea for Employment Supervision in the City Schools," 15; Elias Tobenkin, "Chicago's New Crop of Young Workers: Public School Graduates Face Life," *Chicago Tribune*, June 2, 1912, A5; Ella Flagg Young, "Lucy L. Flower Technical High School," *Fifty-Ninth Annual Report of the BOE, 1913*, 270, CBEA.

19. The first vocational guidance counselors in the public schools all worked under the supervision of the School of Civics and Philanthropy at the University of Chicago. Along with Davis, they included Bertha Van Hove (Woman's Club Lincoln Center), Ethel Kawin (Chicago Woman's Aid), Mary Preston (Hull House), Rachael Gallagher (Englewood Woman's Club), Raymond C. Booth (Chicago Association of Commerce), and a "Miss Culkin." See "Vocational Supervision," *Sixtieth Annual Report of for BOE, 1914*, 204, CBEA; "Meeting Minutes—Civics and Philanthropy," May 1911–March 1918, 110, 118, box 12, folder 110, Chicago Woman's Aid Records, UIC Special Collections. The Vocational Guidance Bureau is now the Center of College and Career Counseling. "Vocational Guidance in Chicago," in *The General Federation of Women's Clubs, Twelfth Biennial Convention, 1914, Chicago, IL* (Bureau of Information, 1914), 469–73.

20. Letter reprinted in Anne S. Davis, "A Brief Statement of the Work of the Vocational Bureau," *Proceedings of the National Vocational Guidance Association, Richmond, Virginia, December 7–9, 1914* (1915), 53–54, digitized by Internet Archive; "Vocational Guidance," *Sixtieth Annual Report of the BOE, 1914*, 347, CBEA; Davis, "What Chance Has a Kid Got, Anyway?" *Chicago Tribune*, December 2, 1914, 15; "Schools to Aid Graduates in Getting Their First Job," *Chicago Tribune*, June 23, 1914, 10.

21. Patricia Carter, "Guiding the Working-Class Girl: Henrietta Rodman's Curriculum for the New Woman, 1913," *Frontiers: A Journal of Women Studies* 38 (2017): 128.

22. Julia Lathrop, "Some Items to Be Considered in a Vocational Guidance Program," *Proceedings of the National Vocational Guidance Association*, 49–50, Scholarship and Guidance Association Records, UIC Special Collections.

23. Ella Adams Moore, "Reports of Committees—Report of the Committee on Vocational Supervision," *Journal of Addresses and Proceedings of the National Education Association of the United States, July 7–14, 1917, Portland, Oregon*, vol. 55, 625, digitized by Google. Also see W. Carson Ryan Jr., "Recent Growth," in *Vocational Guidance and the Public Schools*, Bulletin No. 24 (US Government Printing Office, 1918), 36.

24. Tera Eva Agyepong, *The Criminalization of Black Children: Race, Gender, and Delinquency in Chicago's Juvenile Justice System, 1899–1945* (University of North Carolina Press, 2018), 11; Jane Addams, "Social Control," *The Crisis*, 1911, 22–23; Khalil Gibran Muhammad, *The Condemnation of Blackness: Race, Crime and the Making of Modern Urban America* (Harvard University Press, 2010), 122–24.

25. T. Arnold Hall, "Guiding the Nation's Youth," *Journal of Negro Life*, December 1930, 374. Also see Charles Goodwin Woodson, "Vocational Guidance," in *The Mis-Education of the Negro* (Associated Publishers, 1933), 101–10. See Anne Meis Knupfer, *Toward a Tenderer Humanity and a Nobler Womanhood: African-American Women's Clubs in Turn-of-the-Century Chicago* (New York University Press, 1996).

26. Ruth Bartlett, Vocational Guidance Bureau, "A Study of Beauty Culture in Chicago," *Occupational Studies*, no. 12 (Board of Education, 1926), CBEA; Nancy Green, interview notes on Dorothy Harris, n.d., box 1, folder "Interviews 1922–1975, Black," Nancy Green Papers, CHM; Patricia M. Wright, self-completed interview form, n.d., "Interviews 1917–1939, White," Nancy Green Papers, CHM. On Black women in the beauty industry, see Tiffany M. Gill, *Beauty Shop Politics: African American Women's Activism in the Beauty Industry* (University of Illinois Press, 2010).

27. Louise DeKoven Bowen, "Employment of Colored Women in Chicago," *The Crisis*, 1, no. 3 (January 1911): 24–25.

28. Edith Abbott and Sophonisba Breckinridge, *Truancy and Non-Attendance in the Chicago Schools* (University of Chicago Press, 1917), 461. By 1917, only 23,582 public school students out of 350,197 attended high school (less than 7 percent). See "Table 1: Enrollment, 1917–1918," *Sixty-Fourth Annual Report of the BOE, 1918*, 191, CBEA.

29. Ella Adams Moore, "Trade Training Need Emphasized," *Chicago Tribune*, December 25, 1912, 8; "An Experiment in Vocational Supervision," April 1917, 2, box 5, folder 49, Scholarship and Guidance Association Records, UIC Special Collections; Abbott and Breckinridge, *Truancy and Non-Attendance in the Chicago Schools*, 264; "Meeting Minutes—Civics and Philanthropy," May 1911–March 1918, 110, 118, box 12, folder 110, Chicago Woman's Aid Records, UIC Special Collections; Scholarship and Guidance Association Records, UIC Special Collections; Ella Adams Moore, "Report of the Vocational Supervision League to the Efficiency Committee of the Chicago Woman's Club," Club Minutes, April 14, 1917, 4, box 25, Chicago Woman's Club Records, CHM.

30. Davis, "A Brief Statement of the Work of the Vocational Guidance Bureau and the Joint Committee on Vocational Supervision," 53.

31. The camp was funded by Arthur Spiegel, son of the mail-order businessman Joseph Spiegel, who founded the Spiegel catalog in 1865. "Camp Sunset Lodge," *Reform Advocate* 57, no. 23 (July 12, 1919): 715–16, digitized by Google; "Office Report for Directors Meeting, October 19, 1920," 1, box 5, folder 43, Scholarship and Guidance Association Records, UIC Special Collections.

32. Kenneth M. Gold, "From Vacation to Summer School: The Transformation of Summer Education in New York City 1894–1915," *History of Education Quarterly* (Spring 2002): 18–49.

33. Wanda A. Hendricks, *Fannie Barrier Williams: Crossing the Borders of Region and Race* (University of Illinois Press, 2013), 98.

34. Elizabeth McDonald left the juvenile probation force in 1907 to found the Louise Juvenile House and Industrial School, which took in boys charged with both dependency and delinquency by the Cook County Juvenile Court. The Louise Juvenile Home closed in 1920. See Anne Meis Knupfer, *Reform and Resistance: Gender, Delinquency, and America's First Juvenile Court* (Routledge, 2001), 48–49; Knupfer, "African-American Facilities for Dependent and Delinquent Children in Chicago, 1900 to 1920: The Louise Juvenile School and the Amanda Smith School," *Journal of Sociology and Social Welfare* 24 (September 1997): 202.

35. "Meeting Minutes—Civics and Philanthropy," May 1911–March 1918, 110, 118, box 12, folder 110, Chicago Woman's Aid Records, UIC Special Collections; Anne Meis Knupfer, "Professionalizing Probation Work in Chicago, 1900–1935," *Social Service Review* 73, no. 4 (1999): 481–82; "Delinquent Girls," *Sixtieth Annual Report of the BOE, 1914*, 385, CBEA; Knupfer, *Reform and Resistance*, 185 (table 1).

36. Knupfer, *Reform and Resistance*, 49–50. See Ethel and Irene Kawin Papers, UIC Special Collections.

37. "America's Only Woman Judge Is Doing a Big Work," *New York Times*, May 25, 1913: SM4; unpublished radio speech, November 3, 1923, 2, box 6, folder 76, Mary Bartelme Papers, UIC Special Collections. For more on Mary Bartelme, see Harry G. Hershenson, *Mary Bartelme: First Woman Judge in Illinois Courts* (Illinois State Historical Society, 1924); Estelle B. Freedman, "Mary Bartelme," in *Notable American Women: The Modern Period: A Biographical Dictionary*, ed. Barbara Sicherman and Carol Hurd Green (Belknap Press of Harvard University Press, 1980), 60–61.

38. "America's Only Woman Judge Is Doing a Big Work"; court transcript, G.H., December 28, 1925, 2, box 6, folder 74, Mary Bartelme Papers, UIC Special Collections; Knupfer, *Reform and Resistance*, 83–98.

39. Knupfer, *Reform and Resistance*, 189 (table 5), 193–94 (table 9); court transcript, B.L., September 6, 1922, 2, box 6, folder 73, Mary Bartelme Papers, UIC Special Collections.

40. Emily Thorp Burr, "Activities of the Vocational Adjustment Bureau for Girls," *National Vocational Guidance Association Bulletin* 2 (October 1923): 115–16. By the 1920s, women oversaw the juvenile court cases of girls in other US cities, including Memphis and Washington, DC. See Jennifer Trost, *Gateway to Justice: The Juvenile Court and Progressive Child Welfare in a Southern City* (University of Georgia Press, 2005), 170; Estelle Freedman, *Maternal Justice: Miriam Van Waters and the Female Reform Tradition* (University of Chicago Press, 1996).

41. H. W. Lytle and John Dillon, *From Dance Hall to White Slavery: The World's Greatest Tragedy* (Charles C. Thompson Co., 1912); Ewen, *Immigrant Women in the Land of Dollars*; Peiss, *Cheap Amusements*; Randy McBee, *Dance Hall Days: Intimacy and Leisure Among Working-Class Immigrants in the United States* (New York University Press, 2000); Enstad, *Ladies of Labor, Girls of Adventure*; Elizabeth Alice Clements, *Love for Sale: Courting, Treating, and Prostitution in New York City, 1900–1945* (University of North Carolina Press, 2006).

42. Ella Adams Moore, "Conserving the Children of Working Age," in *National Education Association of the United States, Addresses and Proceedings of the Fifty-Fifth Annual Meeting Held in Portland, Oregon, July 7–14, 1917* (National Education Association, 1917), 646–47; Chicago Vice Commission, *The Social Evil in Chicago*, 150.

43. "College Education Necessary in Life," *Chicago Defender*, June 30, 1917, 1; Hicks, *Talk with You Like a Woman*, particularly chap. 6.

44. Addams, *The Spirit of Youth and the City Streets* (Macmillan, 1910), 51; "Jane Addams Pleads for Wayward Girls," *New York Times*, December 9, 1911, 7; Chicago Vice Commission, *The Social Evil in Chicago*, 269, 42, 45; Anne Dwyer, "The Morals Court of Chicago," *Institution Quarterly* (September 30, 1916), reprinted in *Social Hygiene* 3, no. 1 (January 1917): 144, digitized by Google.

45. "America's Only Woman Judge Is Doing a Big Work," SM4; "She Lists Silk Stockings Among Causes of Delinquency of Girls," *Washington Post*, November 28, 1915, E15; court transcript, October 30, 1922, 5–6, box 6, folder 74, Mary Bartelme Papers, UIC Special Collections.

46. Chicago Vice Commission, *The Social Evil in Chicago*, 32; Erica L. Simpson, "Latest Fashions," *Chicago Defender*, November 21, 1914, 6.

47. Court transcript, L.D., March 3, 1923, box 6, folder 74, Mary Bartelme Papers, UIC Special Collections. Bartelme initially sentenced Linda to the House of the Good Shepherd, a Catholic carceral school for girls that was subsidized under the Girls' Industrial Schools Act of 1879. For more on the history of Catholic industrial schools in Illinois, see Suellen Hoy, *Good Hearts: Catholic Sisters in Chicago's Past* (University of Illinois Press, 2006).

48. Court transcript, L.D., March 3, 1923, box 6, folder 74, Mary Bartelme Papers, UIC Special Collections.

49. Anne Davis, Vocational Guidance Bureau, "A Study of Beginning Office Positions for Young Women," *Occupational Studies*, no. 5 (Board of Education, 1924), Vocational Guidance Bureau Records, CBEA. On gender and office work in the Progressive Era, see Lisa M. Fine, *The Souls of the Skyscraper: Female Clerical Workers in Chicago, 1870–1930* (Temple University Press, 1990); Susan Hartman Strom, *Beyond the Typewriter: Gender, Class, and the Origins of Modern Office Work, 1900–1930* (University of Illinois Press, 1992); Julie Berebitsky, *Sex and the Office: A History of Gender, Power, and Desire* (Yale University Press, 2012); Angel Kwolek-Folland, *Engendering Business: Men and Women in the Corporate Office, 1870–1930* (Johns Hopkins University Press, 1994).

50. Davis, "A Study of Beginning Office Positions for Young Women," 3; Davis, "Preliminary Report on Opportunities of Employment in Chicago Open to Girls Under Sixteen," 35, 38; Davis, "A Brief Statement of the Work of the Vocational Guidance Bureau and the Joint Committee on Vocational Supervision," 53.

51. "Business Course in the High Schools," *Chicago Defender*, May 4, 1918, 7; "Colleges Reject a Negro Pupil," *Chicago Defender*, September 28, 1912, 1; St. Clair Drake and Horace R. Cayton, *Black Metropolis: A Study of Negro Life in a Northern City* (Harcourt, 1945), 225.

52. Addams, *A New Conscience and an Ancient Evil*, 214. Also see Fine, *Souls of the Skyscraper*, 58.

53. Mary King, "For and by Business Girls: Work or Go to School?" *Chicago Tribune*, August 27, 1916, E2.

54. Mary King, "For and by Business Girls: Well Dressed Girl," *Chicago Tribune*, June 1, 1919; "In the Office: Stenographers Too Extravagant," *Chicago Tribune*, June 25, 1907, 11; "Fair Office Girls Refuse to Marry," *Chicago Tribune*, June 11, 1905, B8; Strom,

"Flappers and Feminists: Women's Office Work Culture in the 1920s," in *Beyond the Typewriter*, 367–415; Mary Eleanor O'Donnell, "Fighting Cost of Living: A Stenographer's Way," *Chicago Tribune*, May 24, 1913, 10; "Should Girls Be Stenographers?" *Chicago Tribune*, April 28, 1907, E5; "In the Office: Stenographers Too Extravagant," 11.

55. Berebitsky, *Sex and the Office*, 21–59.

56. "Part VIII—Statistical Reports: Table Five," in *Fifth Annual Report of the Federal Board for Vocational Education* (US Government Printing Office, 1921), 240; Emil Hohn, "The Status Functions and Duties of the Principal and Administrative Staff of Public Industrial Schools for Adolescents" (PhD diss., New York University, School of Education, 1929), 68–69; "Women in Wartime," *Chicago Daily Tribune*, February 16, 1918, 11. See Arthur F. McClure, James Riley Chrisman, and Perry Mock, *Education for Work: The Historical Evolution of Vocational and Distributive Education in America* (Associated University Presses, 1985), 67–68; "Telephone Girls for Oversea Services," *National Society for Vocational Education Newsletter*, no. 1 (March 1918): 5.

57. "The Scholarship Committee," *Vocational Supervision League Bulletin*, March 1, 1918, box 5, folder 50, VSA, UIC Special Collections. See Fine, *Souls of the Skyscraper*; Lynn Dumenil, *The Second Line of Defense: American Women and World War I* (University of North Carolina Press, 2017). Although many scholars place the feminization of office work near the turn of the twentieth century, census data reveals that most office jobs, particularly the work of bookkeepers and cashiers, were not dominated by women until 1930. See Strom, *Beyond the Typewriter*, 18, 49. For more on the feminization of office work, see Margery Davies, *Woman's Place Is at the Typewriter: Office Work and Office Workers, 1870–1930* (Temple University Press, 1982); Kwolek-Folland, *Engendering Business*.

58. Marguerite Stockman Dickson, *Vocational Guidance for Girls* (Rand McNally, 1919), 199.

59. Drake and Cayton, *Black Metropolis*, 225–30; "Business Course in the High Schools," 7.

60. "Report of the Superintendent," *Sixty-Fourth Annual Report of the BOE, 1918*, 190, CBEA.

61. Court transcript, E.N., August 30, 1922, box 6, folder 73, Mary Bartelme Papers, UIC Special Collections.

62. David R. Roediger, *The Wages of Whiteness: Race and the Making of the American Working Class* (Verso, 1991); David R. Roediger, *Working Toward Whiteness: How America's Immigrants Became White* (Basic Books, 2005).

CHAPTER SIX

1. Neva Sexton and Irene Roloff, "Leader in Homemaking Education," *Delta Kappa Gamma Bulletin* 24 (Spring 1958): 34; "Statement of Miss Adelaide S. Baylor," *Hearing Before the Committee on Education, House of Representatives, Seventieth Congress, First Session on H.R. 9201 (H.R. 12241), February 7, March 20, and 21, 1928* (US Government Printing Office, 1928), 28; Adelaide S. Baylor, *Vocational Education in Home Economics: Twelve Years of Home Economics Education Under the National Vocational Education*

Acts, Vocational Education Bulletin No. 151, Home Economics Series No. 12 (US Department of the Interior, June 1930), 2.

2. On the Smith-Hughes Act, see Herbert M. Kliebard, *Schooled to Work: Vocationalism and the American Curriculum, 1876–1946* (Teachers College Press, 1999), 135; David Carleton, *Landmark Congressional Laws on Education* (Greenwood Press, 2001), 40; Michael Thier, Joshua Fitzgerald, and Paul Beach, "Partitioning Schools: Federal Vocational Policy, Tracking, and the Rise of Twentieth-Century Dogmas," in *Educating a Working Society: Vocationalism in Twentieth-Century American Schools*, ed. Glenn P. Lauzon (Information Age, 2019), 15–32.

3. On the AHEA, see Sarah Stage and Virginia B. Vincenti, eds., *Rethinking Home Economics: Women and the History of a Profession* (Cornell University Press, 1997); Rima Apple, *Perfect Motherhood: Science and Childrearing in America* (Rutgers University Press, 2006); Megan J. Elias, *Stir It Up: Home Economics in American Culture* (University of Pennsylvania Press, 2010); Carolyn M. Goldstein, *Creating Consumers: Home Economists in Twentieth-Century America* (University of North Carolina Press, 2014); Danielle Dreilinger, *The Secret History of Home Economics: How Trailblazing Women Harnessed the Power of Home and Changed the Way We Live* (W. W. Norton, 2021).

4. On Americanization and public schools in the 1920s, see David Tyack, *Seeking Common Ground: Public Schools in a Diverse Society* (Harvard University Press, 2003); Frank Van Nuys, *Americanizing the West: Race, Immigrants, and Citizenship, 1890–1930* (University of Kansas Press, 2002); Diana Selig, *Americans All: Cultural Gifts Movement* (Harvard University Press, 2008); Jeffrey Mirel, *Patriotic Pluralism: Americanization Education and European Immigrants* (Harvard University Press, 2010); Kathryn L. Wegner, "Constructing Citizenship: Schooling Chicago's Youth, 1900–1940" (PhD diss., University of Illinois at Chicago, 2010). On education and empire, see Clif Stratton, *Education for Empire: American Schools, Race, and the Paths of Good Citizenship* (University of California Press, 2016).

5. Carleton, *Landmark Congressional Laws on Education*, 76. Also see Marvin Lazerson and W. Norton Grubb, *American Education and Vocationalism: A Documentary History, 1870–1970* (Teachers College Press, 1974).

6. D. M. Hughes, *Report of the Commission on National Aid to Vocational Education*, vol. 2: *Hearings Before Commission* (US Government Printing Office, 1914), 2011–212. Also see George J. Kourpa, "Retooling the School: Vocational Education and the Origins of Federal Funding for Local Public Schools" (PhD diss., University of Virginia, 2014); Charles A. Prosser, *Vocational Education in Democracy* (Century Co., 1925), 424 (I 85.722), Newberry Library, Chicago, IL.

7. General Correspondence, letter from Cleo Murtland to Agnes Nestor, February 18, 1914; letter from Woodrow Wilson to Agnes Nestor, February 17, 1914, Harriet Reid to Nestor, February 24, 1914; Ella Flagg Young to Nestor, February 18, 1914: box 1, folder 7, Agnes Nestor Papers, CHM.

8. *Report of the Commission on National Aid to Vocational Education*, vol. 1 (US Government Printing Office, 1914), 28, 47.

9. "The Need for Vocational Education," *Report of the Commission on National Aid to Vocational Education*, vol. 1, 23–24.

10. *Report of the Commission on National Aid to Vocational Education*, vol. 1, 41–42.

11. Agnes Nestor, *Woman's Labor Leader: An Autobiography* (Bellevue Books, 1954), 151–52.

12. "Statement of Leonora O'Reilly, National Women's Trade Union League," in *Report of the Commission on National Aid to Vocational Education*, vol. 2, 195, 203.

13. "Statement of Mr. Charles Winslow, Bureau of Labor Statistics," in *Report of the Commission on National Aid to Vocational Education*, vol. 2, 108; "Proposed Legislation," in *Report of the Commission on National Aid to Vocational Education*, vol. 1, 78–80; "The Need for Vocational Education," 16.

14. *Twelfth Biennial Convention of the General Federation of Women's Clubs, June 9 to June 19, 1914, Chicago, IL* (General Federation of Women's Clubs, 1914), 145, 167, 622; Mrs. Franklin P. Iams (Lucy V. Dorsey), "Department of Legislation," *The General Federation of Women's Clubs Magazine* 15, no. 4 (April 1916): 23.

15. Lynn Dumenil, *The Second Line of Defense: American Women and World War I* (University of North Carolina Press, 2017); Helen Louise Johnson, "Club Programs in War Time," *Journal of Home Economics* 9, no. 2 (February 1917): 473.

16. Horace Mann Towner, quoted in Jane Bernard Powers, *The "Girl Question" in Education: Vocational Education for Young Women in the Progressive Era* (Routledge, 1992), 68.

17. William Stull Holt, *The Federal Board for Vocational Education: Its History, Activities and Organization* (Appleton, 1922), 15; *Thirteenth Biennial Convention of the General Federation of Women's Clubs, May 24 to June 2, 1916, New York, NY* (General Federation of Women's Clubs, 1916), digitized by Hathi Trust.

18. See James J. Davis, US Department of Labor, "Vocational Education," in *Handbook of Labor Statistics, 1924–1926* (US Government Printing Office, 1927); Carleton, *Landmark Congressional Laws on Education*, 64. See Tracy L. Steffes, *School, Society, and State: A New Education to Govern Modern America, 1890–1940* (University of Chicago Press, 2012); Kourpa, "Retooling the School." Legislation passed by Congress in 2018 (Perkins V) empowered states to distribute $1.4 billion toward vocational programs based on local need. US Congress, House, Strengthening Career and Technical Education for the 21st Century Act, HR 2353, 115th Congress, introduced in House, May 4, 2017, www.congress.gov/115/plaws/publ224/PLAW.

19. Subsequent vocational education legislation has reinforced the rights of states to set their own goals for what is now called "career and technical education" with support from federal funds. This is true of Kennedy's Vocational Education Act of 1963, which maintained the collaboration between state and federal education officials on matters of vocational education established by the Smith-Hughes Act. Holt, *The Federal Board for Vocational Education*; Steffes, *School, Society, and State*.

20. Federal Board for Vocational Education, "Range in Program," in *Ninth Annual Report to Congress of the Federal Board for Vocational Education* (US Government Printing Office, 1925), 55. For state funding statistics, see "Table III," and "Part VIII—Statistical Reports: Table Five," in *Fifth Annual Report of the Federal Board for Vocational Education* (US Government Printing Office, 1921), 144–45, 240. Also see Carleton, *Landmark Congressional Laws on Education*, 64–65; Kyle P. Steele, "The Give and Take of Vocationalism at the Local Level: Administrative and Student Perspectives on Milwaukee's Interwar High Schools," in *Educating a Working Society*, ed. Lauzon, 132.

21. "Board of Vocational Education—Annual Report," *Thirty-Fifth Biennial Report of the Superintendent of Public Instruction of State of Illinois, July 1, 1922–June 30, 1924* (Schnepp & Barnes Printers, 1924), 330, 333, digitized by HathiTrust.org; E. A. Wreidt, "Types of Courses in Industrial Education," *State of Illinois Board for Vocational Education*, Bulletin No. 12 (August 1919): 1–6; Wreidt, "Illinois Legislation for Vocational Education," *Chicago School Journal* 2, no. 1 (September 1919): 17, Newberry Library, Chicago, IL; "Special School for Office Boys Will Be Opened," *Chicago Daily Tribune*, September 18, 1917, 14; "Continuation Idea in Chicago," *Christian Science Monitor*, September 19, 1919, 14; Edwin C. Cooley, "Chicago's Continuation School System," *Chicago Schools Journal* 2, no. 2 (October 1919): 10–11, Newberry Library, Chicago, IL; State Treasurer Records, Vocational Education Fund Records, 1918–1937, box 104.032, Illinois State Archives, Springfield, IL; "Vocational Grants in Illinois," *Chicago Schools Journal* 1, no. 5 (January 1919): 20–21, I407.16, Newberry Library, Chicago, IL; Edward Kossel, "A Historical Study of Vocational Education in the Chicago Public and Technical and Vocational High Schools, 1917–1963" (PhD diss., Loyola University Chicago, 1965), 56; Francis Blair, *Thirty-Sixth Biennial Report of the Superintendent of Public Instruction of State of Illinois, July 1, 1924–June 30, 1926* (Illinois State Journal Co., 1927), 265.

22. "States Which Have Passed Continuation School Laws," *Women's Wear Daily*, August 17, 1920, 59; Isaac Owen Foster, "The Continuation School" (thesis, University of Illinois, 1922), 7, appendix I, 115; Walter S. Deffenbaugh and Ward W. Keesecker, *Compulsory School Attendance Laws and Their Administration*, Bulletin No. 4, Office of Education (US Government Printing Office, 1935); Federal Board for Vocational Education, *Program for Training Part-Time-School Teachers*, Bulletin No. 85: Trade and Industrial Series No. 24 (June 1923), v, 4.

23. John Clarke, "Letter to the Editor," *Afro-American*, June 14, 1930, 6; "Workers Tell U.S. Official of Threats," *Chicago Defender*, August 10, 1929, 3; "Wendell Phillips to Open Evening School," *Chicago Defender*, September 15, 1923, 4; Miriam Noll, "The Illinois Law on Part-Time Schools," *Labor Bulletin* (July 1926): 7; St. Clair Drake and Horace Cayton, *Black Metropolis: A Study of Negro Life in a Northern City* (Harcourt, 1945), 221–22.

24. Cora I. Davis, "Board of Vocational Education—Annual Report," *Thirty-Second Biennial Report of the Superintendent of Public Instruction of State of Illinois, July 1, 1916–June 30, 1918* (State Publishers, 1919), 113, 163; Blair, *Thirty-Sixth Biennial Report of the Superintendent of Public Instruction of State of Illinois, July 1, 1924–June 30, 1926*, 264.

25. Regina E. Groves, "A Commercial Curriculum for the Part-Time School" (thesis, University of Wisconsin, 1926), 13; Drake and Cayton, *Black Metropolis*, 225–30; "Business Course in the High Schools," *Chicago Defender*, May 4, 1918, 7.

26. "States Which Have Passed Continuation School Laws," 59; Foster, "The Continuation School," 7, appendix I, 115; Walter S. Deffenbaugh and Ward W. Keesecker, *Compulsory School Attendance Laws and Their Administration*, Bulletin No. 4, 1935, Office of Education (US Government Printing Office, 1935).

27. Noll, "The Illinois Law on Part-Time Schools," 7; Deffenbaugh and Keesecker, *Compulsory School Attendance Laws and Their Administration*, 73.

28. Federal Board for Vocational Education, "Board of Vocational Education—Annual Report, 1924," 349–54.

29. Mary E. Sweeny, "Mid-Winter Meeting with the NEA," *Bulletin of the American Home Economics Association* Series 6, nos. 3–4 (September–December 1920): 2. On the AHEA, see Stage and Vincenti, *Rethinking Home Economics*; Apple, *Perfect Motherhood*; Elias, *Stir It Up*; Goldstein, *Creating Consumers*; Dreilinger, *The Secret History of Home Economics*.

30. See Stage and Vincenti, *Rethinking Home Economics*.

31. "States Relations Services: Industrial Education," in *Fifth Annual Report of the Federal Board for Vocational Education* (US Government Printing Office, 1921): 105–221; "Supervision," in *Fifth Annual Report of the Federal Board for Vocational Education*, 71; "Statement of Miss Adelaide S. Baylor," *Hearings Before the Committee on Education, House of Representatives, Seventieth Congress, First Session on H.R. 9201 (H.R. 12241)* (US Government Printing Office, 1928), 27.

32. Anna L. Burdick served as the special agent for women and girls until the 1930s. "Women Voters Demand Industrial Justice," *Life and Labor* 10, no. 1 (January 1920): 78; "Home Making Leads," *Life and Labor* 10, no. 1 (January 1920): 119; Women's Bureau, US Department of Labor, *Second Annual Report of the Director of the Women's Bureau for the Fiscal Year Ended June 30, 1920* (US Government Printing Office, 1920), 7; Mary Anderson, "Adjustments to the City," in O. Latham Hatcher, *Rural Girls in the City for Work: A Study Made for the Southern Woman's Educational Alliance* (Garrett & Massie, 1930), 120.

33. "Part VIII—Statistical Reports: Table Five," 240; Federal Board for Vocational Education, *Directory of Trade and Industrial Schools*, 1930.

34. Gladys Alee Branegan, "Home Economics Teacher Training Under the Smith-Hughes Act, 1917–1927," *Contributions to Education*, no. 350 (Teachers College, Columbia University, 1929), 42, 100; American Home Economics Association, "Anna E. Richardson," in *Home Economists: Portraits and Brief Biographies of the Men and Women Prominent in the Home Economics Movement in the United States* (American Home Economics Association, 1929), 60; Anna E. Richardson and Esther McGinnis, *Home Economics and Education for Family Life* (American Home Economics Association, 1932), 21, 30–32; "South Aids Vocational Training," *Chicago Defender*, April 7, 1923, 3.

35. "Negro Education," *Federal Board for Vocational Education Yearbook 1923* (US Government Printing Office, 1924), 308–10; Alabama Department of Education, *Vocational Education Under the State and Federal Acts, 1922–1927* (Brown Printing Co., 1922), 62–73. Also see Dreilinger, *The Secret History of Home Economics*.

36. Nancy Green, "For Girls Only: History of a Chicago Public High School" (unpublished essay, n.d.), 19, Nancy Green Papers, CHM; for the new Flower Tech building, see Ruby Oram, "The Lucy Flower Technical High School for Girls, Chicago, IL" (Property SG100000960), National Register of Historic Places Nomination Form, June 1, 2017.

37. Doris Clark Cheatam, recorded interview with Nancy Green, August 29, 1983; Nancy Green, interview notes on Ms. Steward, former assistant principal: box 1, folder "Lucy Flower," Nancy Green Papers, CHM.

38. "Statement of Miss Louise Stanley," in *Federal Aid for Home Economics: Hearings Before the Committee on Education, House of Representatives Sixty-Sixth Congress Third Session on H.R. 12078, February 4, 1921* (US Government Printing Office, 1921), 5–15, digitized by Hathi Trust.

39. Black women in the South faced the same Jim Crow voting restrictions that had disenfranchised Black male voters since the Fifteenth Amendment of 1870. See Rosalyn Terborg-Penn, *African American Women in the Struggle for the Vote, 1850–1920* (Indiana University Press, 1998); Faye E. Dudden, *Fighting Chance: The Struggle over Woman Suffrage and Black Suffrage in Reconstruction America* (Oxford University Press, 2011); Martha S. Jones, *Vanguard: How Black Women Broke Barriers, Won the Vote, and Insisted on Equality for All* (Basic Books, 2020).

40. Lynn Dumenil, "The New Woman and the Politics of the 1920s," *OAH Magazine of History* (July 2007): 22–26; Kristi Anderson, *After Suffrage: Women in Partisan and Electoral Politics Before the New Deal* (University of Chicago Press, 1996); Eleanor Flexner and Ellen Fitzpatrick, *Century of Struggle: The Woman's Rights Movement in the United States* (Harvard University Press, 1996); Ellen Carol DuBois, *Woman Suffrage and Women's Rights* (New York University Press, 1998).

41. "Statement of Mrs. Maude Wood Park," in *Federal Aid for Home Economics*, 24; "Statement of Mrs. Raymond B. Morgan," in *Federal Aid for Home Economics*, 41.

42. "National Organizations That Have Endorsed the Fess Bill," in *Federal Aid for Home Economics*, 16.

43. "States Relations Services: Industrial Education," 105–221; "Supervision," 71; "Statement of Miss Adelaide S. Baylor," in *Hearings Before the Committee on Education, House of Representatives, Seventieth Congress, First Session on H.R. 9201 (H.R. 12241)* (US Government Printing Office, 1928), 27.

44. Adah Hess, Year: 1930; Census Place: Springfield, Sangamon, Illinois; Page: 13A; Enumeration District: 0032; FHL microfilm: 2340294; Year: 1940; Census Place: Marquette, Marquette, Michigan; Roll: m-t0627-01786; Page: 14B; Enumeration District: 52-25.

45. Commission on the Reorganization of Secondary Education of the National Education Association, *Cardinal Principles of Secondary Education* (Bureau of Education, US Government Printing Office, 1918), 11–16, 17, 27; Kourpa, "Retooling the School," 190; Wegner, "Constructing Citizenship," 168; Diane Ravitch, "Tot Sociology: Or What Happened to History in the Grade Schools," *American Scholar* 56, no. 3 (1987): 343–54; Mirel, *Patriotic Pluralism*; Van Nuys, *Americanizing the West*.

46. Mae M. Ngai, *Impossible Subjects: Illegal Aliens and the Making of Modern America* (Princeton University Press, 2004); Desmond S. King, *Making Americans: Immigration, Race, and the Origins of the Diverse Democracy* (Harvard University Press, 2009); Lia Lynn Yang, *One Mighty and Irresistible Tide: The Epic Struggle over American Immigration, 1924–1965* (W. W. Norton, 2020).

47. R. V. Harman, H. R. Tucker, and J. E. Wrench, *American Citizenship Practice* (University Publishing, 1924), 20; Hannah M. Harris, *Lessons in Civics for the Six Elementary Grades of City Schools*, Bulletin No. 18 (US Bureau of Education, 1920), 15, 46–47.

48. G. Bauerself, "Technical Work in the High Schools," in *Annual Report of the Superintendent of Schools* (1925), 118, CBEA; Franklin Bobbitt, "The Actual Objectives of the Present-Day High School," *School Review* 28, no. 4 (April 1921): 261; "What the Schools Should Include," *Annual Report of the Superintendent of Schools* (1926), 104, CBEA; Frank Cody, "Americanization Courses in the Public Schools," *Chicago Schools Journal* 1, no. 5 (January 1919): 5, I 407.16, Newberry Library, Chicago, IL; "Public

Education Is for . . . ," in *Annual Report of the Superintendent of Schools* (1926), 22; "Citizenship," in *Annual Report of the Superintendent of Schools* (1926), 103, CBEA; "A Proposed Program of Social Studies in the Secondary Schools," *American Economic Review* 12, no. 1 (1922): 67–70. Also see Wegner, "Constructing Citizenship," 99–111.

49. Department of Home Economics, University of Illinois, "Syllabus of Home Economics for the High Schools," *University of Illinois Bulletin* 24, no. 48 (1927): 13, 83–86; Branegan, "Home Economics Teacher Training Under the Smith-Hughes Act, 1917–1927," 118; "Course in Home Economics for the Junior High Schools" (1929), 1–3, CBEA; Frances Bailey, "The Progress of Home Economics in the Secondary Schools, 1917–1927" (PhD diss., University of Chicago, 1928), 68.

50. Adah Hess, "Home Economics Education Shows Rapid Growth in Illinois High Schools," *Educational Press Bulletin*, March 1936, 4; Department of Home Economics, University of Illinois, "Syllabus of Home Economics for the High Schools" (1927), 13, 83–86; "Course in Home Economics for the Junior High Schools" (1929), CBEA; Bailey, "The Progress of Home Economics in the Secondary Schools, 1917–1927," 20–26; Hess, "Home Economics Education Shows Rapid Growth in Illinois High Schools," 4. On how these programs prepared female students for a lifetime of consumer citizenship, see Goldstein, *Creating Consumers*.

51. Board of Education, Denver Public Schools, "Home Economics: Grades Ten, Eleven, and Twelve," *Course of Study Monography*, no. 13 (Denver Public Schools, 1925), 14–20; Annie Robertson Dyer, "The Administration of Home Economics in City Schools: A Study of Present and Desired Practices in the Organization of the Home Economics Program" (PhD diss., Teachers College, Columbia University, 1928), 82.

52. "Statement of Miss Edna N. White," in *Federal Aid for Home Economics*, 37; "Statement of Miss M. Lillian Williamson, in *Federal Aid for Home Economics*, 27–29; "Statement of Miss Alice Bradford Wiles," in *Federal Aid for Home Economics*, 45–46; "Statement of Mrs. Nellie E Blakeman," in *Federal Aid for Home Economics*, 33.

53. Baylor, *Vocational Education in Home Economics*, 1.

54. Baylor, *Vocational Education in Home Economics*, 2.

55. Carrie Lyford, Federal Board for Vocational Education, "Occupations of Negro Girls and Women," *Federal Board for Vocational Education Bulletin: Home Economics Series*, 5–6.

56. Elizabeth Cohen, *Semi-Citizenship in Democratic Politics* (Cambridge University Press, 2009); Lyford, "Occupations of Negro Girls and Women," 5–6, 57.

57. Lyford, "Occupations of Negro Girls and Women," 5–6, 57; Linda Marie Fritschner, "Servants or Ladies: The Differential Implementation of a Federal Mandate," *School Review* 85, no. 2 (1977): 287–96; Federal Board for Vocational Education, "Range in Program," 55, 144–45.

58. Cohen, *Semi-Citizenship in Democratic Politics*; Lyford, "Occupations of Negro Girls and Women," 5–6, 57.

59. Victor K. Houston, *Hearings Before the Committee on Education, House of Representatives, Seventieth Congress, First Session on H.R. 9201, February 7, March 20–21, 1929* (US Government Printing Office, 1928), 36–37; "Girls in Japan Get Homemaking Ideas," *New York Times*, October 2, 1948, 12; *Ninth Annual Report to Congress of the Federal Board for Vocational Education*, part I (US Government Printing Office, 1925),

53; Branegan, "Home Economics Teacher Training Under the Smith-Hughes Act, 1917–1927," 38; Stratton, *Education for Empire*.

60. Baylor, *Vocational Education in Home Economics*, 135–39.

61. Baylor, *Vocational Education in Home Economics*, 135–39.

62. Mrs. A. L. Andrews, "An Introduction," *Women of the Pacific, Being a Record of the Proceedings of the First Pan-Pacific Women's Conference Which Was Held in Honolulu from the 9th to the 19th of August 1928, Under the Auspices of the Pan-Pacific Union* (Honolulu, 1928), 7; Louise Stanley, "Home Economics and Education," in *Women of the Pacific*, 48–49; Baylor, *Vocational Education in Home Economics*, 139.

CONCLUSION

1. Cristina Viviana Groeger, *The Education Trap: Schools and the Remaking of Inequality in Boston* (Harvard University Press, 2021); Jon Shelton, *The Education Myth: How Human Capital Trumped Social Democracy* (Cornell University Press, 2023).

2. Carolyn M. Goldstein, *Creating Consumers: Home Economists in Twentieth-Century America* (University of North Carolina Press, 2014).

3. William H. Johnson, "Opening the Ellen Richards Trade School," *Illinois Vocational Progress* 3 (February 1946): 95–96; Elsie Gruel, "Look Your Best," *Illinois Vocational Progress* 9 (February 1952): 69; "300 Enrolled in New Girls' Trade School," *Chicago Tribune*, September 5, 1945, 15.

4. Sophia A. Theilgaard, "Lucy Flower," n.d., box 1, Nancy Green Papers, CHM; Sophia A. Theilgaard, "The Lucy Flower Technical High School for Girls" (unpublished diss., 1938), 17, 31, box 1, Nancy Green Papers, CHM; "Lucy Flower School Offers Nurse Course," *Chicago Tribune*, September 6, 1955, 10; "Lucy Flower Trains Home, Office Girls," *Chicago Tribune*, February 25, 1954, 4.

5. Anne Davis, "A Study of Beauty Culture in Chicago," *Occupation Studies*, no. 12 (1926), Vocational Guidance Bureau Records, CBEA; Nancy Green, interview notes on Dorothy Harris, n.d., box 1, folder "Interviews 1922–1975, Black," Nancy Green Papers, CHM. Also see "Adds a Frill to the School Bill," *Chicago Tribune*, January 18, 1933, 11; "Beauty Culture Defended," *Chicago Tribune*, January 21, 1933, 12; Johnson, "Opening the Ellen Richards Trade School," 95–96; Gruel, "Look Your Best," 69; "300 Enrolled in New Girls' Trade School," 15.

6. Nancy Green, "For Girls Only: History of a Chicago Public High School" (unpublished essay, n.d.), 18, Nancy Green Papers, CHM; Green, interview notes on Joan Howell Lawson, n.d., box 1, folder "Interview 1922–1975, Black," Nancy Green Papers, CHM.

7. "Sex Discrimination and Sex Stereotyping in Vocational Education," *Hearings Before the Subcommittee on Elementary, Secondary, and Vocational Education of the Committee on Education and Labor, House of Representatives, Ninety-Fourth Congress, March 17 and April 21, 28, 1975* (US Government Printing Office, 1975); US Census, Census Population Studies, "Table A-1: School Enrollment of the Population 3 Years Old and Over, by Level and Control of School, Race, and Hispanic Origin: October 1955 to 2020"; "Table A-2: Percentage of the Population 3 Years Old and Over Enrolled in School, by Age, Sex, Race, and Hispanic Origin: October 1947 to 2020"; Marilyn Steele, "Prepared Statement of Marilyn Steele, PhD, Director of Planning and Community

Activities, Flint, Michigan," *Hearings Before the Subcommittee on Elementary, Secondary, and Vocational Education* (1975), 23.

8. "Statement of Marilyn Steele," *Hearings Before the Subcommittee on Elementary, Secondary, and Vocational Education* (1975), 9, 12.

9. Lynn Y. Weiner, *From Working Girl to Working Mother: The Female Labor Force in the United States, 1820–1980* (University of North Carolina Press, 1985), 3, 7; "Statement of Nancy Perlman, Treasurer of the National Coalition of Labor Union Women," *Hearings Before the Subcommittee on Elementary, Secondary, and Vocational Education* (1975), 26.

10. "Statement of Nancy Perlman, Treasurer of the National Coalition of Labor Union Women," 28.

11. Kathleen Burns, "Coed Entry into Lane Tech Gets Mixed Reaction," *Chicago Tribune*, February 7, 1971, N3; Robert Enstad, "1,500 from Lane Tech March in Protest of Coed Admissions," *Chicago Tribune*, March 3, 1971, 3; Trina Kakacek, email message to author, October 15, 2024. For an excellent history of the controversies surrounding coeducation in higher ed during this period, see Nancy Weiss Malkiel, *"Keep the Damned Women Out": The Struggle for Coeducation* (Princeton University Press, 2016).

12. "Black Student Population Sets Record High in City," *Chicago Defender*, December 8, 1970, 4; Elizabeth Todd-Breland, *A Political Education: Black Politics and Education Reform in Chicago Since the 1960s* (University of North Carolina Press, 2018); "Illinois," *Directory of Public Elementary and Secondary Schools in Selected Districts: Enrollment and Staff by Racial/Ethnic Group* (US Department of Health, Education, and Welfare/Office for Civil Rights, Fall 1972), 316. See "History," Lane Tech College Prep High School, https://lanetech.org/about/history; Peter Kendall, "Curriculum Clash Divides Lane Tech," *Chicago Tribune*, March 19, 1990, S1.

13. Lucy Flower Vocational High School's building—the "school built around the girl"—today houses the Al Raby High School for Community and Environment. For more on the later history of Flower Tech, see "Menu for Success," *Chicago Tribune*, May 22, 1994, H2; Ruby Oram, "The Lucy Flower Technical High School for Girls, Chicago, IL" (Property SG100000960), National Register of Historic Places Nomination Form, June 1, 2017. For more on Chicago school closings in the early 2000s, see Mallika Ahluwalia, "CPS Schools Opened and Closed, by Year," *Chicago Reporter*, February 24, 2006; "A Generation of School Closings," WBEZ Chicago, December 3, 2018, https://interactive.wbez.org/generation-school-closings; Kathryn M. Neckerman, *Schools Betrayed: Roots of Failure in Inner-City Education* (University of Chicago Press, 2007); Carl A. Grant, Anna Floch Arcello, Annika M. Konrad, and Mary C. Swenson, "Fighting for the 'Right to the City': Examining Spatial Injustice in Chicago Public School Closings," *British Journal of Sociology of Education* 35, no. 5 (2014): 670–87.

Index

Abbot, Edith, 128, 132–33
Abel, Mary Hinman, 74–75
accounting, 103–4, 112. *See also* commercial education; office work
Addams, Jane, 2, 5–6, 36, 46, 52–53, 55, 64, 75, 82, 100–101, 105–6, 111–12, 115, 117, 128–31, 136, 143, 147–48, 151, 182
African Americans: in Chicago, 3–4, 166, 179, 191; and child labor, 47–48, 69; and citizenship, 158, 179–82; in courts and carceral schools, 9–11, 16–18, 27–28, 38–39, 141, 143; and domestic science/home economics, 12, 72, 74–76, 87, 94, 114, 171, 174; at Flower Tech, 120–23, 137, 172, 188, 191; and public education, 3–4, 8, 91, 98–99, 105, 113; and urban reform, 5–6, 8, 46, 50, 63, 126, 130, 136, 139–40; and the workforce, 2, 34–37, 106, 130–31, 151–52, 167. *See also* Great Migration; race
age. *See* childhood
age-of-consent laws, 8
Agnes Scott Women's College, 169
Albert G. Lane Technical High School for Boys (Lane Tech), 104–5, 107, 190–91
Alpha Kappa Alpha, 130
Altgeld, Peter John, 31, 44
alumni: and Flower Tech, 118–23, 137; and vocational education, 150, 190–91. *See also* Association of Collegiate Alumnae (ACA)
Amanda Smith Industrial School for Colored Girls, 38–39
American Federation of Labor (AFL), 101, 103, 159

American Home Economics Association (AHEA), 12, 75, 158, 168–75, 178, 180–82, 187. *See also* home economics
Americanization, 158, 175–82. *See also* citizenship training
Amigh, Ophelia, 31–34, 40
Anderson, Mary, 169–70
apprenticeships: for boys and men, 20, 99, 103, 166; for girls and women, 101, 117, 138
Archard, Eliza, 17–18
Armour Institute, 87
Association of Collegiate Alumnae (ACA), 128, 173
attendance. *See* school attendance; truancy

Back of the Yards (neighborhood), 187. *See also* stockyards
Barrows, Alice, 135
Bartelme, Mary, 140–41, 144–46, 150, 152
basketball, 59, 63–64. *See also* physical culture
Baylor, Adelaide Steele, 157
Beveridge, Helen Mar Judson, 17–20, 32–33. *See also* Girls' Industrial Schools Act; Illinois Industrial School for Girls; Ladies' Industrial Schools Association (LISA)
Beveridge, John Lourie, 17
Black Metropolis (neighborhood), 4, 99, 105, 120. *See also* African Americans; Great Migration; South Side (neighborhood)
Bloomfield, Meyer, 127

Board of Education. *See* Chicago Board of Education (BOE)
bookkeeping, 144. *See also* commercial education; office work
Boston, 3, 7, 17–18: commercial education for boys, 104–5; domestic science movement, 74, 82–83; Trade School for Girls, 107–8; Women's Municipal League, 35
Bowen, Louise DeKoven, 137
boys: and child labor, 47–48, 55; citizenship training, 160, 176; and continuation schools, 165–67; definition of "boyhood," 7–8, 19–20, 68–69; and manual training, 72–73, 80–81, 84–85, 89, 91, 95; physical culture, 58–61; and vocational education, 7, 103–5, 110–12, 189–91. *See also* childhood; girls
Boys' Manual Training School Act of 1883, 19–20
Bradwell, Myra, 17
"bread and roses" (speech), 64
Breckinridge, Sophonisba, 108–9, 128, 132–33, 136
Bridgeport (neighborhood), 118
Bronzeville (neighborhood). *See* Black Metropolis
Brown, Corrine Stubbs, 43, 46
Burdick, Anna L., 169
Bureau of Education, 157, 174–75
Bureau of Home Economics, 174, 187
Bureau of Labor Statistics, 127, 159

carceral schools: for boys, 19–20, 79; and domestic service, 16, 21–26, 87; for girls, 2, 6–7, 9, 15–41, 145–46; parole and indenture from, 32–34; racism in, 27–29, 34–39, 141, 146; and truancy, 44, 140, 187. *See also* Illinois Industrial School for Girls; Illinois State Training School for Girls
Catholic schools, 6, 55, 120, 152
charity groups, 17, 132, 139
Chicago Board of Education (BOE): childhood health, 57, 59–60, 94; child labor regulation, 46, 53–56; domestic science movement, 78–81, 84–85, 90–91; establishment of, 43; vocational education, 97, 99–103, 107, 113–14, 116, 121, 150, 176, 187, 191; vocational guidance, 11, 133–34, 138–40; women board members, 2, 6, 10, 43–44, 79–83, 88, 105
Chicago Commons, 62–66, 118
Chicago Defender, 90, 105, 120, 143–44, 147
Chicago Department of Health, 60, 62, 92, 94. *See also* health
Chicago Normal School, 86, 88, 113, 117
Chicago School of Civics and Philanthropy, 108, 128, 132. *See also* University of Chicago
Chicago Stock Exchange, 23
Chicago Times, 1, 43
Chicago Tribune, 22, 24–25, 64–66, 68, 79–80, 84, 109, 129, 132, 148
Chicago Urban League, 136
Chicago Vice Commission, 125, 130–32, 142–44
Chicago Woman's Aid, 133–34
Chicago Woman's Club (CWC), 5, 17, 22–23, 26, 43–44, 49, 59, 74–75, 79, 82–84, 87, 98–99, 107–17, 122–25, 128, 137, 140, 178. *See also* women's club movement
Chicago Women's Trade Union League. *See* Women's Trade Union League (WTUL)
Chicago World's Fair. *See* World's Columbian Exposition
childcare, 17, 92–93, 95, 171, 179, 181, 190; childcare classes, 2, 71, 157, 167, 171, 179. *See also* "little mothers" courses
Child Federation of Philadelphia, 92
childhood: definition of term, 3, 7–9, 20, 42, 65, 67, 167, 187; and health, 49, 57, 60–62; and race, 8, 51–52. *See also* boys; girls
child labor: contradictions in reform, 72, 91–93, 181; and gender, 10, 46–49, 62–68, 127, 141; and health, 57–65; and race, 8, 10, 49–52; regulations on, 1–5, 7, 42–49, 52–56, 99–100, 165–67; and vocational guidance, 134–36

Child Labor Law of 1903 (Illinois), 53–56, 67–69
Children's Bureau (US), 135
"child saving" (term), 8. *See also* dependency; "worthy poor" (term)
Child Study Committee. *See* Department of Child Study
Chisholm, Shirley, 189
Christopher, Walter Scott, 57, 60. *See also* Department of Child Study
citizenship training: and gender, 42, 50–51, 173, 176–79; for immigrants, 3, 51, 126–27, 175; and race, 12, 74, 152, 158, 179–82; and vocational education, 159–60, 165–68. *See also* Americanization
City Club of Chicago, 127
Civil War, 4, 17, 33, 43, 75
clubwomen. *See* women's club movement
Coalition of Labor Union Women, 190
coeducation, 111–12, 190–91
colleges and universities: and business, 147; and domestic science, 72–77; and home economics, 158, 160, 162, 164, 169–71, 174; and teaching, 98–100, 113, 120, 122–23
commercial education, 38, 98, 103–7, 123, 147, 150, 161, 167, 186. *See also* office work; stenography
Commission on Federal Aid to Vocational Education, 159–62. *See also* Smith-Hughes Act
Compulsory Attendance Law of 1903 (Illinois), 53, 55. *See also* school attendance
continuation schools, 2, 12, 157, 165–70, 175, 178, 182–83. *See also* Smith-Hughes Act
Cook County Court for Delinquent Girls, 140, 144–46, 152. *See also* Cook County Juvenile Court; delinquency
Cook County Juvenile Court, 19, 39, 55, 126, 140–43. *See also* juvenile courts
Cook County School of Nursing, 189. *See also* nursing (profession)
cooking: in carceral schools, 21–23, 28–30, 39; in kitchen garden schools, 23–26; in public schools, 82–90, 113–14, 116, 161, 172. *See also* domestic science; home economics
Cooley, Edwin G., 103–5, 107, 110
cosmetology, 137, 171, 187–88
Crane, Richard T., 80
Crane Tech. *See* Richard T. Crane Technical High School for Boys
The Crisis, 92, 136
Cusack, Helen (Nell Nelson), 1–2

Davis, Anne, 132–34, 137–40, 142, 146–47, 150
Davis, Cora, 166–67, 171
degenerative theory, 59–61, 69. *See also* eugenics
delinquency: definition of term, 8–9, 145; and gender, 7, 26–34, 54, 61; and juvenile courts, 140–46; and race, 16, 27–28, 37–39; and sex, 126–34; and the workplace, 37, 146–50. *See also* Cook County Juvenile Court
Department of Child Study, 57–61
Department of Sanitary Science (Department of Household Administration), 76. *See also* University of Chicago
dependency: definition of term, 19–20, 26–27; and gender, 20; and race, 8–9, 16, 27–28, 38–39, 47. *See also* "worthy poor" (term)
Dewey, John, 88
Dickson, Marguerite Stockman, 35, 151
domestic science, 2, 7, 10, 71–77, 82–96, 108–10, 112–13, 158, 161, 166, 169, 172, 174. *See also* home economics
domestic service: and domestic science, 86–91; jobs in, 2, 11, 21–22, 25, 28, 34; and race/racism, 4, 34–39, 151, 172, 180, 182, 186–87; and "the servant problem," 9, 16, 21–26; training in carceral schools, 21–26, 28, 32–34
Doolittle Elementary School, 91
Dorsey, Lucy V., 162
Douglas Commission. *See* Massachusetts Commission on Industrial and Technical Education
dressmaking: education for, 5, 10, 35, 38, 85, 97, 103, 111–12, 116–18, 132, 137, 161,

dressmaking *(cont.)*
  170–71, 177, 187; jobs in, 36, 101, 105–6; and race, 106, 137. *See also* needle trades
Dwyer, Anne, 143

Education Amendments Act of 1972. *See* Title IX
educators. *See* teachers
Edwards, Richard, 44. *See also* Edwards Law
Edwards Law, 44, 46, 48, 52, 209n10
elementary schools (public), 41–69, 71–98
elites. *See* upper-class women
Ellen Richards Trade School for Girls, 187–88
Emanuel Settlement, 63
embroidery, 85–86, 108, 132, 146. *See also* needle trades
Englewood (neighborhood), 118
ethnicity, 2, 63, 85, 88, 152, 175, 180. *See also* immigration
eugenics, 42, 50, 52, 57–58, 63, 69. *See also* degenerative theory
exercise. *See* physical culture

factory inspection, 1, 5, 44–47, 49, 53–55. *See also* child labor; Florence Kelley; Workshop and Factories Act
Federal Board for Vocational Education, 163–66, 169, 179, 181. *See also* Smith-Hughes Act
Fess, Simeon D., 159, 173
Fess Home Economics Amendment (Fess Amendment), 173–74, 178
Flower, Lucy, 79–81, 116
Flower Tech. *See* Lucy Flower Technical School for Girls
Frake, Evelyn Allen, 84

Galton, Francis, 50
Garfield Park (neighborhood), 99, 121–22, 137, 171
garment industry, 1, 4, 42–43, 52–54, 77–78, 130, 132, 144, 147; education for, 103–8, 117–19, 161, 171–72, 177; strikes of 1910, 115–16. *See also* dressmaking; needle trades
General Federation of Women's Clubs (GFWC), 162–63, 180, 182. *See also* women's club movement
Geneva (Illinois), 16, 29–31, 33, 38, 40, 141, 145. *See also* Illinois State Training School for Girls
George-Reed Act, 178–79, 183
Germany, industrial competition with, 100, 107, 159–60
germ theory, 72–73. *See also* domestic science
girls: and carceral schools, 41–70; and child labor, 41–57, 62, 136; and citizenship training, 170–72, 176–77; definition of "girlhood," 7–9, 19; and delinquency, 26–34, 127–34, 138–49; and domestic science, 78–95; and eugenics, 49–52; and high schools, 118–23; and home economics, 166–68; and office work, 146–54; and physical culture, 59–68; and race, 9–10, 27–29, 34–39, 136–37, 179–82; and resistance to school reform, 11, 15, 113–15, 172, 189. *See also* boys; childhood
Girls' Industrial Schools Act of 1879, 19–21, 26
Glenwood Manual Training School for Boys. *See* Illinois Manual Training School for Boys
Great Chicago Fire, 16–17
Great Depression, 187
Great Migration, 3–5, 34–35, 38, 40, 80; migrant girls, 35, 122, 130, 143. *See also* African Americans
guidance counseling. *See* vocational guidance

Hampton Normal and Agricultural Institute, 179
Harbert, Elizabeth Boynton, 17
Harper's Bazaar, 78
Hawai'i, education for girls, 157–58, 180–83, 187
health: and child labor, 46–47, 54; courses in, 3, 62–65, 78–86, 158; and

domesticity, 71–77, 86–87, 179–80; exams in school, 57–62, 151; and "little mothers," 65–68, 91–95; and reproduction, 9–10, 41–42, 49–53
Hedger, Caroline, 62–63, 65–67, 69, 92–93
Henrotin, Ellen Martin, 1, 23–24, 26–27, 32, 37, 43–44, 75, 87, 115, 125
Hess, Adah, 171, 174, 176–77
higher education. *See* colleges and universities
high schools (public), 97–123, 134–39, 147, 151–52, 171–72, 176–79, 187–92
Hill, Lucille Eaton, 59
Hill, Thomas (T.) Arnold, 136
Hine, Lewis, 47–48
Holt, Charlotte, 29
home economics, 7, 12, 72, 75, 97, 157–58, 161–64, 166–83, 185, 187–90. *See also* American Home Economics Association (AHEA); domestic science
homemaking: and Americanization for girls, 175–83; use of the term, 169. *See also* American Home Economics Association (AHEA); domestic science; home economics
household arts, 10–11, 99, 112–16, 146, 177, 185; use of the term, 90–91, 174. *See also* domestic science; home economics
housekeeping: and domestic science, 71–76, 82, 86–87; and domestic service training, 18, 21–26, 28, 33, 37–39, 86–87. *See also* domestic science; home economics
Houston, Victor, 180
Hughes, Dudley, 159–60, 162–63. *See also* Smith-Hughes Act
Hull House, 4, 36, 46, 52, 63–64, 71, 111, 117, 128, 135; Hull-House Trade School for Girls, 117; Practical Housekeeping Center, 82–83. *See also* Addams, Jane; settlement houses
Hungerford White, Annie, 24
Huntington, Emily, 21, 23
Hyde Park (neighborhood), 83–84, 90
hygiene. *See* health

Illinois Federation of Women's Clubs, 53
Illinois Industrial School for Girls, 9, 16, 18–20, 21–28, 32, 34, 36–38; move to Park Ridge, 37
Illinois Manual Training School Boys (Glenwood), 19–20, 79
Illinois State Normal University, 166
Illinois State Training School for Girls, 9, 15–16, 26–35, 37–39, 141, 145, 187
Illinois Women's Alliance (IWA), 42–44, 46–47, 49
Illinois Woman's Suffrage Association (IWSA), 17
industrial education, 104, 110, 158, 160–63, 173, 178. *See also* National Society for the Promotion of Industrial Education (NSPIE); vocational education
industrial schools. *See* carceral schools
International Brotherhood of Electrical Workers, 117
International Ladies' Garment Workers Union (ILGWU), 115
International Ladies' Glove Workers Union, 101
immigration, 2–5, 41, 46, 50–51, 55, 57, 63, 152, 175–77, 180. *See also* Americanization; ethnicity

Johnson, Helen Louise, 163
Johnson-Reed Act, 175
Journal of Industrial Education, 24
Judson, Philo, 17
juvenile courts, 7, 11, 38, 140–43. *See also* Cook County Juvenile Court
juvenile delinquency. *See* delinquency

Kawin, Ethel and Irene, 140
Kehew, Mary Morton, 100–101
Kelley, Florence, 5–6, 10, 44–49, 51–53, 55, 65, 69, 71, 77, 82
Kingsbury, Susan M., 99
Kirk, Eleanor, 78
Kitchen Garden Association, 23–25, 40
Kozminski Elementary School, 83

Ladies' Home Journal, 78
Ladies' Industrial Schools Association (LISA), 17–20, 26, 39

lampshade design, 121, 146. *See also* needle trades
Lancaster Industrial School for Girls (Massachusetts), 29
Lane Tech. *See* Albert G. Lane Technical High School for Boys
Lapp, John A., 159
Lathrop, Julia, 29, 135
League of Jewish Women, 139
League of Women Voters (LWV), 158, 173–74, 178
Levee District, 130. *See also* redlight district; sex work
Lewis, Dora S., 181
"little mothers" classes, 10, 65–67, 91–94, 157, 181, 185
Lucy Flower Technical School for Girls, 11, 98–99, 116–22, 133, 137–38, 150, 166, 171–72, 177, 186; change to Flower Vocational School, 188–89, 191; relocation to Garfield Park, 120, 229n45
Lyford, Carrie, 179–80

MacFadden, Bernarr, 57–58. *See also* physical culture
MacMillan, Daniel, 60
Manhattan Trade School for Girls, 107–9, 159, 161, 170
manhood. *See* masculinity
Mann Act (White Slave Traffic Act), 131. *See also* "white slavery" hysteria
manual training: and carceral schools, 19–20; and masculinity, 104; and public schools, 72, 80–81, 84–85, 89, 95, 99
Manufacturing Belt, 4, 21, 42, 75, 93, 163
Marshall, Florence, 108, 121, 159
masculinity, 20, 46, 57–59, 81, 104–7, 127. *See also* boys
Massachusetts Commission on Industrial Education (Douglas Commission), 99–100, 103
Massachusetts Institute of Technology (MIT), 73–74, 76
"maternalism" (term), 6–7, 31, 42, 74
Matthews, Victoria Earle, 130
McClees, Mary, 23
McCormick, Cyrus H., Jr., 80

McCormick, Nancy, 83
McDonald, Elizabeth, 140
meatpacking, 4, 54, 64, 118, 166. *See also* stockyards
medical exams. *See* health
middle class: definition of, 5; high school enrollment, 98, 100, 103–5, 110, 114; views on childhood, 8, 46–47, 65, 69; views on domesticity, 16, 36, 72, 75, 77–79, 81, 85, 84–88, 90, 92, 175; views on leisure, 25, 63–65, 142, 144; views on respectability, 86, 131, 142, 177. *See also* respectability
millinery, 36, 38, 97, 101, 105–6, 121, 147, 161, 187. *See also* needle trades
Montgomery, Louise, 41–42, 51–52, 54, 62, 69
Moody's Evangelical Church, 79
Moore, Ella Adams, 138
"mother blame" (term), 31
motherhood: education for, 1–2, 9–10, 37, 41–69, 91–95, 171–72, 181–82. *See also* "little mothers" classes

National American Woman Suffrage Association (NAWSA), 173
National Association for the Advancement of Colored People (NAACP), 94, 136
National Child Labor Committee (NCLC), 47–48
National Council of Women Voters (NCWV), 173
National Household Economics Association (NHEA), 75–77, 86–88, 90, 95
National League for the Protection of Colored Women (NLPCW), 130
National Society for the Promotion of Industrial Education (NSPIE), 100–101, 103, 109, 158–59
National Vocational Guidance Association, 135
National Women's Trade Union League. *See* Women's Trade Union League (WTUL)
needle trades, 9, 11, 36–37, 79–80, 85, 97–99, 102–3, 105–7, 112–13, 116, 118,

121–23, 132, 137–28, 146–48, 177. *See also* dressmaking; garment industry; millinery
Negro Fellowship League, 121
Neilson, Nell. *See* Cusack, Helen
Nestor, Agnes, 97–98, 101–3, 106, 109–10, 115, 117, 123, 157, 159, 161–62, 164, 174, 189
"new woman" (term), 59
New York City, 4, 7, 20–21, 25, 43, 46, 52, 65, 115–17, 130, 142–43; Board of Health, 54; public schools, 3, 54, 63, 82, 90, 93, 107–9, 128, 135, 176; and Smith-Hughes Act, 165, 170
Northwestern University, 62, 140
nursing (profession), 39, 120, 162, 188–89

office work: anxieties about, 11, 104–7, 123, 126–27, 131, 146–50; education for, 9, 98, 114, 165, 167, 188; preference for, 25, 106, 147, 152, 186; racism in, 35–38, 151–52. *See also* commercial education; stenography
O'Reilly, Leonora, 109, 161

Page, Carroll S., 159, 161
Pan-Pacific Women's Conference, 182
parens patriae, 20, 31
parents, 3, 5, 18–20, 44, 47, 51, 65, 72–73, 81, 85–86, 105, 113, 118–22, 152, 179, 181, 186; education for, 62–63, 134–35; perspectives of, 31–32, 54–55, 67–68, 90–91, 136–37, 143, 166
Park Ridge Industrial School for Girls. *See* Illinois Industrial School for Girls
Parsons, Frank, 127
Perkins, Dwight, 89
Perlman, Nancy, 190
physical culture (education), 42, 57–59, 62–63, 65, 81, 112, 187
piecework, 62, 106
police, 15, 18–19, 27, 54–55, 127
probation (juvenile), 11, 126, 140–44, 146, 154
Prosser, Charles, 159
prostitution. *See* sex work
protective legislation, 51, 69, 101
Provident Hospital, 76

public education: expansion of, 3–4, 7. *See* Board of Education (BOE); elementary schools; high schools; school attendance
public health, 10, 52, 60, 62, 72–73, 75–77, 82, 84, 86, 88, 91, 93–95, 158, 187, 189. *See also* health

race: and child labor, 47–48, 69; and citizenship, 152, 158, 175, 179–82; and delinquency, 16, 27–28, 37–39; and domestic labor, 4, 34–39, 151, 172, 180, 182, 186–87; and eugenics, 42, 50, 52, 57–58, 63, 69; and public education, 3–4, 8, 91, 98–99, 105, 113. *See also* African Americans
Raymond Elementary School, 90
redlight district, 121, 125, 128, 130–31, 136. *See also* sex work
respectability, 2, 6, 35–36, 79, 86, 123, 131, 152, 167, 177; and race, 3, 8, 74, 120, 143. *See also* middle class
Richards, Ellen Swallow, 73–76, 158, 187
Richardson, Anna E., 169, 174
Richard T. Crane Technical High School for Boys, 104–5, 107, 111
Robins, Margaret Dreier, 77, 102–3, 109–10, 117
Roche, John A., 43–44
Rodman, Henrietta, 135
Roosevelt, Theodore, 100, 104
Rumford Kitchen, 74–75. *See also* World's Columbian Exposition (Chicago World's Fair)
Rush Medical College, 62

Schneiderman, Rose, 64, 103
Scholarship and Guidance Association, 139. *See also* Vocational Supervision League (VSL)
scholarships, 7, 11, 127, 138–39, 151–54. *See also* vocational guidance
school attendance: as child labor regulation, 42–49, 52–57, 68–69; and continuation schools, 167; and immigrant parents, 67–68, 186; laws, 2–3, 10; in public high schools, 100, 134, 137, 165

School of Civics and Philanthropy, 108, 128, 132. *See also* University of Chicago
schools. *See* carceral schools; elementary schools; high schools; public education
secondary education. *See* high schools
servants. *See* domestic service
settlement houses, 4–5, 8, 10, 41, 46, 62–64, 68–69, 75–76, 82, 98, 109, 118, 123, 130, 132, 185
sewing classes: in carceral schools, 15, 18, 22; in public schools, 78–81, 85–86, 107–8, 113, 116. *See also* domestic science; needle trades
Sewing School Association, 79
sexual assault, 2, 29, 34, 36, 40, 47, 125–26, 131, 143, 151
sexual delinquency. *See* delinquency
sex work, 18, 26, 29, 125–29, 131, 136, 138, 143–44, 147, 154
Sheppard-Towner Act, 173
Sickels, Emma Cornelia, 74–75
Smith, Amanda, 38. *See also* Amanda Smith Industrial School for Colored Girls
Smith, Hoke, 159–60, 162–63; *See also* Smith-Hughes Act
Smith-Hughes Act, 12, 157–75, 178–83, 188, 190
Snow, Mary, 90
Society for the Promotion of Physical Culture and Correct Dress, 59
South Loop (neighborhood), 28, 116
South Side (neighborhood), 4, 72, 83, 89, 99, 105, 118, 120–22, 136, 166, 176. *See also* Black Metropolis
Spafford, Ivol, 171
Stanley, Louise, 172–74, 182
Starr, Ellen Gates, 46
State Board of Charities (Illinois), 19, 36, 39
State Guardians for Girls, 26–34, 39
State Training School for Girls. *See* Illinois State Training School for Girls
Steele, Marilyn, 189
stenography: courses in, 5, 9, 39, 112, 124, 127; popularity of, 126, 132, 146–54. *See also* commercial education
Stickney, Elizabeth, 83

St. Joseph's Polish School, 55
stockyards, 4, 41, 51, 55, 62, 66, 75, 84, 93, 118, 165, 187. *See also* Back of the Yards; meatpacking
Stock Yards National Bank, 83
St. Pierre Ruffin, Josephine, 74
strikes (labor), 65, 103, 115
Sunset Lodge Camp, 138–39
sweatshops, 5, 44, 77
Sweeny, Mary E., 168

Taft, William, 135
Talbot, Marion, 76
Taylor, Graham, 64
teachers: college training programs, 76, 160, 162, 164–65, 169–71, 173, 181; in public schools, 43, 59–60, 73, 78–80, 85–86, 88, 90, 100, 114, 118, 167–77, 188
technical education. *See* vocational education
tenements, 5, 10, 36, 46, 71–73, 76–78, 81–82, 84–86, 88, 92, 95, 118
Title IX, 189–91
Towner, Harriet Elizabeth, 163
Towner, Horace Mann, 163
trade education, 97–108, 115–18, 158–62, 164–66. *See also* vocational education
Training School for Active Women Workers, 117–18. *See also* Women's Trade Union League (WTUL)
Triangle Shirtwaist Factory Fire, 52, 116
truancy, 3, 44, 46, 54, 67–68, 91, 167
Tuskegee University, 39, 76, 171

United Garment Workers (UGW), 115
universities. *See* colleges and universities
University of Chicago, 41, 84, 88, 108, 128, 138, 166, 169. *See also* Chicago School of Civics and Philanthropy; Department of Sanitary Science
University of Hawai'i in Honolulu, 181
University of Illinois, 171, 189
University of Missouri, 173
upper-class women, 2, 16, 33, 75, 80, 108, 115; and the "servant problem," 21–26

vacation (summer) schools, 139
vagrancy, 26, 28, 47

vice reform, 125–36, 140–43, 154. *See also* Chicago Vice Commission

vocational education: in carceral schools, 15, 17–18, 37–38; in elementary schools, 91; and gender anxiety, 103–7; in high schools, 97–123, 125, 145, 147; in settlement houses, 46, 117–18; and the Smith-Hughes Act, 157–83; and Title IX, 189–92. *See also* commercial education; home economics

vocational guidance, 7, 11, 30, 35, 100, 125–55, 172, 185–87, 189; Chicago Vocational Guidance Bureau, 126, 134–39, 142–42, 146–47, 151–52; Vocational Adjustment Bureau for Girls, 142

Vocational Supervision League (VSL), 11, 126–40, 151–55. *See also* vocational guidance

Wallace, Emma Gilson, 26
Washington, Booker T., 39, 76
Washington, Margaret Murray, 76
Waters, Adah M., 38
Wellesley College, 59, 117
Wells, Dora, 116–17
Wells-Barnett, Ida B., 120
Wendell Phillips High School, 121, 141, 147
Wendell Phillips Settlement, 63, 136
white-collar work. *See* commercial education; office work
"white ethnics" (term), 152
White Rose Home, 130. *See also* Matthews, Victoria Earle
"white slavery" hysteria, 7, 11, 125–26, 131–32, 134, 136, 142, 147, 152–54
Wickens, Margaret Ray, 30
Willard, Harriet J., 22–23
Wilson, Woodrow, 158–59, 163
Wilson Industrial School for Girls, 23
Winchell Continuation School, 166–67. *See also* continuation schools
Winslow, Charles, 159, 162
Woodlock, Mary, 175

Woolman, Mary Schenck, 108
Woman's Christian Temperance Union (WCTU), 23–25
Woman's City Club (WCC), 128, 137
Woman's Era, 74
Women's Bureau of the Labor Department, 169
women's club movement, 5–8, 17; Black clubwomen, 5, 74, 87, 120, 139; education reform, 2, 22–24, 43–44, 52, 59, 74–75, 79, 83–84, 87, 110, 115–16, 123, 126–28, 138, 162; Smith-Hughes Act, 157, 162–64, 182. *See also* Chicago Woman's Club (CWC); "maternalism"
Women's Trade Union League (WTUL): and federal education policy, 159, 161, 169, 174; and protective legislation, 51; and public school reform, 97–103, 105–10, 113–15, 117–18, 120, 122–23
work certificates, 42, 52–56, 60–62, 67–68, 121, 127–28, 134, 138, 151, 168. *See also* school attendance
working class: boys, 7, 20, 47–48, 53, 55, 61, 72–73, 81, 91, 160, 165–66, 98, 103–5; definition of, 5–6; families and parents, 4–5, 18–29, 31, 54–55, 65, 76–79, 109, 118–22, 186, 190; leisure activities, 5, 9, 64, 142–43. *See also* middle class; parents
Workshop and Factories Act, 44, 46, 50, 52
World's Columbian Exposition (Chicago World's Fair), 26, 74–75, 116
World War I, 2, 7, 11–12, 98, 106, 108, 113–14, 121, 126, 138–39, 150–52, 154, 158–59, 163–65, 168–71, 175–77, 179, 182–83, 185, 189
World War II, 187–89
"worthy poor" (term), 8, 18, 20, 23, 25, 47, 49, 138
Wreidt, A. E., 165

Young, Ella Flagg, 6, 44, 82, 88–93, 97, 110–12, 116–18, 120, 133, 159, 167

www.ingramcontent.com/pod-product-compliance
Lightning Source LLC
Chambersburg PA
CBHW022046290426
44109CB00014B/996